THE 3M
WAY TO
INNOVATION

THE 3M WAY TO INNOVATION

Balancing People and Profit

ERNEST GUNDLING

Foreword by Jerry I. Porras

KODANSHA INTERNATIONAL
Tokyo • New York • London

Published by Kodansha International Ltd., 17–14 Otowa 1-chome, Bunkyo-ku, Tokyo 112–8652, and Kodansha America, Inc.

Distributed in the United States by Kodansha America, Inc., 575 Lexington Avenue, New York, New York 10022, and in the United Kingdom and continental Europe by Kodansha Europe Ltd., 95 Aldwych, London WC2B 4JF.

First edition, 2000

1 2 3 4 5   03 02 01 00
ISBN 4–7700–2476–2

To
my mother and father
for their love and patience

CONTENTS

ACKNOWLEDGMENTS

This book was inspired by a chance meeting with Roger Appledorn, 3M Corporate Scientist. In 1996 I entered his office for a consulting interview. My job was to talk to him and others about how innovation takes place in St. Paul, and to look for ways that such practices could stimulate innovative efforts at Sumitomo 3M, the company's joint venture in Japan. Appledorn's energy, enthusiasm, and obvious affection for the company and his work have somehow stayed with me, even after his retirement. His home-brewed presentation materials on innovation have also become the core for the chapter on technical innovation.

Other 3Mers have been particularly helpful along the way. Harold Wiens, now Executive Vice-President for Industrial Markets, Tony Gastaldo, Vice-President for Asia Pacific, Masayuki Ichikawa, Director of Staff Marketing at Sumitomo 3M, and Steve Pusey of 3M Corporate Marketing all provided support and encouragement at a time when the book project was still just an idea. Once the research was under way, John Schroeder and Katherine Hagmeier from 3M Public Relations, and Camille Anderson of Corporate Marketing set up interviews with 3M employees in St. Paul. Shin'ichiro Hinokuma, Masashi Katoh, and Keiko Tsurumi arranged interviews in Asia. Steve Pusey provided a list of contacts for 3M Europe.

A number of 3Mers have been kind enough to read the entire English manuscript and offer comments and suggestions that significantly expanded my knowledge of the company: John Schroeder, Dick Lidstad, Bill Coyne, Barry Dayton, and Bill Allen. Bill Coyne, 3M Senior Vice President for Research and Development, was generous with original source materials and particularly influential in shaping my thinking. At no time in the writing process did I feel a loss of editorial freedom. It says something about 3M that these readers, while never hesitating to voice disagreements, always left me to form my own opinions, including criticisms of the company.

There are many 3M interviewees to thank, both for their specific comments and for the general spirit of their remarks. It is rare and even a bit unnerving for a consultant accustomed to analyzing more troubled companies to encounter so many people with a generally positive outlook on their jobs and their employer. I apologize in advance to other contributors who are not mentioned here and to those whose stories did not survive the editorial process; the original manuscript had to be pared down considerably to make it a manageable length.

Interviewees, listed in alphabetical order, included: Giulio Agostini, Margaret Alldredge, Bill Allen, Richard Anthony, Karon Armstrong, Ron Baukol, Tony Bellis, David Braun, Bill Coyne, Barry Dayton, Veronique Delpla-Dabon, Livio DeSimone, Ikuko Ebihara, Ronald Faas, Robert Finocchiaro, Simon Fung, Rainer Goldammer, Kay Grenz, David Hagen, Patrick Hager, Timm Hammond, Chuck Harstad, Anthony Hoffman, Kim Johnson, Marty Kenner, Amy Krohn, Pratib Kumar, Richard Lidstad, Michael Linnerooth, Barbara Lother, Richard Minday, Howard Miners, Geoff Nicholson, Iwao Nishida, Ward Petrich, Antonio Pinna Berchet, Alphonsus Pocius, Steve Pusey, Keith Roddan, Milind Sabade, Shigeru ("Lefty") Sato, H. C. Shin, Gene Shipman, Wendy Stanton, Ian Tansey, Arlan Tietel, Jean Waller, Joseph Ward, Rick Weiss, and Thomas Wollner.

Hiroshi Kagawa, a long-time colleague and friend who is the primary author of the Japanese edition, conducted other interviews in India, Japan, Singapore, and Thailand, uncovering a wealth of good stories and examples. Meimei Fox served very ably as a research assistant throughout the interviewing and initial writing process. She carried out a number of interviews on her own and contributed to the historical research and drafting of the manuscript for chapter two. Other colleagues at Meridian Resources were tolerant of my extended absences, mental as well as physical.

Clifford Clarke, a valued mentor and former boss, provided my initial introduction to 3M in 1987; he graciously consented to the use of interview data generated during my time at his firm. Kuniyaki Ura and Barry Lancet, executive editors at Kodansha, have capably guided the publishing process from start to finish.

Finally, Professor Jerry Porras of Stanford University has been remarkably generous and helpful in shaping this book. In the midst of his busy schedule he has been kind enough to meet several times, to offer wise advice on the type of presentation that would have the greatest appeal to a business audience, and to provide successive rounds of insightful critical comments on the manuscript. His interest in 3M and in this project has been more important than he may know to this first-time author who appeared on his doorstep with little more than a series of favors to ask of him.

The best efforts of all of these good people notwithstanding, I have undoubtedly still been guilty of errors, omissions, and conceptual flaws for which I take full responsibility. I hope that my own shortcomings in the course of assembling the material are sufficiently outweighed by the value of the subject matter.

NOTES ON CITATIONS AND TITLES

In addition to the research conducted expressly for this book, the text draws upon more than two hundred interviews conducted with 3M employees over the last ten years in connection with a variety of consulting projects. Because the personal confidentiality of these interviews was guaranteed, I have not cited individual sources in the text. Chapters five and six are particularly dependent upon these sources. Most of the verbatim comments have appeared in internal reports to the company. My thanks to 3M for permission to use these materials, and to individual interviewees in the United States and Asia (China, Japan, Korea, Malaysia, Singapore, Taiwan, and Thailand) for their frank and constructive comments.

In referring to 3M employees, I have chosen by and large not to use formal, social, or academic titles such as Dr., Mr./Ms., or Ph.D., although I am well aware that many people possess advanced degrees and other impressive credentials. The company typically works on a first name basis except where there are major differences of hierarchy involved, and the use of such titles did not seem to me to convey the proper atmosphere. The lack of titles here in no way lessens my respect for these individuals, and I ask forgiveness from those who think it would have been better to refer to them in a different way.

FOREWORD

Only occasionally in the history of organizations does a company like 3M rise above the masses and become truly great and enduring. Just as rarely does anyone capture the very essence of the methods used by that company to attain and preserve such greatness. In this book, Ernest Gundling accomplishes the unusual. He has probed the depths of 3M's operations and identified the approaches to managing innovation so fundamental to its continuing success.

Every company seeks the keys to innovation, but few find them. Over the decades 3M learned how to be innovative and today they use that skill to great competitive advantage. Gundling identifies significant examples of 3M innovation, describes them in vivid detail, then conceptualizes their key underlying processes. As a student of visionary organizations, I believe developing frameworks that explain *why* particular management approaches work constitutes the most important contribution any scholar can make.

Far too many authors simply describe an interesting and perhaps highly effective best practice without offering enough technical guidance or any descriptions of the underlying principles leading to its success. As a result, when readers attempt to apply the best practice to their own organization they find the ideas do not quite fit their reality and require significant adaptation. But what should be modified? In which direction might the modification best head? What might the modification look like? These and many more questions remain unanswered.

By presenting key underlying principles organized into useful frameworks, Gundling captures the essence of what makes a book like this so useful. Detailed descriptions of innovation processes followed by detailed explanations of why they work give readers a clear idea of the possibilities and provide the tools needed to invent a workable approach for their own organization.

The reader can expect not only to be entertained by exciting examples of highly effective organizational practice but also to be taught how to implement change. Gundling expertly builds ever more complex frameworks that can truly guide any manager in the development of an innovation-rich environment. Creating innovative behavior requires numerous organizational changes. A wide variety of key components of a company must be brought into alignment with the goal of promoting innovative behavior. Concepts must guide the process of reshaping the work setting so that it continuously stimulates and supports creativity, risk taking, and learning from mistakes—all necessary behaviors for innovation to occur.

As an ex-engineer I am always attracted to conceptual frameworks represented in visual form, believing that "if I can't draw it, I don't understand it." Gundling has more than satisfied my penchant for graphical presentation. He cleverly translates most of his frameworks into creative charts and drawings that help the reader better understand and remember them. The notion that a picture is worth a thousand words plays itself out very well in this work, and I expect that many readers will find the illustrations invaluable.

I think you will find this book can help you build a more innovative organization. It won't be easy, but Gundling's effort will make the journey much less difficult and, in the end, more rewarding.

Jerry I. Porras
Lane Professor of Organizational Behavior and Change
Graduate School of Business
Stanford University
Stanford, California

October 1999

INTRODUCTION

Business trends move uncannily like the world of fashion. Although we may prefer to think that restructuring, mergers and acquisitions, quality control, and scientific management have all been strategic responses to market imperatives, this succession of trends also resembles a generational fashion parade of long and short skirts, bell-bottoms and baggy pants. Such trends have their virtues and certainly seem important while they take center stage, but in retrospect they often look like a closet full of outdated clothes. It is unclear what lasting value has been created for customers, employees, shareholders, and local communities—not to mention what damage might have been done.

In the long run, what is most consistently critical to the creation of value for commercial enterprises is innovation. A company can cut expenses only so much, imitate somebody else's inventions only so far, or dress up a homely pig in only so many ways before its customers and competitors catch on. Honest profit is earned most readily when the products or services that an organization offers are viewed by customers as new and highly desirable. To do that requires innovation, or whatever else it happens to be called at the time. American corporations appear to be increasingly aware of the value of innovation, as they are expanding their research and development investments at several times the rate of national economic growth.[1]

Those who really want to learn about innovation—how it happens, what sustains it, how it contributes to business results—will eventually find their way to Minnesota Mining and Manufacturing, commonly known as 3M. An unassuming Midwestern enterprise with roots in Minnesota's farming country, 3M is also arguably the most innovative company in the world. Indeed, countless visitors now come to 3M each year, many impelled by the fashionable notion of "benchmarking," to examine its innovation practices.

Dick Lidstad, a big, jovial man who came out of a line job to finish his career as 3M's Vice-President of Human Resources, describes what happens on these benchmarking visits. A group of visitors arrives that typically includes several senior executives plus some of their staff members. They have asked to spend a few hours or a day at the company's headquarters in St. Paul, Minnesota. 3M, fulfilling the role of good host, has lined up five or six people from different functions to try to respond to their questions. Yet, in spite of 3M's Midwestern hospitality, the visitors may go away feeling frustrated. Lidstad comments:

> They want to take away one or two things that will help them to innovate. They always listen politely, and have heard about some of our typical practices like the Fifteen Percent Rule. We say that maintaining a climate in which innovation flourishes may be the single biggest factor overall. As the conversation winds down, it becomes clear that what they want is something that is easily transferable. They want specific practices or policies, and get frustrated because they'd like to go away with a clear prescription.[2]

Innovation is not brought into existence with a silver bullet, a magic pill, or even a well-intended benchmarking trip. At 3M, as elsewhere, it is the product of a complex environment. The company's outstanding gift, according to Lidstad, is its skill at nourishing an overall working climate in which a variety of innovative factors converge and support each other. There is a distinctive ecology of innovation, 3Mers (3M employees) claim, that produces a dazzling variety of new products each year.

Other writers have ably addressed the subject of innovation in general terms, comparing the activities and best practices of market leaders, including 3M.[3] But there are few in-depth studies of innovation within a single enterprise—and none of 3M itself—that examine the complex fabric of success and failure, invention and ideology, that constitute a whole innovation system. This book outlines key elements of 3M's system as well as how they interact with one another in the company that is perhaps the world's best example.

Jim Collins and Jerry Porras, authors of *Built to Last: Successful Habits of Visionary Companies*, paid 3M perhaps the ultimate compliment when they stated in their 1994 work that "if we had to bet our lives on the continued success and adaptability of any single company in our study over the next 50 to 100 years, we would place that bet on 3M."[4] What is it about 3M innovation that could enable it to prosper well into the next century and outlive most of us who are alive today?

3M's Global Innovation Credentials

3M has a consistent track record of innovative activity that goes back to the early part of this century and has led to the creation of whole new industries. The company currently manufactures more than fifty thousand different products, and is a global leader in a highly diverse range of markets, from industrial abrasives to electronics, specialty chemicals to health care.

3M's St. Paul headquarters now orchestrates a worldwide presence in nearly two hundred countries, including sixty-plus subsidiaries. There are substantial research activities and local manufacturing operations in a number of these locations. More than half of 3M's $15 billion in sales, as well as nearly half of its seventy thousand employees, come from outside of the United States.

A few additional facts help to confirm 3M's credentials as a world-class innovator along with its ongoing commitment to innovation:

3M INNOVATION CREDENTIALS

New Products as a Percentage of Sales: 30 percent of sales come from products new to the market within the past four years.

Pacing Plus: The approximately 35 new technology programs that 3M has targeted for accelerated investment generated sales of $1 billion in 1998 (up about 50 percent from the previous year) hold a long-term market potential of $6 billion.

Patents: 3M gained 611 patents in 1998; it normally ranks among the top 10 U.S. companies in patents granted.

Technology Platforms: 30 proprietary 3M technology areas produce multiple products for multiple markets.

Research & Development: 3M invests more than $1 billion a year, and has 7,100 employees engaged full-time in technical research and development.

Capital Spending: The company spent $1.4 billion in 1998 to finance expansions and improvements in manufacturing as well as other areas.

Financial Results: 3M's balance sheet is rock solid, with annual

---

operating income of nearly 17 percent of sales, a generous return on stockholders' equity of 26 percent, return on invested capital of 16 percent, high-quality debt rating, and more than 40 years of consecutive dividend increases.[5]

Recent Awards: National Medal of Technology; Presidential Award for Sustainable Development; Malcolm Baldrige National Quality Award (Dental Products Division); Heroes of Chemistry Award; Les Trophees de l'Environment (3M France); Argentine National Quality Award (3M Argentina).

3M has placed in the top ten on Fortune magazine's list of America's most admired companies in ten of the fifteen years in which Fortune has published the list. Fortune calls it "the Cal Ripken of corporate consistency."[6] Another recent survey of U.S. executives, comparing their attitudes toward forty-eight top U.S. companies, found strong support for 3M's innovative credentials among its industry peers. When asked to rate which U.S. companies had the most aggressive research and development programs, and which would best be able to adapt to future market conditions, the executives rated 3M number one in both categories. 3M's high ratings in these areas were accompanied by other strengths perhaps less commonly associated with innovation—an intriguing phenomenon that we will explore later. Among the items on which 3M received high national survey ratings were[7]:

Item	Ranking Among 48 Top U.S. Companies
Aggressive research and development programs	1
Best able to adapt to future market conditions	1
Leaders in recognizing corporate social responsibilities	3
Reputation for offering high-quality products or services	2
Ability to attract, retain, and develop high-quality employees	3
Establish and demand high standards of ethical business practice	3
Responsive to environmental concerns and problems	1
Companies with which your company would be willing to do business	1
Companies you would be willing to recommend as an employer to a colleague or friend	1
General favorability	1

Challenging Common Ideas about Innovation

The 3M case is so interesting in part because it calls into question much of the current wisdom about innovation shared by corporate leaders and consultants:

- **Standard Wisdom, Item 1:** *Specific innovative practices can be readily benchmarked and imported into other environments.*

  Importation of specific innovation practices could have zero impact, provide the illusion of progress without substance, or even do real damage. The eager benchmarker may be importing a plant or insect that had a positive role in its host environment but turns into a pest in another. What are the natural support and control mechanisms which enable a flower to thrive in one soil without growing wildly out of control? The 3M example demonstrates that innovative practices are part of a complex system where numerous factors work together in symbiotic fashion to support the creation of new products.

- **Standard Wisdom, Item 2:** *Companies need to establish a market-in or product-out innovation strategy that fits the requirements of their market.*

  There is no preferred approach to innovation at 3M. Market-in and product-out approaches, as well as numerous hybrid forms, are all present, and each seems to be an important contributor to the company's innovation repertoire. Businesses that ought to benefit most from close attention to customer needs have achieved some of their greatest successes through the introduction of products that customers have never heard of, while disciplined market research has been brought to bear in new technology fields that are still being defined. 3Mers are eclectic and opportunistic, preferring what works over what ought to work.

- **Standard Wisdom, Item 3:** *The best way to foster innovation in a large, established organization is to create an internal "skunkworks"—that is, an entrepreneurial unit insulated from the potentially stifling influence of regular operating procedures, systems, management personnel, and corporate culture.*

3M strives to make innovative practices part of its corporate mainstream. The company's unofficial motto seems to be, "Every employee a skunk." Rather than isolating or protecting entrepreneurial units, the company brings to bear the full leverage of its corporate systems at the first reasonable opportunity. Then it plucks out the successful but shy innovators, drags them into the spotlight, and turns them into the equivalent of corporate rock stars. Employees in all professions are encouraged to become innovators or at least to support innovative activity.

- **Standard Wisdom, Item 4:** *Real innovation comes through a revolutionary breakthrough, or paradigm shift.*

    Revolutionary breakthroughs turn out to be a rare and relatively small part of the innovation repertoire at 3M. A close look at the company's successful innovations reveals that they originate from multiple directions: revolution, evolution, new paradigms, and old paradigms. Experience suggests that innovation can spring from the womb of an old cash cow as readily as from an exciting new paradigm.

- **Standard Wisdom, Item 5:** *Innovation is the product of strategic management actions.*

    Strategic management actions often get in the way of innovation. Another key 3M lesson is when not to manage—when to let the forces of innovation simmer in their own juices without active intervention, however strategic or well-intended. The major temptation in any innovation effort is to force geese to sing in sweet chorus, or apple trees to bear fruit in the springtime.

■ The Wheel of Innovation

So how does innovation actually take place at 3M, and of what practical use can it be to those who want to foster innovation elsewhere?

As Dick Lidstad, the host for so many benchmarkers, confesses, "The truth is that a lot of the stuff we do won't necessarily work in another company without modification. When we try and explain that, it creates more frustration. They don't really believe that we're leveling with them—it's almost as if they think we are trying to hide something."[8]

What 3M does offer, however, is a model of how an innovation system works in its full-blown maturity, with a host of congruent factors combining to generate thousands of new products each year. Several primary components make up 3M's innovation system, which is depicted here in the form of a wheel. The different elements of the innovation process are highlighted in the upper half of the diagram. Multiple fields of support and application exist as well—they are portrayed in the lower half. These various features form the spokes of the wheel; at its hub is a blend of contemporary management practices with the legacy of 3M history and corporate culture.

3M's Innovation Wheel

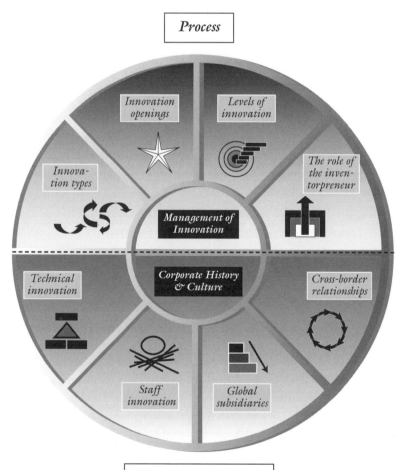

Each chapter of this book sheds light on a particular part of the wheel. Chapter one lays out the fundamental innovation processes. Chapter two looks back at 3M history and the influences that have shaped its corporate culture. Chapters three through six turn to the fields of support and application. The core theme of how to balance deliberate management techniques with the more organic elements of 3M corporate history and culture is addressed at various points throughout the book, and summarized in chapter seven. Chapter eight, the final chapter, examines how the innovation system portrayed by the wheel is positioned to address the business environment of the future.

Although it is unwise to lift out specific 3M practices and transplant them without adaptation into a different environment, fundamental principles of the 3M system are well worth examining. Indeed, the model of 3M's innovation system that is presented here transcends the particular forms assumed by its various elements. Others can benefit by considering how their own organizations might create localized versions of 3M's Innovation Wheel. For companies that are just beginning to think about how to innovate more successfully, the 3M model offers a conceptual road map; companies that seek to improve systems already in place may prefer to use it as a diagnostic tool to analyze their own strengths and weaknesses. At the end of each chapter, key questions are provided to stimulate the process of applying 3M innovation principles elsewhere.

■ Managing Innovation for the Future

While there can be no disputing 3M's position as one of the world's greatest innovative organizations, the future viability of its celebrated business model is hardly guaranteed. Financial results for 1998 were uncharacteristically mediocre. Net income, after four years of double-digit increases, actually fell slightly, with currency exchange losses turning a small increase in sales into a slight decrease. The company's stock price plummeted, dropping 30 percent from its previous highs.

3M's global presence, which provided major growth opportunities in past years, has also left it exposed to economic downturns in Asia and Latin America. Some Wall Street analysts say that the problems go deeper—that earnings should be stronger even when international issues are factored out. Notes one, "It's not a worse-managed company than five years ago, but the world is a lot more competitive and they haven't raised the benchmark as much as they should have."

3M, from this analyst's point of view, ought to be looking for bench-marks rather than serving as one.[9]

3M continues to exude its distinctive brand of quiet self-confidence, even as it turns up the heat on its operations and presses for greater internal efficiencies. Management has avoided drastic measures to boost financial performance of the kind favored by Wall Street, regarding them as short-term fixes that could ultimately do more harm than good. Most 3Mers feel that the current economic troubles will turn out to be a minor disturbance rather than a sea change—but not everyone is so sure.

As additional information is presented in subsequent chapters, another central issue will be whether 3M's distinctive brand of innovation can retain its modestly revolutionary edge. What keeps 3M's best and brightest awake at night, and what are they doing about it? We will try to peer into the future of innovation at this most innovative of firms. 3M has been a dependable paragon of U.S. business practices for decades. Where it goes from here will have significant repercussions for how we approach future innovation challenges.

1

The Innovation Process

It is impossible to spend even an hour at 3M without hearing about innovation. The company's official vision statement is to be THE MOST INNOVATIVE ENTERPRISE IN THE WORLD. Unofficially, it seems that almost every 3Mer has a pet project or some team activity that is focused on promoting innovation in his or her particular area.

3M's basic definition of innovation is arrestingly straightforward. Innovation is:

> *New ideas + action or implementation which results in an improvement, gain, or profit.*

Employees are quick to point out that this is not the same thing as creativity. Innovation is more than just a bright idea; it is an idea that gets implemented and has a real impact.[1] In other words, somebody has to make it happen.

Even though the definition of innovation is simple enough, many sophisticated processes contribute to transforming ideas into reality. This chapter looks at:

- *Types of innovation*
- *Pivotal openings* that transform humdrum research routines into moments of sudden insight
- *Organizational levels* at which innovation takes place
- *The innovation champion*, or what 3M calls the "*inventorpreneur*"

Management is naturally involved in each step along the way, and its role will be touched on briefly here, with a fuller treatment given in later sections of the book.

3Mers relish the chance to share their company's innovation stories: the countless tales of people who somehow defied the odds and the status quo, stumbled, tried again, persisted, and finally succeeded. Examining such stories in relation to each element of the innovation process will help to reveal how innovation actually takes place.

Three Types of Innovation

There are several distinct types of innovation. The first, most radical, type gives birth to a brand new business or industry (Type A). 3M has done this in the past with coated abrasives, Scotch tape, magnetic recording tape, and reflective signage.[2] The second type of innovation, Type B, "changes the basis of competition." Such innovations create a new competitive position or niche within an established field. The third is a line extension, which produces an incremental advance. Offering 3M's Post-it notes in multiple shapes and colors is a simple example of extending a product's life and market.

Each type of innovation involves a different kind of customer interaction: Type A transcends existing customer desires by serving needs that have not yet been articulated. Type B breakthroughs may originate in a research laboratory before they are matched with customers' needs, while Type C innovation is often closely aligned with explicit customer needs.

Three Innovation Types

Type A:
New Market
or Industry

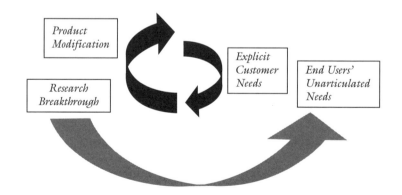

Product Modification

Research Breakthrough

Explicit Customer Needs

End Users' Unarticulated Needs

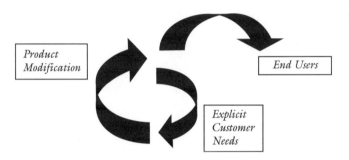

Type B:
Changing the
Basis of
Competition

Type C:
Line Extension

 From Ribbons to Respirators: Nonwoven Fibers

Nonwoven materials are a classic example of what 3M calls a technology platform—a set of core technologies that are used in inventing a family of related products for different businesses. A nonwoven is a mass of fibers that is assembled into a web and bonded together through any of several techniques, including one similar to the process for making cotton candy.

3M's nonwoven technology dates from the late 1930s, when a researcher named Al Boese ran a late-night experiment. Boese took a machine that heated and kneaded rubber—one step in the manufacture of adhesive for tape—and in place of rubber ran clumps of cellulose acetate fibers through the machine's rollers. He found that the machine could flatten and bind the fibers, creating a new nonwoven material.

In spite of the best research efforts of Boese and his co-workers over the next decade, there were no immediate practical applications for this discovery. On two occasions in the late 1940s, management recommended ending the research. Finally, a third management review gave Boese's team just three months to find a marketable application for his nonwoven technology.

In desperation, Boese thought of creating a decorative ribbon by bonding lustrous threads to a nonwoven web. Using a dime-store comb and sewing machine bobbins, he put together a contraption to lay parallel fibers onto the web. Further tinkering and equipment upgrades led to a nicely finished product called the Sasheen decorative ribbon—and a quarter-million yards of sales in its first year.[3]

Sasheen Decorative Ribbon

New investments in web-making equipment in the 1950s spawned fresh products. Decorative ribbons eventually led to floppy disk liners and insulation tapes. Another prominent product family that emerged was Scotch-Brite materials, including the scrubbing pads that have become a familiar feature in most American households. Simon Fung, a Senior Research Specialist in the Nonwoven Technologies Center, tells the story of one more nonwoven product family called Melt Blown Webs:

At first they intended to make a bra cup out of Melt Blown Webs, and even obtained a patent, but it didn't work out. However, at that time surgeons were using fiberglass masks, and someone had the idea to turn the bra cup into a surgical mask! This idea really took off. Another attempted product application was to skim the fat off chicken soup, as the nonwoven fabric would pick up oil but not the other liquid. This concept didn't go very far either, but it led to a material that could be used to clean up oil spills.[4]

Dave Braun, a researcher in the Occupational Health and Safety area, recounts his own early role in this convoluted trail of innovation. One of his first breakthroughs was to redefine the product possibilities by redesigning the machine which formed the material.

I developed a way to make a wide web out of blown microfibers. Rather than simply forcing the material through the machine, I made the machine itself bounce back and forth, creating two sets of parallel fibers. They said it wouldn't work. . . . [but] I eventually sold my idea, got support, took it to the next level, and got more support. You just need a little money and a little support to nourish an idea through its earliest stages. The more original an idea, the more fragile it is. It needs breathing space. There's no precedent, no infrastructure.

Braun's wide web technology was put to use in making 3M respirators. His next invention was the Particle Loaded Web. He incorporated particles into the microfibers by holding them over his machine and letting them fall into the fibers. This technique fully activated the particles—a critical feature in allowing respirators to filter well. 3M's new respirators were thus very effective at filtering toxic fumes, even mercury. Braun and his colleagues then developed ways to put electricity into the fibers so they would attract dust like a magnet. Now the respirators worked six times better than before, and 3M could make them lighter and more comfortable to wear.[5]

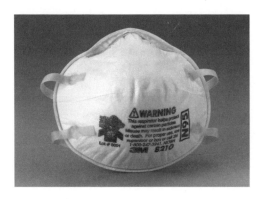

Respirator
Made from
Nonwoven
Material

3M's surgical masks, face masks, and respirators are still significant contributors to its medical and occupational health and safety businesses. With manufacturing or assembly facilities in seven countries, 3M provides respirators that meet government safety standards worldwide. The company supports the products by offering worker safety education to help customers meet local government requirements. Nonwoven fiber technology is mature enough that its development has actually been mapped out (see Appendix D)—not all of the thirty-odd 3M technology platforms have such a venerable history.

This partial history of 3M's nonwovens business provides glimpses of all three innovation types. Type A, the creation of a new market or industry, occurred when Al Boese finally found a practical use for his nonwoven fiber even though no customers were breaking down his door demanding Sasheen decorative ribbons. This proved to be only the first of myriad applications for his new technology: 3M has since been able to change the basis of competition numerous times in nonwoven product lines by applying a string of research breakthroughs to meet explicit customer needs (Type B). Dave Braun, for instance, accomplished this when he electrified the fibers in a respirator to make it more effective and easier to wear. Line extensions, Type C, occur every time 3M puts out a different configuration or color of floor cleaning pads, another nonwoven product, to meet customer needs.

These three innovation types can be applied to different kinds of customer relationships—existing customers, new applications with existing customers, and new customers—to produce a matrix of possibilities. The matrix, with a few 3M examples selected from among those mentioned thus far, looks like this:

Innovation and Customer Applications		*Existing Customer & Application*	*Existing Customer & New Application Areas*	*New Customers & Markets*
	Type A—New Business			• Sasheen Decorative Ribbons • Oil Sorbent Nonwovens
	Type B—Change the Basis of Competition		• Respirators with Improved Function • Respirators Plus User Training	
	Type C—Linear Extension	• Floor Cleaning Pads in New Configurations and Colors		

NOTE: This sort of matrix is used by 3M management personnel to consider the potential of a given technology and to develop marketing strategies. Of course, some applications overlap between different categories, and their status changes over time.

Solutions before Problems?

One striking characteristic of these innovation examples is that it seems just as common to have a solution in search of a real-world problem as an orderly succession from problem to solution. Al Boese produced his new nonwoven material long before he figured out how to make decorative ribbons with it—indeed, the ribbons were a desperate afterthought. In similar fashion, a later generation of nonwoven researchers was fooling around with skimming oil off chicken soup—a marginal problem, at best—before they applied their technological solution to the worthy purpose of cleaning up oil spills. (3M's oil sorbents proved their worth in the wake of the Exxon Valdez disaster in Alaska.)

At the same time, there are more conventional examples where 3Mers did identify a problem first and then created the solution. 3M's corporate advertising campaign—based on the motif of 1: NEED, 2: SOLUTION, 3M: INNOVATION—sometimes does reflect the true sequence of events. The improvements made in 3M's respirators and the user training were both initiated in response to customer input.

Solutions may come before problems because a researcher simply can't foresee the range of possible applications for a new technology. There is also some correlation between the sequence of solution/problem and different types of innovation. "This is a great technology with lots of interesting properties. What can we do with it?" is a pattern of thinking that is conducive to revolutionary breakthroughs, tapping into unarticulated customer needs (Type A). On the other hand, more predictable or immediately useful forms of innovation result from the mind-set, "Here is what our customer really wants. How can we meet that need?" (Types B or C).

The relationships among 3M's researchers, marketers, and salespeople are akin to a loosely choreographed courtship dance. It doesn't matter so much whether the solution arrives before the problem or vice versa, as long as they do link up somehow. Certain romances between solutions and problems turn out to be almost comical mismatches, but a different combination of partners can turn a failed romance into a blissful marriage—a solution and a problem that seemed destined to meet. The trick seems to be to ensure sufficient circulation among prospective partners so that failure can ultimately lead to success.

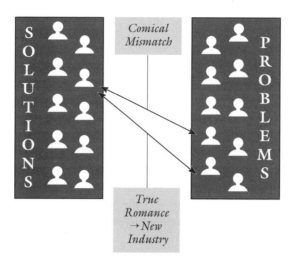

*The Solution/
Problem
Dating
Game*

Observation to Inspiration

In most innovation stories there is a critical juncture where a fresh connection is made—a nagging puzzle is suddenly seen in a new light. The pattern begins when a researcher has come to an impasse beyond which he or she cannot go without a leap into the unknown. After frontal attempts at a solution prove futile, the would-be innovator must settle down for a long siege, watching, waiting, and probing for some fortuitous opportunity.

Before spelling out what happens next, it is worth considering the chain of events that produced another 3M technology platform.

 ### Reinventing the Company: Microreplication

Microreplication, like nonwoven materials, is a core 3M technology. It had its start in the late 1950s when Roger Appledorn, who later became a renowned 3M corporate scientist, invented a new type of optical lens. 3M regarded overhead transparencies as a promising area for business development and sought to boost transparency sales by offering a lightweight, economical overhead projector for schools. Appledorn provided the solution, replacing the standard, heavy glass lens with a plastic lens that had microgrooves in its surface in order to focus light and increase brightness while decreasing overall weight. He had discovered that changing the surface characteristics of a material could dramatically alter its performance.

As 3M researchers further developed microreplication technology, they were able to produce some of the smallest and most precisely shaped structures ever made, with characteristics that are measured in nanometers. Such microstructured surfaces turned out to have physical, chemical, and optical properties with extremely useful applications. For example, 3M's Traffic Control Materials Division makes products which have the highest level of reflectivity on the market, thanks to their unique surface structures.

An outstanding recent application came about when 3M's microreplication scientists began to ponder a frequent complaint of laptop computer users: laptop batteries don't last long enough. According to Robert Finocchiaro, Technical Director of the 3M Microreplication Technology Center, "Most people think the solution is to increase the battery life. We said, use less battery power! How? By making the display use less power with a film that enhances the screen's brightness."

3M's team came up with Brightness Enhancement Film (BEF), made with a precisely calibrated surface structure that magnifies the brightness of backlit flat panel displays enough to extend battery time significantly. Two 3M scientists, Rick Dryer and Sandy Cobb, discovered the film. Dryer used to keep film samples in his pocket, and happened to be looking at his films while in the bathroom. He noticed how light was reflected at selected angles of incidence and transmitted at others, which led him to new insights about how a film with the proper structure could enhance the lighting of a laptop display.

The most exciting frontier for microreplication, however, lies in integration with other established 3M technologies. 3M's Trizact abrasives belts, introduced within the last few years, have revolutionized the industrial abrasives market, already a 3M stronghold. Once again, a couple of persistent 3M researchers sparked this transformation. Mike Mucci and Jon Pieper from the Abrasives Systems Division combined their skills in an attempt to develop a different type of abrasive: not the ordinary resin impregnated with alumina and attached to a paper backing, but a three-dimensional surface composed of microscopic pyramids with imbedded particles. Performance advantages would stem from the fact that microsurface ridges wear down more slowly and renew themselves with less build-up of detached particles and debris.

Magnified Microreplication Surface

Mucci and Pieper faced the usual obstacles of other job responsibilities and no formal project designation, so they drew upon the Fifteen Percent Rule (the 15 percent of work time in which 3M employees can pursue their own ideas). They borrowed equipment and expertise from 3M's Central Research Process Technology Laboratory, and later benefited from the award of two successive 3M Genesis Grants, which provide funds for personnel and equipment. They became notorious for the clamor they made with endless sanding trials on golf club heads and plumbing fixtures. The two of them also commandeered a retired manufacturing line elsewhere—partly at the urging of other 3Mers involved in producing precision optics materials who wanted a respite from the noise and dust of abrasives experiments. Access to this manufacturing line greatly accelerated their development process.

A presentation to the Microreplication Technology Center brought strong management support, the loan of master tools, and new team members who contributed technical and project management skills. Corporate designation as a high-priority program made fast-track development possible. Early product performance was disappointing, so more people joined the project, adding experience in areas such as light curing methods. Eventually, nine 3M laboratories contributed to the creation of Trizact abrasives belts, an astonishing display of internal cooperation and resource sharing. One project team member remarked that, when seeking extra expertise or equipment, "We never had to ask twice." The result of this collective effort was an abrasive belt with two to three times the life of traditional abrasives, capable of faster cut rates and more uniform finishes. One successful application has been in the manufacturing of jet turbine blades.

Today, another research and development focus in microreplication is semiconductor wafer polishing. Pilot results showed that 3M's new abrasives offer advantages in planarization of wafer surfaces and waste disposal. Initial trials produced flatter and more uniform wafer surfaces at much higher rates than conventional products.

The project's current manager calls these structured abrasives a "process revolution and a product revolution. . . . When we first started we didn't see the full scope of the product. There are still many applications that have not yet been thought of and many other market areas where we can change the basis of competition." Robert Finocchiaro is even more ambitious. He regularly brings specialists from a wide variety of other technical disciplines into his Microreplication Technology Center in the search for applications to different 3M technology areas. "I feel that we will reinvent every 3M product with microreplication," Finocchiaro says. "We can change the surface and make a difference."[6]

Five Openings to Innovation

In both the nonwoven materials and the microreplication stories, there are five distinct events, or "openings," by which the innovator moves from impasse to solution.

1. The most direct path is to build an incremental *bridge* beyond previous accomplishments: respirators made from nonwoven materials are improved by adding particles to absorb gases, or an electrical charge to capture dust.

2. A second route, which requires a broader intuitive leap, is the pattern of *association* which can link bra cups to respirators or chicken soup to oil sorbents.

3. Sometimes *stimulation* from an outside source is required to generate an unprecedented approach, such as bringing mechanical engineers into an optics meeting to explore new ideas for microreplication.

4. The answer to a seemingly insoluble puzzle may lie right in front of our noses and can be realized if only we allow a complete *reversal* of previous assumptions, turning our conceptual structures inside out. Rather than trying to build a better laptop battery like everyone else, why not enhance the illumination of the screen and enhance the efficiency of current battery power?

5. Finally, the *combination* of technologies may open up a whole new world of possibilities: contributions from nine different laboratories led to the revolutionary hybrid of industrial abrasives and microreplication technologies.

Five Innovation Openings

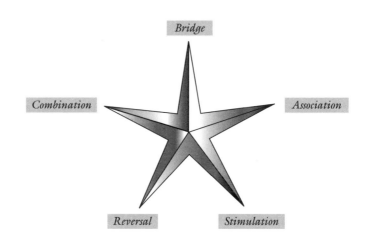

Levels of Innovation

Innovation can take place on many levels. Besides original technical innovation that is generated within a company, there is also the adaptation of knowledge from another source, as with the modifications Roger Appledorn made to existing technology to produce an overhead projector lens in plastic. Moreover, innovative approaches can be taken to organizational efforts as well as to dealings with customers, distributors, and regulators. 3M's development program for HFEs (hydrofluoroethers) provides an illustration of the tremendous momentum which derives from innovative efforts on all of these levels, often simultaneously.

A New Product Home Run: CFC Substitutes

When the depletion of the ozone layer became a major issue, legislation phasing out the use of CFCs (chlorofluorocarbons) led to the development of 3M's HFEs, which are designed to replace CFCs and other ozone-depleting substances. Richard Minday, lab manager of 3M Chemicals, describes the origins of this development project:

> 3M had been selling PFCs [perfluorinated chemical products] for many years into specialty electronic testing, cooling, and manufacturing applications. In the early nineties, the U.S. government ordered that CFCs be phased out by January 1996. PFCs were initially sold by 3M as CFC replacements in a number of areas, but there was environmental and regulatory concern with these replacement products as well due to their long atmospheric lifetimes. HFEs, therefore, were born out of desperation.

In late 1993, 3M formed a cross-functional team of chemists, engineers, and managers to develop a better CFC replacement. The pressure was intense, as many competitors were also investing in the same kind of project. This Phase I team first interviewed customers, influential industry figures, and regulators about the performance, safety, and environmental features they would want in a CFC replacement. Wayland Holloway, another team member, notes, "Instead of inventing a product first and finding a market for it later, we based our innovation entirely on customer needs."

The Phase I team then went to work feverishly to build a new molecule, synthesizing over one hundred compounds. They utilized a variety of time-compression techniques, developing testing methods that enabled them to gain a great deal of information from very small quantities of actual material. Predictive computer modeling was used to gauge key chemical properties that would affect the molecule's performance, safety, and environmental features.

In the summer of 1994, after less than a year at work, the team discovered the hydrofluoroether molecule. Its properties were exceptional: low toxicity, short atmospheric life, low global-warming potential, and superior performance at key applications such as cleaning and coating. Dr. Mario Molina of the Massachusetts Institute of Technology (MIT), one of the discoverers of the ozone layer hole and a Nobel Prize winner, determined the environmental reactivity of the molecule, which showed the HFEs to have outstanding environmental properties in comparison with other materials containing fluorine.

At this point, with the government's 1996 deadline drawing near, the project really began to gear up. A Phase II team of ten to twelve core people, plus some adjunct members, was put into place. The members included a process development expert, a patent representative, a synthetic chemist, engineers, and representatives from the manufacturing, regulatory, sales and marketing, technology service, and toxicology areas. A researcher from 3M's Japan subsidiary joined the team for what was to become a two-year stay, and European involvement was also solicited.

Everything was done in parallel. The Phase II team already had enough information to set about extensive testing, and it was reasonably certain, based on predictive toxicology modeling, that the test results would be positive. So some team members simultaneously began to work on patent applications, while another subgroup started on manufacturing process design. Several members addressed the product life cycle issue by setting in motion a recycling program either to re-purify used HFEs or to dispose of them in a nonhazardous way. The team also started a dialogue with the Environmental Protection Agency (EPA), describing its commercial intentions and potential product benefits. As one team member comments, "We made a proactive decision to treat the regulatory body as a key account and to work with them. . . . There is a tendency to think of regulations as uncontrollable external factors. Viewed differently, you can turn them into an opportunity."

At this stage, 3M recognized the HFE introduction program with Pacing Plus (see page 46) status and began to pour in more resources. Three additional teams, each headed by a member of the Phase II introduction team, were set up to investigate particular product applications for HFEs. (One potential application, for instance, was cleaning and drying precision parts in industries such as aerospace, computers, and electronics.) Eventually, more than forty 3Mers were involved in simultaneous efforts to develop, market, and provide technical support for the HFE product family.

All of the teams continued to seek customer input, with testing at customer sites helping both to develop specific applications and to pre-sell the product. Informational seminars were offered for distributors and their customers.

The HFEs were officially launched in May 1996 at the Precision Cleaning Show in Anaheim, California. They were quickly approved by the U.S. Environmental Protection Agency as well as regulatory bodies in Japan and Europe. Actually, 3M's HFEs have been the only CFC replacements to be approved by the EPA without restrictions, which counts as a ringing endorsement. 3M was invited to make a presentation on HFEs at an annual EPA Ozone Protection Conference, and the team that discovered this product family was given the "Heroes of Chemistry" award by the American Chemical Society in 1997.

The entire process, from the discovery of the molecule to product introduction, took only twenty-two months—lightning speed in an industry where the average time required to introduce a new chemical is four years. 3M's sense of urgency turned out to be justified: the company filed its patents just one month before a research company in Japan discovered the same molecule.

Today, 3M's HFE project continues to be a corporate priority; global sales are projected to exceed $100 million by the year 2000. The primary negatives that have emerged so far are that costs are too high for some applications, while the company simply can't make enough product to keep up with demand—not necessarily a bad problem to have. Substantial investments are being made to expand production capacity. Meanwhile, the search goes on for other applications. Efforts are under way, for example, to develop an application for HFEs in secondary loop cooling technology designed to replace traditional CFC-based refrigerants.[7]

■ ■ ■

3M's HFE teams did much more than invent a successful new technology. Team members also innovated at the organizational level, applying sophisticated project management and teamwork practices that turned out to be indispensable in patenting the technology and bringing the product to market ahead of the competition. Innovative thinking was applied to marketing through the simultaneous product testing and presales approaches undertaken with customers, and the seminars held for distributors. And an innovative partnering approach to government regulators helped to bring quick regulatory approval and positive publicity. Innovative activity on each of these levels arguably had a compounding effect, producing results more profound than any single action could have.

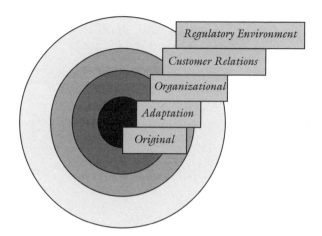

*Levels of
Innovation*

Regulatory Environment

Customer Relations

Organizational

Adaptation

Original

Unpredictability vs. Order

One organizational challenge posed by innovation efforts is achieving a balance between the unpredictability of basic research and the need for structure and discipline in bringing a new product to market. Anyone familiar with innovation knows how essential it is to move fluidly from the sometimes chaotic realm of creative discovery toward orderly implementation, and then back again. Both are essential: innovation is, by definition, new ideas + their implementation. But too much of either leads to dysfunction.

So as 3M's HFE project moved from Phase I to Phase II, the team makeup changed: research scientists skilled at ferreting out new molecules from a jumble of variables gradually ceded project control to people with skills in more predictable fields like manufacturing or patent protection. The beauty of the HFE effort, besides its commercial success, was the smooth handoff from discovery to implementation, with both processes carefully integrated and for a time running in parallel.

The mutual frustration of researchers and salespeople common to most industries stems from their working on polar ends of the same process. 3Mers enjoy recounting how Art Fry and Spence Silver, the discoverers of Post-it notes, received a discouraging response from the marketing people about the commercial prospects for their invention. They had to resort to guerrilla warfare—distributing free pads of

Post-it notes inside the company until the staff was hooked—so that the product's potential appeal was recognized. Marketing and salespeople may counter with sad tales of quixotic research ventures that never connected with real customer needs. The best examples of 3M's success stories involve researchers from corporate labs and Tech Centers who are speaking directly with customers, while marketers are on the lookout for unarticulated customer needs that may be served by still nascent technologies.

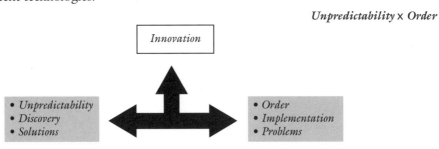

Unpredictability x *Order*

Innovation

- *Unpredictability*
- *Discovery*
- *Solutions*

- *Order*
- *Implementation*
- *Problems*

The Role of the Inventorpreneur

3Mers have adopted the word "inventorpreneur" to describe outstanding innovators. The term signifies that the inventor's work is not over after the act of discovery. Rather, that is when inventorpreneurs must embark on a long list of tasks to ensure the transition to implementation:

> An inventorpreneur is one who invents or creates a new product that fulfills a defined need; promotes the new opportunity or product; manages, organizes, and assumes many risks in establishing a new business based on that product.[8]

 From Exile to Innovation Ambassador: The Aldara Cream Story

Richard Miller, a manager in 3M's Pharmaceuticals Division lab, has discovered a new product line that represents a marked departure from 3M's more traditional businesses such as nonwoven materials. His discovery consists of a new class of therapeutic agents known as immune response modifiers; the first product of this class is called Aldara cream, a treatment for external genital and perianal warts. Whereas nonwovens technology has benefited over the years from many contributors (including Boese, Braun, and Fung), Miller is the unquestioned champion of a new technology which he invented and almost single-handedly kept alive.

Drug research is an inherently risky and expensive proposition, and Miller's superiors were initially doubtful about his technology's prospects. As Miller himself admits, "The success ratio is something like 10,000 to 1." Unimpressed by his early research findings, 3M officially terminated Miller's project and placed him on the unassigned list, the company's in-house version of temporary unemployment.

At this point it would have been easy simply to accept another project, but Miller had a stubborn streak a mile wide and more than a decade long. Invoking 3M's so-called Fifteen Percent Rule, he persisted in his research efforts. Understating the case considerably, Miller notes that he was "fairly consumed by the project, trying to keep it alive." He won official reinstatement for the program in 1983, but it was another ten long years before the project received Pacing Plus designation in 1993.

Today, Aldara cream has been approved for marketing in the United States and is awaiting review by regulatory agencies in other countries. It shows high commercial promise, and could eventually lead to a broader family of immune response modifiers with potential applications against keratosis, basal cell carcinoma, viral infections, and Hepatitis C. Sales for Aldara cream alone are projected to exceed $100 million annually within a few years. In acknowledgment of his belief in an idea and uncommon persistence, Miller was selected for the 3M Innovator Award and named the 3M Global Ambassador of Innovation for a year.[9]

■　■　■

Like Richard Miller, an inventorpreneur must not only have a good idea but also function as its chief cheerleader and salesperson. He or she must be able to seek out and persuade others to lend the resources necessary to take a project to the next stage. Even modest successes at this point make it necessary to obtain further resources, be it from colleagues who may be willing to offer their help or from managers who require tangible evidence that the investment will be worthwhile. Then the whole process of drumming up support begins again on a greater scale, while the inventorpreneur must sustain the technical momentum of the project and organize the resources won thus far. Risks increase with each step, as more people and money are on the line.

As a new technology area becomes too complex and logistically demanding for one individual to manage, a team of inventorpreneurs may be required. Successful programs tend to accumulate their own groundswell of volunteer momentum. Positive management signals such as Genesis Grants or Pacing Plus designation can help to turn this groundswell into a tidal wave.

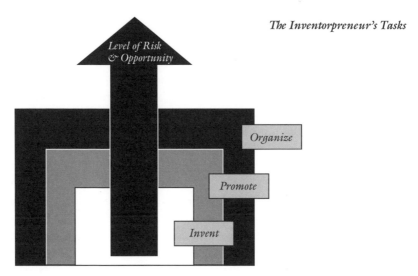

The Inventorpreneur's Tasks

Level of Risk & Opportunity

Organize

Promote

Invent

Managing Innovation

A number of 3M management practices that cut across diverse disciplines play a key role in keeping the innovation engine humming. A brief discussion of some influential practices follows; innovation management strategies are discussed more fully in chapter seven.

■ The Goldilocks Principle

Imagine yourself as a 3M manager. Chances are, especially if you are in a technical area, that you have a number of very bright people with advanced academic degrees working for you, many of them with years of solid service at 3M. Chances are that some of them are old friends. You have set goals for the group in line with the objectives of your boss and the corporate objectives. Progress is gradually being made toward achieving these objectives, there are several promising new product development projects in the works, and a few individuals are spending a lot of their time on projects about which you have your doubts. Everyone wants money and resources, while these are naturally in short supply. You have carefully listened to each person's presentation of his or her progress, and have carefully studied the available data on projected results—only to conclude that it is mostly guesswork. Now you have to place your bets, and your own future depends on the results.

If there is any single principle that 3M management will turn to whenever presented with this kind of dilemma, they will typically shoot right down the middle: not too hot, not too cold, but *just* right. 3Mers are constantly talking and debating with one another about balance—not about whether balance in itself is a good thing, for this is assumed, but how to strike the proper balance, particularly when you don't exactly know where you are going or how to get there. Long-term investments have to be balanced with short-term profits, invention with implementation, intuition with marketing data. And everyone shares the imperative to preserve 3M's "tradition of innovation," itself a paradox.

Different managers certainly have different perspectives, depending upon how close they are to the business side of 3M and how personally accountable they will be for this quarter's results. Their common craft, however, is to seek out the middle ground—finding, reconciling, and integrating opposites.[10] It is refreshing to see 3M managers who practice this craft deliberately and with considerable skill—who are trying hard not to overmanage their people. 3Mers who ask a manager to finance a good idea may find that he or she is surprisingly willing to offer support. But what comes next bears careful listening: "I can only give you a little bit of seed money; here are the names of a few other people you might want to go talk to; and by the way, there are a few things that I expect from you in return. Come back and let me know when you've made some progress. . . ."

■ Structured Serendipity

One sure bet for 3M managers who want to get the maximum out of their people is circulation. There are so many different ideas and technologies bubbling up in the company that bringing people together often generates unexpectedly positive results. In the days when the company was smaller, this was accomplished by the lab manager who reserved Friday afternoons as show-and-tell time, supplying the coffee and doughnuts.[11]

Now, with hundreds of 3M buildings and locations around the United States and the world, circulation is no longer so easy. Managers do their best to get people together through meetings, conferences, cross-functional teams, computer software, databases, and so forth. What is even more important, however, is to foster an environment where employees feel free to seek out the input of persons from completely different parts of the company, and where the individuals who are contacted are ready to share generously what they know. This, too, is best not overmanaged. Such contacts are most likely to succeed when there is just enough structure to enable them to occur on a voluntary basis—the challenge is how to create the right degree of structure for serendipitous encounters to occur.[12]

■ Stretch Goals

Stretch goals are a management tool used to foster innovation by setting out ambitious and quantifiable targets. There are only a handful of 3M corporate goals, several of them concerned with financial performance: earnings per share, return on capital, return on stockholder's equity. One other goal, however, is specifically targeted at "stretching" the pace of innovation: at least 30 percent of annual sales should come from products introduced in the last four years.

The company takes this target seriously. A few years back, the objective for new product sales as a percentage of revenues was stretched from 25 percent in five years to 30 percent in four years, and this new goal was met for the first time in 1997. But it is a goal that must be met again every year, and is applied to every part of 3M's business. This keeps up the pressure to innovate constantly. A recent refinement, intended to establish an even greater sense of urgency, is that 10 percent of sales should come from products that have been in the market for just one year.

3M has become increasingly aware that innovation is time sensitive. A study cited by Dr. Bill Coyne, senior vice president and head of Research and Development, suggests that overspending on a new product can turn out to be far less costly than a delay in its introduction. "It doesn't do us any good to have the best technology if we wait long enough for the next best to get good enough," Coyne says. He and his top management colleagues are now placing their own biggest bets on products that they expect will redefine industries and customer expectations, thereby leapfrogging the competition. And they are determined to move quickly: a new stretch goal is to halve the time it takes to bring products to market.[13]

■ Trial by Fire

Another standard managerial duty, which takes on a distinctive form at 3M, is to hold people's feet to the fire to produce results. It is easy to criticize management figures who tried to put an end to now-celebrated 3M products such as masking tape, Post-it notes, nonwoven technology, or immune response modifiers. According to some, however, there are still lots of pet projects around that should have been killed a long time ago.

There is actually a curious correspondence between the delivery of such "do-or-die" ultimatums and creative breakthroughs that lead to new product applications. While the researchers may not feel at the time that management is doing them a favor, the threat to terminate their work forces them to find innovative ways to move their ideas out of the laboratory and into the hands of paying customers.

L. D. DeSimone, the current CEO, tells the story of how he himself tried five times to terminate the development of Thinsulate material, a type of nonwoven insulation that is now used in jackets, gloves, and sleeping bags. It turned out that he had made an error of judgment, and that the material did have considerable business potential. But the obvious relish with which DeSimone describes his own blunders suggests that he was pleased to have been proved wrong, and that he was happier still to have pushed the supporters of Thinsulate's technology to the point where they had to prove him wrong or give up.

■ The Benevolent Blind Eye

3M managers must be a tolerant lot because even repeated attempts to get rid of apparently half-baked ideas can be met with stubborn noncompliance. Moreover, the company fully sanctions that stubbornness.

The meaning of 3M's famous Fifteen Percent Rule is not that everyone looks at their watches and calculates an hour and twelve minutes out of each eight-hour day to use for projects of their own making. In fact, the earliest form of the rule was simply the freedom for 3M lab employees to work on ideas outside of assigned projects at coffee breaks, lunch, and after hours. It turns out that some employees spend a lot more than 15 percent of their time bootlegging their own ideas, even when this is calculated on the basis of a twelve-hour day. Others find themselves too busy or contented with assigned projects to make more work for themselves.

Bill Coyne, the Research and Development head, confesses:

> The 15 percent part of the Fifteen Percent Rule is essentially meaningless. Some of our technical people use much more than 15 percent of their time on projects of their own choosing. Some use less than that; some use none at all. The number is not so important as the message, which is this: the system has some slack in it. If you have a good idea, and the commitment to squirrel away time to work on it, and the raw nerve to skirt your lab manager's expressed desires, then go for it.[14]

The real significance of 3M's Fifteen Percent Rule, then, is that employees have the *right* to spend some of their office time working on unassigned tasks; they are encouraged to do what they think is best for the company. And it is the obligation of 3M managers to turn a blind eye to this activity so long as other duties are performed adequately. They must remain patient, sometimes even when promised deadlines slip or a sure-fire idea turns out to be a loser, while the perpetrators optimistically move on to new projects.

Managers may go so far as to throw a protective blanket over their organization at a delicate stage in the development of a technology. They invoke a kind of group-based version of the Fifteen Percent Rule, actively protecting subordinates from the scrutiny of outsiders who have blunt, probing questions about expenditures, deadlines, market research, and projected business results. Some managers have even been known to assist employees with a promising idea not only by deliberately overlooking what is going on nearby, but also by quietly aiding and abetting a team's bootlegging efforts, helping them to find ways around the official project approval system and its rules. In fact, there is always some degree of covert R&D going on at 3M;

a savvy and respected manager can keep others from gaining access to low-profile projects that do not require a large financial investment.

■ Pacing Plus

With so many products and technologies, it is easy to spread resources around too thin and not achieve innovative breakthroughs of sufficient size or with enough speed to win in the marketplace. "Make a little, sell a little" and "a mile wide and six inches deep" are expressions that 3Mers use to describe their own failings in this area.

Pacing Programs were top management's first attempt to establish a priority system. But the tug of so many good ideas chasing after resources multiplied the number of such programs beyond the original intent. A second, more effective attempt at picking out and nourishing the most promising opportunities is the Pacing Plus designation. The roughly thirty Pacing Plus programs at 3M are defined as those which:

- Change the basis of competition in new or existing markets
- Offer large sales and profit potential, with attractive returns on investment
- Receive priority access to 3M resources
- Operate in an accelerated time frame
- Employ the best available product commercialization processes[15]

Pacing Plus is the most powerful management tool now used by 3M to support and reinforce an idea with strong potential. Several of the examples mentioned earlier in this chapter have received Pacing Plus designation. There are many other more modest tools in the manager's toolkit as well, such as internal grants and various forms of reward and recognition for innovators.

The Hero's Journey

It isn't easy to establish a unified vision for a company with fifty thousand products and thirty different technology families, including offerings in nearly every major industry. "Most innovative enterprise" and "preferred supplier" are general enough to fit everyone, but by themselves they would be empty abstractions. 3M's sparse vision statement is given substance by the shared belief of employees in a deep-rooted article of faith: the notion that one person who has a bright idea and who is willing to work hard enough to turn it into reality can make a difference.

3M's vision is revalidated from time to time with stirring new success stories. Company managers try to celebrate such triumphs with congratulations, even if it means acknowledging their own doubts and lack of support for the idea. A few such examples go a long way toward energizing ambitious innovators who are just stepping onto the inventorpreneurial path. It is a good thing for the company and the people in it to believe in a kind of hero's journey, in which the creator of a revolutionary idea persists through trials and disappointments to ultimately prevail. As one researcher puts it, "You assume that if you have a good idea, it has a home at 3M."

The actual circumstances in which innovation occurs are complex and varied: disappointments far outnumber triumphs, and time simply runs out on many dreams. Prominent recent successes like the HFE project, with its five cross-functional teams, time-compression techniques, and critical path computer software, seem to have outgrown the original myth of the individual innovator, even though they echo it in collective form. The creative Big Bang gets most of the glory, but it takes more people and more effort to steer an idea through to product release and full realization of its commercial potential—much innovative activity is still of the more mundane implementation or line extension variety.

It is appropriate to enshrine the rebellious spirit of 3M's corporate heroes because this is the hardest part of the "tradition of innovation" to preserve. 3Mers are not the nutty nanosecond warriors of Tom Peters' recent works who constantly revel in chaos and are ready to turn the world upside down. They tend to show up for work every day, carry out the fundamental responsibilities of their jobs, and stick around to work at 3M for an entire career. But then they have one or two projects going on the side which are pretty darn interesting. . . .

Something about being close to innovative activity gives people a gleam in their eye—the urge to innovate is a quintessential human characteristic. Certainly there are few greater pleasures than seeing one's ideas come to fruition. 3M is set up to make that happen. Even the people whose projects ultimately fail feel better for having tried, and it is good to be around people who are making the attempt. Geoff Nicholson, a member of 3M's prestigious Carlton Society and now head of Corporate Technical Planning, observes: "Innovative people . . . breathe spirit and life into everyone around them."[16]

	Discipline	Balance	Support & Reinforcement
3M Innovation Management: Sample Tools	Stretch Goals	The Goldilocks Principle	The Benevolent Blind Eye
	Trial by Fire	Structured Serendipity	Pacing Plus
			The Hero's Journey

Key Questions To Ask About Innovation

The Innovation Process

1. Does everyone in your organization know how to define innovation: new ideas + action that produces results?

2. Are you utilizing all three innovation types: A) Creating a New Market or Industry, B) Changing the Basis of Competition, and C) Line Extension?

3. Are you practicing the five innovation openings: bridge, association, stimulation, reversal, combination?

4. Is innovation occurring at all levels: original, adaptation, organizational, customer relations, regulatory environment?

5. Who are the inventorpreneurs in your workplace? How can you or your team do the work of an inventorpreneur or find ways to support such activities?

6. Do managers know how to balance support for innovation with healthy discipline—e.g., the "benevolent blind eye" along with "trial by fire"?

2

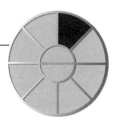

The Birth of Innovation at 3M

*Along with some outstanding successes, we've had some resound-
ing flops. . . . But even the flops are valuable in certain ways.
As someone once said: you can learn from success, but you have
to work at it; it's a lot easier to learn from a failure.*
—Lewis Lehr, former 3M CEO

3M's innovation processes and strategies have evolved from a distinctive corporate history and culture. It is worth a journey into the
past in order to appreciate both the company's approach to innovation
and what it can offer to other organizations. In contrast to the present
day's reliance on massive R&D investments, increasing technical spe-
cialization, and refined procedures for new product development, the
origins of 3M innovation lie in rather homely, frontier values such as
the stubborn refusal to quit, a respect for individual initiative, and a
willingness to learn from the most miserable of failures.[1]

3M's Early Days: Coping with Failure

Given the early history of the company, it is surprising that Minnesota Mining and Manufacturing survived its first years of existence at all. With only limited financial resources and the strength of
their own commitment to fuel them, 3Mers eventually succeeded in

transforming a pile of worthless rubble into a gold mine. They could hardly have imagined that their small Midwestern sandpaper operation, which could not afford to pay its president for his first eleven years in office, would grow into a global company with sales of more than $15 billion by 1998. 3M was such a marginal enterprise at the outset that only one of the founders, John Dwan, remained alive and invested long enough to make money off the venture. Perhaps the adversity 3M faced during those years helped to make it the innovative company that it is today, for it served to teach the employees then and now a valuable lesson: success can emerge from failure.

3M was founded on a mistake. In 1902, five businessmen contributed $5,000 apiece to purchase land which they believed to contain the mineral corundum, in Crystal Bay, Minnesota. At the time, corundum was considered an excellent natural abrasive and was used to make the grit on sandpaper. Since an increasing number of industries were requiring sandpaper in some phase of production, 3M's founders thought that they could make a business out of quarrying the corundum and then selling it to grinding-wheel manufacturers. Soon, however, they were to discover that the "corundum" in their mine was actually another mineral not even fit for abrasive work.

The Minnesota Mining and Manufacturing Company got off to a slow start. Mining did not begin until January of 1904. Shortly thereafter, the company made its first—and last—bulk sale of the mineral from the Crystal Bay mine. With misplaced confidence, 3M officers awarded themselves considerable salaries, but these had to be discontinued only months later as no further sales were made. By the end of that year, 3M stock was being traded for two shots of whiskey at local bars, and cheap whiskey at that.

Then, out of the blue, one of 3M's stockholders came to the rescue of the struggling company. Edgar Ober believed that rather than selling corundum to other abrasives companies, 3M itself should manufacture abrasives. He convinced a good friend and wealthy businessman, Lucius P. Ordway, to invest. In 1905, with the agreement of the founders, the two men from St. Paul purchased 60 percent of 3M's shares and took control of the company. Ober became president. That same year, they bought an old flour mill in Duluth and converted it into a sandpaper factory.

3M's struggles were not yet over, however. Even with the sandpaper manufacturing operations up and running, the company sank further and further into debt. Expenses far exceeded revenues. Worse yet, the managers confirmed that sandpaper could not be made from the "corundum" in the Crystal Bay mine. They were forced to purchase the cheapest abrasive material they could find, Spanish garnet, even though it made poor sandpaper. To make matters still worse, the general manager engaged competitors in an ongoing price war that destroyed all chances of turning a profit.

Edgar Ober

These early problems were compounded by old-fashioned bad luck. Even now, most 3Mers know the story of a particularly unfortunate event that occurred one day in 1910.

Construction of a new 3M plant in St. Paul had only just been completed. General manager Hull and sales manager Bush decided to take inventory before operations started. In order to keep an accurate count they piled the heavy bags of mineral for sandpaper production eight

Sandpaper Factory, Duluth

high in the center of the factory's first floor. That night the watchman quietly made his rounds, noticing nothing out of the ordinary. Suddenly, a tremendous noise emanated from the interior of the building. He jumped in alarm and ran inside to investigate. With wonder he gazed at a gaping hole in the floor: the first floor of the new factory had collapsed under the weight of the stacked bags, which now rested in the basement below. 3M's brand new factory had to be rebuilt before production had even begun. Fortunately, President Ober continued to work without salary and Lucius Ordway continued to invest tens of thousands of dollars in the failing operation. Then a young man by the name of William McKnight joined the company, and soon began to come into his own. Thanks to the dedication of these and other early 3M employees, business eventually improved.

In 1914, 3M began production of a synthetic abrasive named Three-M-ite. The product doubled company sales in just two years and served to establish 3M's reputation as a serious competitor in the sandpaper business. The new product enjoyed tremendous popularity with the growing automotive industry and was considered the best metal-working abrasive available. In fact, the Three-M-ite abrasives quickly became 3M's best-selling product.

So it was that 3M finally turned a profit. In 1916, after fourteen years of operation, management was able to pay its first dividend to shareholders.

The William McKnight Era: Quality and R&D

*More than any other person, Mr. McKnight was responsible
for 3M's early survival and growth. He instituted many of the
basic management policies which still guide the company and
will continue to do so for the foreseeable future.*
            —Harry Heltzer, former 3M CEO

*Long before the rest of the world was talking about policies like
empowerment and the importance of research and development,
quality, product diversity, and patent protection, Mr. McKnight
was making sure they were at the cornerstone of 3M.*
            —L. D. DeSimone, current 3M chairman
            of the board and CEO

William McKnight joined the young and struggling Minnesota
Mining and Manufacturing Company right out of school in
1907. His cost control, sales, quality, and human resources philosophies
would play a crucial role in growing 3M from an upstart sandpaper
manufacturer into a highly respected and profitable organization. The quiet,
thoughtful twenty-year-old came from a humble background. Born to a
South Dakota farming family, McKnight had to work his way through
school. He had not even completed his six-month course at Duluth
Business University when 3M hired him as assistant bookkeeper.

McKnight rose quickly to a position of leadership at 3M. He was made
the company's first cost accountant in 1909 thanks to his careful control
of company expenditures. Only two years after that, McKnight was promoted to Chicago sales branch office manager. At the age of just 28, he
was appointed general manager for sales and manufacturing by Ober.
McKnight was soon promoted again to vice president, then to president
of 3M. Notwithstanding his success, McKnight always remained humble
and dedicated to the company. It is reported that he said of himself, "I know
I am not any smarter than anyone else, but I think I put in a lot more time."

As a salesman, McKnight found that his customers constantly complained about the poor quality of 3M's sandpaper. When he asked repeatedly for the factory to improve the products, no one would respond. At
one point in 1914, customer complaints exploded: granules were falling
off the sandpaper at an unusually rapid rate. 3M manufacturing people
were frantic. No one could determine the cause of the disaster, until an
alert worker pointed out that the mineral left an oily film when soaked

in water. It was soon discovered that a shipment of 3M's Spanish garnet had become soaked with olive oil that had spilled in the cargo hold on the voyage across the Atlantic. The oily residue prevented the mineral from adhering to the paper. From that day on, the 3M factory was required to heat all incoming garnet in order to rid it of possible pollutants.

McKnight nevertheless felt strongly that this new heating method was not enough. It took years for 3M to reestablish its customer base and recover from the olive oil fiasco. He demanded that quality be improved in order to ensure the company's long-term success. In 1916, he invested $500 to create a one-room, one-man laboratory to research the manufacturing process and set quality standards. The lab conducted tests to ensure that raw materials, products at various stages of the manufacturing process, and the final sandpaper all met certain criteria. The establishment of this rudimentary quality lab led directly to 3M's ongoing focus on research and development. McKnight encouraged managers to put budget surpluses into cash reserves, product research, expansion, and patent protection, while paying only modest dividends to shareholders. This general mindset still guides 3M today.

3M Legend: McKnight's Obsession with Quality

After years of being required to sell an inferior product to his customers, McKnight became obsessed with quality. Once he was made general manager for sales and manufacturing, he took the concept of quality out to the workers on the factory floor. Upon completion, every batch of sandpaper had to be coded with a series of numbers and letters for inventory purposes. McKnight chose the letters C O M P L A I N T S to use in the code—a constant reminder to workers of the importance of high-quality products.

Shortly after McKnight established the first 3M quality control laboratory, he hired a scientist by the name of William Vievering to run it. One day, McKnight ordered Vievering, the lab's sole employee, to test every roll of sandpaper in the factory. There were over 1,100 rolls; Vievering tested every last one. "The shipping room was a shambles," he recounted later. "But we knew when I got through whether the stuff was good enough to send out, and that's what McKnight wanted to be absolutely sure of."[2]

In 1921, McKnight hired an engineer by the name of Richard P. Carlton to work in the quality lab. Carlton had the distinction of being the company's first technical employee with a college degree. He actually took a pay cut from $200 to $65 a month—the most McKnight could offer at the time—in order to join 3M. Carlton quickly shifted the lab from its trial-and-error style of research to a scientific method of testing products. He believed strongly that not just technical personnel but every individual in the company should understand the importance of research and development.

Carlton published a technical information manual in 1925 to encourage new product research. He wrote:

> No plant can rest on its laurels—it either develops and improves or loses ground. Every idea evolved should have a chance to prove its worth, and this is true for two reasons: 1) if it is good, we want it; 2) if it is not good, we will have purchased our insurance and peace of mind when we have proved it impractical. Our company has adopted the policy, "Research in Business Pays."[3]

Carlton's evangelism had a deep impact on the budding organization. In addition to developing many product improvements on his own, he was well known for his receptivity to almost any idea and his encouragement of creative thinking in others. In later years, when McKnight was elected chairman of the board, Carlton was to become 3M's president.

William
McKnight

In 1937, 3M management, led by McKnight and Carlton, determined that research was the single greatest factor contributing to the company's growth. So the company launched an expanded research program—directing more resources to divisional labs; establishing a new lab devoted to long-range scientific problems (the Central Research Laboratory); and, over the next few years, setting up a New Products Department to investigate new ideas and a Product Fabrication Lab to improve manufacturing methods.

Of course, management knew that not every idea would develop into a marketable product. Yet, they realized that the successes would more than pay for the failures. An estimate made by the company in the 1950s was that every dollar invested in research and product development since 1926 had returned $28 in gross sales. By maintaining supportive management policies that encouraged employees to explore their ideas, 3M generated one successful new product after another.

■ Curiosity and Innovation

William McKnight had an inquisitive streak that has been passed on to subsequent generations of 3Mers. In one case, his curiosity led to the creation of a key family of 3M products. McKnight was curious about a letter he had received from an ink manufacturer requesting samples of 3M sandpaper. "What about sandpaper could possibly interest the man?" he wondered. Rather than sending the samples without question, McKnight instructed a sales manager to contact the letter writer.

Francis G. Okie, it turned out, had invented a waterproof sandpaper after watching his neighbor, a glass worker, struggle with the dust generated during glass sanding. McKnight felt that the product had huge potential, and convinced Okie to sell his invention to 3M and join the company as a researcher.

Launched in 1920, 3M Wetordry sandpaper quickly became a best-selling product. It served automobile manufacturers' need for finishing the paint or varnish on cars, and improved health conditions for factory workers by reducing levels of dust. Sales reached new heights, vaulting 3M to the ranks of the world leaders in the abrasives industry.

Wetordry, an Early 3M Product

While 3M's encounter with Okie and his Wetordry paper may appear like pure luck, the fact is that it was a direct outcome of McKnight's curiosity and desire to generate new products. Several other abrasives manufacturers were presented with the same opportunity when Okie approached them for samples, but none of them bothered to ask "Why?"

■ Listening to Customers

When McKnight was made a salesman in Chicago, he had no sales experience. But he felt that the current sales method of meeting purchasers in factory front offices was a mistake. Instead, he insisted on getting into the back shops to speak with the men who actually used the products. He would demonstrate sandpaper to the workmen, find out what they needed, and report this back to the 3M factory. McKnight's tactic proved so effective that eventually all 3M salesmen were trained to take this approach. In fact, this strategy has led to many of 3M's product innovations throughout the years.

The invention of masking tape is one such story. The year was 1925. A young and inexperienced lab assistant by the name of Richard Drew had just stumbled across an innovative new product idea.

As a lab assistant, Drew made frequent trips to auto refinishing shops to test samples of 3M's new Wetordry sandpaper. On one of these visits he heard an auto refinisher launch into a long string of choice profanities. Drew observed how frustrated the man became while attempting to paint a two-tone finish on a car body. Nothing could keep the paints from running together without also destroying the paint covering the rest of the car. Watching the worker struggle, Drew came up with a solution: a tape that could mask the first area from the second.

In the spirit of innovation, the 3M management team authorized Drew to get to work on the new product and provided funds for his experiments. Drew began at once, testing all sorts of sticky substances for his new tape. After many trials, he created a product called 3M non-drying tape. The tape did prevent leakage; unfortunately, it was not flexible enough for auto workers to use on the curves of car bodies. While not fully satisfied with the quality, industry workers bought the product because nothing else was available.

McKnight, however, started to feel uncomfortable about producing such a low-quality product. "What will be the effects of such quality standards on 3M's reputation?" he wondered. Eventually, he pulled Drew off the masking tape project and reassigned him to his job as a lab assistant. While Drew obeyed, he did not give up thoughts of creating a better masking tape. On his way to pick up some sandpaper material for his boss one day, Drew noticed a roll of sandpaper backing that looked like the answer to his flexibility problem. He grabbed it and took it to the lab for some experiments.

Drew soon abandoned his lab assignment and went back to his experiments with masking tape. McKnight chose to turn a blind eye to Drew's activities. Within a short time, Drew had created an effective masking tape; sales took off and continued to grow steadily for the next decade. Drew's tape was not only innovative and popular but also represented 3M's first diversified product. This one invention led to the development of a whole division devoted to adhesive products, which have become one of 3M's core businesses.[4]

McKnight's Human Resources Philosophy

3M is people, and our opportunity to succeed depends upon the capabilities of our people.
—William L. McKnight

Many of William McKnight's practices and policies made a lasting impression on 3M. We have already noted his emphasis on research as well as on effective quality control methods and sales techniques. Beyond these, some of his most influential contributions—and perhaps those best appreciated inside of 3M—have been in the area of human resources. McKnight believed that, "The best and hardest work is done in the spirit of adventure and challenge."

At a time when such practices were hardly commonplace, 3M treated its work force well. Old age pensions and disability insurance were put into place. McKnight extended a profit-sharing program instituted by his predecessor, Edgar Ober, to include every 3M employee. Then, during the Great Depression, he made 3M one of the first American firms to implement company-sponsored unemployment insurance—this at a time when people stood in line for jobs at twenty-five cents an hour. McKnight once stated:

I think an aggressive, satisfied, keen, virile organization in this company is worth more to the stockholder than brick and mortar, and providing some measure of security in old age, is, in a way, ensuring such an organization.

McKnight practiced a hands-on management style. He was known to walk the factory floor, chatting with employees about projects they were working on. Employees felt comfortable approaching him, for he truly maintained an open-door policy. At one point, all of the senior 3M executives in St. Paul had lights on their office doors, which served as signals to their employees. A red light meant, "Don't come in," and a white light meant, "Come in." McKnight always left his light on white.

McKnight also believed in tolerance and delegation. A statement that he penned around 1948 expresses his views with clarity and brevity. It is the philosophy that many 3M managers still try to live by:

As our business grows, it becomes increasingly necessary to delegate responsibility and to encourage men and women to exercise their initiative. This requires considerable tolerance. These men and women to whom we delegate authority and responsibility, if they are good people, are going to want to do their jobs in their own way. These are characteristics we want, and people should be encouraged as long as their way conforms to our general pattern of operations.

Mistakes will be made, but if a person is essentially right, the mistakes he or she makes are not as serious, in the long run, as the mistakes management will make if it's dictatorial and undertakes to tell those under its authority exactly how they must do their job.

Management that is destructively critical when mistakes are made kills initiative, and it is essential that we have many people with initiative if we are to continue to grow.[5]

This has become the most quoted text in all of 3M. 3M employees also give McKnight credit for the Fifteen Percent Rule because he encouraged managers to allow employees time to work on projects of their own personal interest. This "rule" is as fundamental to 3M's corporate culture as any other HR policy or practice, and it is very much alive today. As recently as 1996, 3M created a new award, called the Innovator Award, to recognize employees for nondirected projects that result in the development of successful new products or technologies.

Unlike companies that change HR policies as management trends come and go, 3M's policies grow naturally out of its history, thanks primarily to William McKnight. The 3M Human Resources Principles can be traced back directly to the forward-thinking views and practices of this early 3M president that have long nourished employee innovation.

3M Human Resources Principles

The people of 3M are the company's most valuable resource. They are the primary means by which 3M goals and objectives will be attained. 3M management, therefore, believes that it is essential to provide an organizational structure and a work climate which will:

- **Respect the dignity and worth of individuals** by encouraging their highest level of performance in a fair, challenging, objective, and cooperative work environment. Individual rights are respected. Timely and open communication to and from employees is encouraged. Supervisors and managers are accountable for the performance and development of the employees assigned to them.

- **Encourage the initiative of each employee** by providing both direction and the freedom to work creatively. Risk-taking and innovation are requirements for growth. Both are to be encouraged and supported in an atmosphere of integrity and mutual respect.

- **Challenge individual capabilities** through proper placement, orientation, and development. Responsibility for development is shared by the employee, by supervisors and managers, and by the company.

- **Provide equal opportunity** for development and equitably reward good performance. Performance is evaluated against objective, job-related criteria and rewarded with appropriate recognition and compensation.

The Divisional Structure

In 1949, McKnight proposed an innovative change in 3M's organizational structure. A few years before, he had given the Detroit Adhesives and Coating Division near-autonomous status, with control of its own finances. When this experiment proved successful, McKnight determined that a decentralized structure would best serve the entire 3M organization. New divisions could easily be added and, he predicted correctly, "There would be no limit to how big we would grow." Each division was given a sales force, a research lab, and responsibility for its own profits. Eventually, the company grew so big that the efforts of its forty-plus divisions had to be coordinated by product or market groupings, but the basic structure McKnight implemented is still in place.

During the period of the reorganization, McKnight shared his management philosophy with the new division managers. Before any business guru used the term "empowerment," McKnight explained the clear benefits of creating an independent workforce by delegating responsibility and rewarding individual initiative. McKnight lived his management philosophy on a daily basis. As a colleague said of him, "He'd back you even when he thought you were wrong. Then you'd work all the harder to make your idea work."

One of McKnight's successors, Ray Herzog, who became CEO and chairman of the board, commented on the invigorating effect that the divisional system has had on 3M employees:

> When we break out these new businesses we appoint a new management team. We give people an opportunity to identify with a new business and become more important to 3M; and we find, almost without exception, that the new division begins growing at a faster rate. We also stimulate the established division to find other new products and markets which will help it meet our growth objectives.[7]

Open-Ended Research: Stumbling in Motion

We've made a lot of mistakes. And we've been very lucky at times. Some of our products are things you might say we've just stumbled on. But you can't stumble if you're not in motion.
—Richard Carlton, early laboratory manager
and 3M president

Over the course of several decades, 3M evolved its research and development program and human resources policies into a process of "stumbling in motion." 3Mers know that most product innovations are a result of a combination of things—hard work, new ideas, timing, and luck. They also know that the process usually involves innumerable disappointments and dead ends. Based on this hard-earned knowledge gained over the years, systems are in place to support constructive stumbling: management encourages employees to explore their ideas, failure is probed for the lessons it offers, and employees are constantly on the lookout for ways to match problems with solutions. Accordingly, opportunities are created that might otherwise have been missed. And in most success stories, along with all of these other factors, sheer persistence in the face of repeated failures continues to be a key ingredient.

■ Persistence Pays Off: Scotchlite Reflective Sheeting

The development of Scotchlite reflective sheeting for highway signs provides an excellent example of 3Mers' willingness to stumble forward while doggedly pursuing a goal. This particular technology paid off—but only after years of research time and many thousands of dollars invested. Scientists began working on the idea in 1937; not until 1949 did they create a profitable product.

The increase in automobile accidents throughout the 1920s and 1930s made auto safety a topic of widespread concern. During an Exchange Club luncheon in St. Paul in the summer of 1937, a highway official suggested to a 3M salesman that the company research how to make highway center striping more visible. The salesman felt that this would indeed make good business, and 3M management, realizing that no other company had yet entered the market, agreed.

An abrasives engineer decided to tackle the problem. He and his fellow lab workers developed their first version of the center striping by covering one side of a double-coated 3M Scotch tape with reflective glass beads; the other side of the tape would adhere to the pavement. The engineers eagerly tested the striping on a street in St. Paul, but when they returned to their test site after the harsh Minnesota winter they found the strips floating about haphazardly. Although it did an excellent job of reflecting light, the striping would not remain attached to the road.

Back to the lab the team went. A year later, the second batch of reflective center striping was ready, and company volunteers helped set the experimental pieces on a St. Paul highway. Once again, however, the striping came loose from the road after a few months of wear and tear.

At this point, many of the engineers wanted to abandon the project. Not only had their striping failed to pass road tests but high production costs made the product too expensive for highway departments. Richard Carlton, then vice president of 3M, would not give up. He suggested shifting the focus from highway center striping to reflective sheeting for road signs. Work began immediately and within a few months 3M had its first Scotchlite sheeting installed on Minnesota road signs.

Yet the project still could not be considered a success. Technically, the reflective sheeting was far from perfect, and it also proved difficult to sell. For the next eight years, the reflective sheeting department lost money. In spite of this lack of profitability, management continued to support its research. Various departments contributed their expertise: Central Research Labs developed high-quality glass beads, the roofing granules division increased the range of colors that could be produced, the abrasives division assisted with coating processes, and the adhesives lab provided knowledge about cementing the beads to the sheeting surface.

Finally, in 1949, twelve years after the research began, the labs made a technical breakthrough. Researchers discovered that coating the glass beads with a thin layer of transparent plastic greatly increased visibility. Sales finally took off as highway departments and state legislatures began recommending the use of 3M's reflective sheeting.[7]

■ The Golden Era of the Fifties: Scotchgard Products

The 1950s are considered the golden era of 3M research, a decade that saw the commercialization of reflective products, printing products, copy machines, fluorochemicals, electrical tapes, magnetic tape, and others. Moreover, a large percentage of innovations made over the next two decades grew directly out of those inventions. 3M earned an enviable reputation as an innovator. By the time it reached its fiftieth anniversary in 1952, 3M's annual sales were well over $100 million, and the company employed more than ten thousand people.

One of the best-known products developed during the 1950s research boom is Scotchgard fabric protector. It provides another example of a fortuitous invention that occurred only thanks to 3M's open-ended research environment. In fact, 3M scientists literally stumbled across the idea in their own labs.

In 1944, 3M had purchased a process for producing fluorochemical compounds from a Pennsylvania State University professor, Joseph Simons. Although there were no applications for the technology at the time, 3M scientists felt certain that the unusual inert materials created with the compounds could be developed into successful products. Over the next ten years, the researchers eagerly attempted to find uses for these fascinating fluorochemicals—but came up with only a few small, unremarkable product ideas.

Then, one day in 1953, a young research chemist named JoAn Mullin stumbled as she was carrying a sample of fluorochemical compound across the room, spilling several drops onto her tennis shoe. Annoyed at the accident, she struggled to clean the substance off her shoe, first with water and soap, then with alcohol and other solvents—but nothing would remove the compound. It occurred to Mullin that this problem had intriguing implications when considered in reverse: if the compound would not come off the shoe, perhaps it could be used as an oil- and water-repellent treatment. The problematic qualities of the compound could actually be made to protect the shoe.

Mullin reported this interesting phenomenon to her colleagues and spoke with her supervisor, but she found that only the supervisor took her seriously. He did some initial testing and shared the test samples with the head of the fluorochemical applications group, who in turn, largely thanks to Mullin's continued prodding, passed the samples on to a talented researcher who was looking for a new project. Mullin, in the meantime, was so discouraged with the lack of a positive response to her idea that she changed to another job within 3M.

But Mullin's idea remained alive. When further testing began to bear fruit, the company started a concerted drive to develop applications for fabric treatment. A year after Mullin's first observation, two other chemists, Patsy Sherman and Sam Smith, became involved. After many struggles these chemists finally succeeded in developing a commercial treatment for wool that had the right balance of properties: it repelled both oil and water, held up when washed, and was inexpensive to manufacture. In 1956, their product, Scotchgard fabric protector, was released onto the market. After four years of mediocre but life-sustaining sales primarily to the Australian wool market, more practical products were developed. Later, in the mid-1960s, Sherman and Smith produced a successful new line of repellents for the permanent-press materials then becoming popular. (This pair would eventually be inducted into 3M's Carlton Society, its most prestigious award for inventors.) The Scotchgard brand became a household name, and the technology 3M had purchased two decades earlier finally paid off.[8]

Today, the initial Scotchgard fabric protector has been expanded into a line with dozens of different products. Experiments with the fluorochemical compounds have continued, becoming the basis of many other key 3M products: Fluorinert liquids for heat transfer, Scotchban treatment for paper, and Light Water fire extinguishing agent, among others. The hydrofluorinated ethers (HFEs) referred to in chapter one as a promising replacement for ozone-damaging CFCs are another outgrowth of fluorochemistry. Dr. Craig Burton, research manager of the Fluorochemical Process and Technology Center, is confident that further innovations lie ahead. "We receive about thirty patents a year based on fluorochemical technology," he says, "and we're a long way from reaching the limits of this technology. Our biggest problem is choosing from all of the opportunities."[9]

■ Hit Product of the Eighties: Post-it Notes

A pivotal event linking 3M's past and present is the invention of Post-it notes. The story of how these detachable, self-sticking notes came into being in the latter part of the 1970s has attained legendary status well beyond company boundaries.

Art Fry, a 3M scientist, was getting frustrated every week at church choir practice. In order to mark the pages of the hymns the choir would be performing that Sunday, he inserted small pieces of paper into his hymnal. But whenever he opened his hymnal, the paper slipped to the floor and Fry lost his place in the book. "If only I could temporarily stick these papers to the page," he thought to himself.

Then an idea suddenly struck him. He remembered attending a presentation by one of his co-workers, Spence Silver, on an impermanent glue that the adhesives researcher had invented. Although Silver could find no uses for his glue and it was considered a failure because of its low adhesive properties, in typical 3M style he shared his discovery in the hope that it would provide the solution one of his colleagues was looking for. It did just that for Art Fry.

Fry worked on his own time to develop a prototype "temporary bookmark." Even with his sample product in hand, though, Fry's work was not over. Next he had to convince the marketing department that people would actually buy these pieces of paper that could be attached to a page and then just as easily removed. Thinking like a true "inventorpreneur," over time he broadened the product concept from bookmark to note paper, vastly enlarging its potential applications. Still, Fry recalls, the going was tough: "It was hard to sell the concept that people needed a notepad that would sell for a premium price compared to ordinary scratch paper."

Fry and his colleagues resorted to a form of guerrilla-warfare tactics, distributing prototype products to office personnel around the company, including administrative assistants who worked for key executives, thereby generating internal demand and repeat orders. Eventually Fry convinced the Commercial Office Supply Division to manufacture Post-it notes. They were released onto the market in 1980. One year later, Fry's invention was honored with 3M's Outstanding New Product Award. Today, Post-it notes are one of the five most popular office products in the United States, and are best sellers around the world.[10]

3M's Historical Values

Although there is no official list of values that derive from 3M's history, the events recounted above certainly embody a consistent group of themes. Scratch the surface of any 3M legend, and you will probably find a subset of the following values, all of which have shaped the company's approach to innovation[11]:

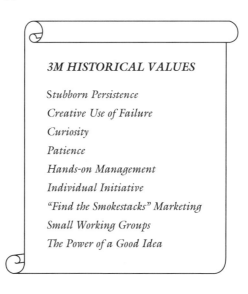

3M HISTORICAL VALUES

Stubborn Persistence

Creative Use of Failure

Curiosity

Patience

Hands-on Management

Individual Initiative

"Find the Smokestacks" Marketing

Small Working Groups

The Power of a Good Idea

Much of what 3Mers say and do may actually sound corny or trite to people well-versed in management theory. There is little in this list of values that has not been presented in scholarly tomes or in the business best sellers stacked on the shelves in airport bookstores. What is striking, however, for observers jaded by association with companies whose values seldom extend beyond plaques on the wall, is that 3M's values are for real. Certainly there are many points where the company and its employees fall short of their own ideals, and there is a constant struggle to keep their innovative heritage alive. But the enthusiasm in the place is still palpable to this day, and even the most hard-boiled onlooker must struggle to avoid being infected by it.

One can only speculate about the influence of a frontier heritage, long Minnesota winters, and the Midwest farming culture in forming values such as stubbornness, patience, and individual initiative. As was mentioned, McKnight himself was the son of a farming family who grew up in a rude log cabin. For decades the company has continued to seek out independent, can-do types in its recruiting practices. But regardless of the origins of such values, a long-term visitor will eventually begin to realize that they are, if anything, understated rather than overstated. When 3M leaders and publications say they want to create a company that employees are proud to be a part of, they are tapping into deep subterranean reservoirs of loyalty and mutual affection. These are priceless resources bestowed by the company's history, and they are its most vital current assets.

Key Questions To Ask About Innovation

Origins of Innovation

1. Does your organization have an oral history of stories that helps employees to learn about innovation?

2. In what way have key corporate leaders contributed to creating an innovative heritage?

3. Are there established corporate values that enable innovators to flourish: stubborn persistence, creative use of failure, curiosity, patience, individual initiative, and so on?

4. How deep do these values run and what sustains and renews them?

3

Forging Technical Innovation

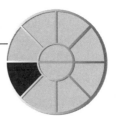

> It's a series of lateral developments. Offshoot and divide, off-
> shoot and divide, that's the thing. . . . We're not choosy. We'll
> make any damn thing we can make money on.
> —Richard Carlton, former 3M president

Each year 3M invests over a billion dollars, or 6.7 percent of its revenues, in research and development. 3M's research establishment employs some seven thousand people, five thousand of them in the United States. Most of these researchers are based in St. Paul, but there is also a significant technical contingent in Austin, Texas, where the electronics, electrical, and telecom businesses are housed. The other two thousand technical staff are located overseas. Sumitomo 3M's lab in Sagamihara, Japan, with a technical force of five hundred, is the largest overseas research site; Germany and the United Kingdom have the next largest research operations.

Technical innovation at 3M is focused on approximately thirty technology platforms (see Appendix C) that yield multiple products for multiple markets. The company's strategy is to build on these platforms while tying them together with a variety of linking systems.[1] Ron Baukol, 3M's head of International Operations, describes the company as an upside-down table with a hundred legs. Each of the legs represents a different business. The thirty technology platforms are the leaves of the table's surface. Three tapes are used to shrink-wrap the structure and hold it together: corporate vision and values, financial goals, and the human resources principles promoted by McKnight.[2]

In reality, 3M is not as static as this metaphor implies. The table legs are constantly growing as they might in an animated cartoon, and new legs appear periodically. Moreover, the legs tend to cross and mingle with one another, creating new businesses.

Several basic company rules stimulate this constant growth and movement. One is the requirement that 30 percent of sales come from products introduced in the last four years. All divisions understand that they must introduce new products to the marketplace on a regular basis. Another rule is that "products belong to divisions, but technologies belong to the company." In other words, while divisions must define products and generate sales, no division has proprietary rights over any technology. All technologies are to be shared freely throughout the organization. The Fifteen Percent Rule is also invoked to justify networking time among researchers, a key ingredient in the innovation process that is often overlooked by commentators.

Up to the mid-nineties it was possible to draw an orderly, if somewhat inaccurate, chart of 3M's research structure. It had three levels corresponding with the three distinct innovation types discussed in chapter one. Division laboratories interfaced closely with customers and developed products to meet current needs. Sector labs cultivated particular technology segments in the three- to ten-year time frame. Central Research, for its part, was devoted to long-term technology development.[3]

3M's Former Research Paradigm

Laboratories	Primary Activities	Time Frame	Innovation Type
Division laboratories	Product development Product control Technical service	Today's business 0–3 years	Line extension
Sector laboratories	Sector technology development	3–10 years	Changing the basis of competition
Central research	New technology development	10+ years	New industries

3M recently revamped the previous structure to create clearer lines of responsibility for growing the company's technology platforms. Tech Centers replaced sector labs and incorporated some functions of the Central Research Labs. Each Tech Center is responsible for preserving and developing one or more technology platforms while also looking for new product applications. 3M's research management has become wary of slipping into the mind-set that business divisions are solely in charge of customer contacts and concrete product development, while nondivisional laboratory people engage in purer forms of research. As Dr. Bill Coyne, head of 3M Research and Development, suggests:

> Technology Centers are developing new products themselves. Divisional labs shouldn't stand between the Tech Center and the customer. And all of the labs are available to everyone. A divisional GM has access to the whole company. Long-range research may have what you need to sponsor a short-range development project.[4]

This organizational redesign is another means to promote constant innovation, discouraging any division from becoming too comfortable with its current product mix, or any researcher from tinkering endlessly with an interesting technology without considering relevant applications. Both ways of thinking do still exist: one corporate lab denizen opined, "3M is trying to turn this technology into money, making new enterprises. . . . I'm corporate R&D, so I have little to do with that." But 3M's labs are ideally viewed as a fluid rather than a solid structure, serving as the oil and the spark in the company's innovation engine—circulating, lubricating, or igniting instead of taking up a fixed position. Thus, Tech Centers are now free to circumvent a stodgy division in order to create a new business, according to Robert Finocchiaro, technical director of the 3M Microreplication Technology Center:

> Ten years ago, the Tech Center's view of the world was completely through the Business Units. We're finding now that our people in the Tech Center should be talking to end-user customers. We ask better questions than field salespeople do. We can serve customer needs better. We're working in the white spaces now, the spaces between existing divisions, which leads to the development of new Business Units. . . . Our field of view is enhanced by customer

contact. We're going back to McKnight's "find the smokestacks" mentality, the roots of 3M.[5]

Another way to envision 3M's research and development complex is as an organic molecular structure, a structure that is less tidy but closer to how the labs interface with one another and with customers.

3M Research & Development:
An Organic Molecular Structure

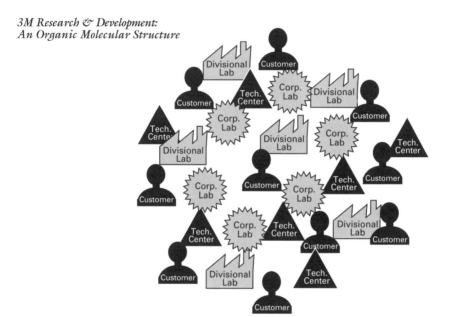

Developing a Technical Community

3M puts a great deal of effort into sustaining the "innovative climate" formed over the course of the company's history, a fact often overlooked by one-day benchmarking visitors. One of the unofficial guardians of that climate has been Roger Appledorn, the distinguished corporate scientist who originated the microreplication technology platform and has thirty-one patents to his name. He cites three vital factors in fostering innovation: culture, communication, and style. Because 3Mers are ushered into this corporate climate by yarns spun and embellished by more senior employees,[6] it is instructive to consider the narration that Appledorn himself has prepared for new members of the company in the United States and abroad.

■ A Classic Tale of Innovation at 3M: Roger Appledorn

The reason I started working at 3M was my need to finance my education. I quickly discovered that 3M was no ordinary company. On the one hand, I never felt out of place or unwelcome. On the other hand, I seemed to be surrounded by numerous heroes. Everyone talked about the accomplishments of people like Dick Drew, the inventor of Scotch tape, George Swenson, the inventor of colored ceramic-coated roofing granules, Bill Lundquist, the inventor of acrylic adhesives, Carl Miller, the inventor of thermographic office copying, and so on.

There was an air of excitement everywhere. Stories were regularly told and shared by all employees about how, in each case, these people made discoveries and worked to build the businesses that were making 3M great. There was a general feeling that anyone had the freedom to do it regardless of who you were, where you worked, or the type of education you had. If you had a good idea or made a new discovery, you too could create a new business within 3M and grow with its successes.

One of my first supervisors and mentors was Emil Grieshaber in the brand new Thermofax Department laboratory. He had a Ph.D. in organic chemistry. One of the first things I learned was—never call him "Doctor!" The second was that he was an extremely hard taskmaster. If you weren't working hard you had better look like it. . . . Although he was extremely tolerant of my irregular hours since I was still attending college, there just weren't any excuses for being tardy or late.

We all had our projects and progress was expected. But if any of us came up with an unrelated idea he would permit us to work on it on our own time. This meant coffee breaks, lunch, after hours, et cetera. Later, this approach became known as the Fifteen Percent Rule. In addition, he reserved Friday afternoons as "Show and Tell" time. He would supply the coffee and doughnuts. For the rest of the afternoon each of us would have the opportunity to talk about our personal project, ideas, or new discoveries. It wasn't long before we discovered that we better do a little homework, for he and the others attending the meeting were sure to ask questions ranging from technical issues to customer needs and market potential.

Our primary research directive at the time was to find a way of improving a thermographic imaging process. 3M was in the throes of pioneering the office duplicating market and had developed the "Thermofax" desktop copier, which was creating the office copying market.

The process relied upon infrared energy to "see" the original and produce the copy. However, the infrared process could not reproduce colored originals or images. Only black infrared inks could be copied.

In the attempt to solve this problem, a process utilizing a transparent intermediate copy had been developed. In looking for new applications for this unique transparent copy, we attempted to project it on a screen using a "view-graph." However, we found the projected image rather poor due to the translucent nature of the infrared-sensitive coating and its light brown color.

While attempting to improve the clarity of the copy film, I chanced upon a new thermographic imaging technology. It was based upon a physical process where the surface of the clear transparent film became highly disrupted and diffuse when heated in the image areas. The disrupted areas appeared white, but when projected the image was jet black against a very clear white background.

Soon after this event, a man in a business suit showed up in the laboratory looking for me and asking for a demonstration. It was our corporate president, A. G. Bush! Somehow he had heard about my discovery and had taken time out of his busy schedule to come all the way over to our lab to see it. There are no words that describe the impact this simple act on his part had on me and on my life.

The Show and Tell group and my supervisor, Emil, thought there must be a market for these transparency films, so we took the proposed product to our marketing and sales people. To our surprise, they didn't think there would be much of a market for it and turned us down.

Undaunted, we made our own sales calls. One evening, on the way home from work, we stopped to see Emma Storstein, the audiovisual director for the North St. Paul public schools. She was so impressed with the demo that she bought our entire supply of transparency film! The next morning, with an order in hand, we proudly met with our sales and marketing group. This was enough to get them thinking that maybe we had something after all.

Things went well for a while, but it wasn't long before it was made clear that to be successful we would need to sell the projector as well. After all, very few people even knew what a "view-graph" was. To solve this problem we contracted with an outside firm to produce our first overhead projector, known as the Model 42.

For the first time we had a total system to sell that included the "Transparency Maker," the "Overhead Projector," and the "Transparency

Films." Sales were starting to be noticed by management and people were being assigned by marketing to concentrate on selling the system.

One day, one of the local salesmen called me and invited me to make a few sales calls with him. What an opportunity! I couldn't wait! All day we made sales calls. My task was to carry the projector for him and assist in the demonstrations. This was quite a task, for the projector weighed over 60 pounds and was in a case that was about 3 feet tall, 1.5 feet wide, and 2.5 feet long. Worse yet, every call we made seemed to be on the third or fourth floor and there was never an elevator to be found. Needless to say, I got the message. It was a neat product, but if we were really going to sell it, it just had to be made lighter, smaller, and much less expensive.

During this period we were developing a vision. We could envision this system replacing the blackboard, not only in schools, but everywhere presentations needed to be made. It really was a better way of presenting information and teaching—and we just knew it. We were convinced that we were going to "revolutionize the education process by developing the overhead projector system" (this became our vision statement), as well as make a major contribution to society.

Marketing wasn't convinced, however. They conducted a market study that showed that even if we were successful in developing the new projector, the size of the market wasn't significant. Further, they concluded that what people wanted was a better blackboard, not a projector using those flimsy Thermofax transparencies. They recommended that the project be shelved.

Fortunately, our new manager, Bert Auger, wasn't convinced by marketing and decided to proceed with the development of a smaller, lighter weight portable projector. To make sure we were on the right track, input regarding the "wanted" design features was solicited from our salespeople. They seemed to want every whip, whistle, and balloon you could think of. We were somewhat dismayed, for our vision was a projector in every classroom, and the schools didn't need all these whips, whistles, balloons, and the added cost.

However, we proceeded with the design and development program anyway, and in September of 1961 a prototype was demonstrated. Nearly all of the design objectives had been met, but when the very high estimated manufacturing costs were reviewed, the division operating committee ordered that the project be shelved—again! This time Bert agreed with them.

Later that day, a rather lively discussion followed with Bert. We continued the argument that what was really needed was a small, light-weight, low-cost projector that would project a good image on the screen and that was all. The customer didn't need or want all the frills the sales and marketing people had asked for.

Bert listened and gave us some additional time to make our case. It wasn't much—only thirty days—but it gave us the time we needed. By November 1 we had a conceptual model designed and prototyped based upon a new "integrated optical design" concept that could drastically reduce costs. It didn't function, but it was enough to buy us some more time. The new date was now January 15, 1962, when we were scheduled to show that it really would work.

Having a working model by the January 15 was the first very ambitious goal. We had only two and one-half months, minus Thanksgiving, Christmas, and New Year. In addition, the key optical components had never been produced before and the technology was totally new to us. One of the key elements to be developed was a new-to-the-world Frensel Lens, for which tooling had to be precision machined.

On January 15, 1962, we presented a "sort-of-working" model to the division operating committee. To our surprise, the good news was that we were given the go-ahead. The bad news was that we had to be in production by August 12 so as to coincide with the national dealer meeting in Florida, where it was planned that we would demonstrate the projector and take orders. If we missed, we would have to wait an entire year before the next dealer meeting could be held.

This was our second and very ambitious schedule, to say the least. But our budget was approved and I started the process to hire the mechanical design people we needed. However, I ran smack-dab into a company hiring freeze and was informed that I couldn't hire anyone!

Lamenting over this dilemma with our purchasing agent, Dick Hewitt, we concluded that what we really needed was the design prints and specifications, and not people. So, why not go outside of the company and have an engineering firm produce these prints and specifications for us? To do this all we needed was a materials purchase requisition to buy the design prints. After all, no freeze had been placed upon purchase requisitions.

This really worked well, but it wasn't long before we tired of driving back and forth between 3M in St. Paul and the engineering firms in Minneapolis. So, we invited the designers to come to 3M, where we gave them temporary passes, a desk, and the necessary equipment, and located them in one of our conference rooms. Before long, we had some fifteen people working with us without a single employment requisition.

(As a side note, we continued to use this technique for some years before I got caught. When it was discovered what we were doing it caused quite a stir, and I was asked to explain my actions to the corporate vice president of research and development, Bob Adams. After listening to a rather lengthy lecture about how I had broken all the rules and policies, I asked if I should have done anything differently. He said, "No, just don't get caught.")

This took care of the design requirements, but we were still short of people to tackle the technical problems that needed to be resolved. One of the great things about 3M is the many ways networking, communication, and interdepartmental assistance are encouraged and established. Through the contacts we had previously established it wasn't long before we had volunteers to provide the technical assistance we needed. In return, we went out of our way to let them share in the vision and ensure that they considered themselves to be one of the team's members. I have lost track of all the pizzas, doughnuts, and pots of coffee I bought in an attempt to reward them for their efforts and contributions.

Somehow, we made it. We finished the design and started production on time. The dealer show in Florida was a hit and we were off and running. The 3M Model 66 Overhead Projector was also a hit in the marketplace, and for a while it was all we could do to keep up with the orders.

But sales suddenly and unexpectedly slowed down, and the whole project was under question again. The problem was that although we had met the goals we had set for ourselves, the prime market we were targeting (schools) didn't have the money and, what's more, the teachers didn't want it. They were stuck in their old ways of teaching and had no desire to change. Yet we were convinced that although they didn't know it, they needed the product and that it would be a benefit to education.

We concluded that it was unlikely that the current educators could be convinced, but what about the students in the teacher colleges? It was here where the new teachers were being trained, and if they could also learn the benefits of the overhead projector, they would carry that knowledge with them when they entered the teaching profession.

However, after a few attempts of trying to sell the colleges on the concept and the products, we found similar resistance and discovered that they didn't have any money either. By this time we had made department status and had been assigned a full-time accountant. In discussing the problem with him, Bert, who was now our department manager, stated, "The only way we are going to get teachers to use overhead projectors is by giving them away." Frank, our accountant, said, "Why not?" He pointed out that it would be considered a charitable donation, the government would allow 3M to take a tax deduction for the value of the projector, and with the additional sales of accessory items and transparency films, we would actually make money. (Who says there aren't innovative accountants?!) We couldn't wait to start giving our overhead projectors away.

The plan was put into action as a part of a program we titled "Assistance Grant to Education," or AGE. To receive a grant of these projectors, the college was required to submit a plan as to how the product would be effectively used in the classroom. A panel of non-3M judges reviewed the proposals and selected those they felt were worthy of the gift.

The program was so successful that subsequent programs titled AGE-II and AGE-III, mainly directed toward primary and secondary schools, were run also. After AGE-III the government determined that this really wasn't fair, and required that only the "actual cost" of the product to 3M could be used as the tax deduction. However, by this time the market had been established, a whole new business had been created for 3M, and we had seen our vision become a reality.[7]

Radical Innovation: Key Elements

Appledorn's tale holds key elements of 3M's most radical innovation practices—those that lead to the creation of new markets and/or industries (Type A innovation as outlined in chapter one). A chance invention occurs and alert researchers sense its potential. A dedicated group forms that finds it has to sidestep other parts of the company and make the first sales themselves. When organizational roadblocks get in the way, the product development group bootlegs outside resources while luring internal volunteers to the team (with pizza and doughnuts). Management tells them to shelve the project, and customers not only decline to articulate their needs but say they don't want the product. Undeterred, the team bargains for more time, sets out to educate buyers (in this case, new teachers), and persuades them to submit plans for effective use of the product. Technological innovation is complemented by a critical piece of innovative accounting. The whole effort is fueled by incredible perseverance and the refusal to take no for an answer.

So, successful innovation is likely to require far more than a single act or process. Here is a diagram of the interlocking chain of innovative actions that led to the creation of a new market in overhead projectors, transparency films, and accessories, one which is still a healthy business for 3M today.

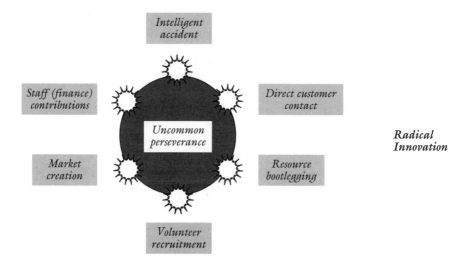

Innovation Management

Roger Appledorn himself draws some conclusions regarding what is required to manage technical innovation successfully. ORGANIZATIONAL CULTURE, the first of the three factors that he lists, has the following characteristics:

- **Heroes** "We had heroes who made it evident that it was possible to be successful in promoting new ideas and starting new businesses and that, if you did, there would be recognition and reward."

- **Freedom** "We not only had the freedom to express our ideas, but it was encouraged and supported."

- **Excitement and anticipation** "There was also excitement and an air of anticipation about what we were doing."

- **Never give up** "When management said no to an idea or program we felt that what they were really saying was: 'In its present form, we cannot accept it. Go back and see if you can't find a way to make it acceptable!' "

- **Value in failure** "If a project turned out to be unsuccessful, there were no recriminations and it was recognized that there was value in failure."

- **Fun** "We really enjoyed the challenge, the long hours, working weekends and holidays. We knew we were really doing something important and valuable. Maybe another reason was the parties we would have at the end of a successful program where everyone was involved from top management down to the technician."

A second set of innovation management skills focuses on COMMUNICATION:

- **Mentoring** "No one said that Emil Grieshaber would be my mentor. He just did it, teaching and guiding me through one-on-one communication, as did so many others at 3M."

- **Clear vision** "It was Emil who saw to it that we had a clear vision that was shared by all."

- **Ambitious goals** "These were always being set. If I felt the goals were too ambitious or wouldn't work, Emil would say, 'I'll bet you a cup of coffee!' (I still can't figure out why I would work so hard for just a cup of coffee.)"

- **Planning** "Setting ambitious goals forced us to do a good job of planning."

- **Opening doors** "Emil and Bert were always opening doors for us."

- **Interface with customers** "They gave us opportunities to interface with customers as well as our own management."

- **Rewards** "There were little rewards like management showing up with a few treats. . . . There were also big rewards, on occasion, like unexpectedly being recognized by one of the formal corporate recognition programs. And finally there was the reward of having your career grow with your program."

Thirdly, there is the elusive but crucial area of MANAGEMENT STYLE:

- **Personal involvement** "You never knew when any of the management team would show up to see what you had accomplished. And it was done regularly."

- **Being a servant** "Frequently, when we were working late, Bert and Emil would show up with a bag full of White Castle hamburgers or a bag full of doughnuts and the next thing I knew they were helping me get my job done! They became my servant or technician."

- **Eliminating barriers** "On many occasions they would help overcome or eliminate barriers that were in our way, like hiring freezes, budget constraints, and so on."

- **Breaking the rules** "On occasion they let us break the rules, knowing it was the right thing to do."

- **Trust and credibility** "We knew we had their trust and we could feel the faith they had in us. When things weren't going well they would make sure we knew what it was and why. For example, when it was recommended that our project be stopped, they maintained a high level of credibility not only by keeping us informed but by involving us in formulating an alternative or solution."

- **Risk-taking** "They knew that we were stretching ourselves technically and time wise. But they supported us and shared the risk."

- **Being a champion** "Champions were all around us and they ensured that we received credit and recognition for our accomplishments."

- **Taking time, giving credit** "Even our president would take time to follow our progress, encourage us, and ensure we received credit and rewards."

- **Empowerment** "The managers were empowered to make constructive decisions. For example, even when the operating committee recommended that the project be shelved, Bert was empowered to give us more time to find a better alternative."

Technical Innovation: Current Examples

Innovation at 3M retains many of the elements present in Appledorn's tale from the 1960s. Indeed, his own distinguished career of more than forty years, which came to an end with his retirement in 1997, has done much to set the pattern for 3M's innovation practices. But along with this continuity there have also been some gradual but very important changes. 3M has grown, and inventorpreneurs have more and better resources at their disposal, but the company vessel is harder to steer in new directions.

■ A New Tape

A Golden Step Award was presented to the creators of Scotch satin tape. This honor goes to product development teams that create profitable new businesses with sales in excess of $10 million during the first year, an impressive feat in any field. Just as with the overhead projector, the new tape was invented because of an inquisitive, alert response to a chance observation.

Pat Hager, a polymer science researcher who works in the Division Lab for office supplies, had long been aware that 3M's old stand-by, Scotch Magic tape, shows up on gift-wrap, slightly marring the appearance of an otherwise perfect package. While working on a project to create an opaque film, Hager happened to use that film to tape a roll of gift wrap together. When he went back to remove the film it took a long time to find it. "I looked closely and thought, 'This could be something,' " Hager remembers.

Soon Hager and his colleagues were working on Scotch satin tape, a new brand of tape that would be virtually invisible on the surface of a gift package. The team had not only to overcome initial opposition of the kind that Appledorn had experienced but also to redirect the sheer momentum of a long-established business. It would have been easy to treat the Scotch tape business as a fat cash cow and look elsewhere for innovation. "There was extreme sensitivity to the idea of a new Scotch tape, because it's such a 3M icon," Hager says. "We needed to convince marketing that we weren't out to destroy it, that it wouldn't cannibalize sales or move consumers out of their comfort zones."

Hager's idea began to take hold after he was paired with Amy Krohn, a senior product engineer with strong team management skills and determination: "We had to push it through," he acknowledges.

Satin tape subsequently became part of an overall film and tape program with Pacing Plus status, which helped the team convince others to invest their time and resources. As the project gathered steam, interest grew and volunteers appeared. Says Hager: "We attracted people not because they were assigned but because they wanted to join. This was something new and different instead of doing similar work for so long. We had fun together."

Hager and Krohn's team was animated by the same excitement and anticipation that Appledorn had felt. Yet they had access to far greater resources than those available to develop the overhead projector. The team was able to draw on the technical resources of colleagues across the company, including a manufacturing plant, engineering designs, and testing support. All this was in addition to the assistance lent by the Film and Light Management Technology Center. The technology arising from the development of Scotch satin tape has spurred continued research in the areas of embossing and optical property management. Hager notes that combining the technology that has emerged in this area with computer imaging "allows you to take my picture, scan it into the computer, and then emboss my face on rolls of tape. . . . This is a whole new world. There are all sorts of ideas between tape and film."[8]

In short, there are now tradeoffs that go beyond Appledorn's earlier days, opening up both opportunities and hazards. Compensating for the stodginess of a hugely successful business are vast technical resources that can propel a new invention into another dimension. Corporate programs such as Pacing Plus help to counter organizational inertia by providing funding and people, yet they have to be carefully meshed with 3M's distinctive heritage of grassroots volunteerism.

■ A Graphic Solution

If you've seen a bus with a forty-foot-long image of a Subway sandwich or a Burger King truck with its sides illuminated by a brightly flaming grill, chances are you've seen 3M's Scotchprint graphics at work. Sales and marketing may have created impediments to Appledorn and his early co-developers, but with Scotchprint the fields of technical research and marketing innovation merge. It took a marketing mind to recognize the potential for advertising on the sides of buses and trucks, and to see how hotels, restaurants, and shops might project an eye-catching image to consumers. It took technical expertise to develop the product that could realize that potential.

Commercial graphics customers want a full range of color options; materials that can withstand both indoor and outdoor conditions; flexibility in size and materials; and the freedom to input and modify their own creative designs and then produce images quickly and inexpensively. Joe Ward, lab manager for Digital Imaging in 3M's Commercial Graphics division, provided the technical solution. His team came up with the Scotchprint electronic graphic system. Different versions of the system exist, but each has a high-resolution color scanner, a host computer that permits the easy manipulation of images, and an electrostatic printer that can handle a variety of materials and sizes. The printers are impressive, with the largest able to accept rolls of film up to fifty-four inches wide and produce full-coverage graphics for a semi-trailer in about twelve minutes, or four hundred wall posters in an hour. An image can be scanned in or imported on disk, modified, and printed out more quickly and cheaply than by traditional printing methods.

Like the overhead projector business begun by Appledorn and his colleagues, Ward's business offers a system with all of the essential components. It is even better than selling overhead projectors and transparency film—or razors and razor blades—because along with the hardware components, 3M's comprehensive package includes a host of other elements such as proprietary software, inks, transfer media, imaging paper, vinyl films, and overlaminates. Different materials are available for specific commercial graphics applications—indoor or outdoor, short-term or long-term, removable or permanent, opaque or back-lit. The company has put in place a comprehensive program to assist vendors with training, certification, business development, technical support, and product warranties, and has built up a large network of certified fabricators using 3M products. It is not difficult to understand why the upgraded Scotchprint 2000 system was another Golden Step Award winner in its first year on the market.

The Commercial Graphics Division that Ward belongs to has departed further from the mostly homegrown development process of the 1960s by setting up strategic partnerships with other high-tech firms. Scotchprint 2000 printers are made by Nippon Steel because 3M found it difficult to make money selling its own equipment in the heavily discounted U.S. market. In the broader market for small-scale thermal ink-jet printers, 3M has partnered with Hewlett-Packard to offer high-quality, weatherable graphics capabilities on low-cost printers.

HP provides the printers and the inks, while 3M contributes the imaging media and overlaminates, along with its 3M Certified Fabricators program. As Ward explains, 3M's strategic priority is the materials onto which the images are printed and preserved.

Appledorn's first customer was a St. Paul school administrator, and product development was focused on the U.S. domestic market. In contrast, Ward's group has constant dealings with its Japanese and American business partners and is field-testing products in three major locations outside of the United States. The Commercial Graphics Division holds an annual global conference where overseas employees can offer their input directly. Sumitomo 3M has a strong position in the Japanese marketplace and has pioneered many aspects of the systems approach that has been used so effectively in the United States. Ward is well aware of the strengths and weaknesses of the division's U.S. and overseas operations, and has spent a good deal of time trying to coordinate these into an optimal global business.[9]

Technical Innovation: Change and Continuity

The greatest change in the process of technical innovation at 3M has been a move from sequential to simultaneous development. However pressed Appledorn and his colleagues may have been in the sixties, and however capricious the factors that caused them to change direction, they followed a step-by-step sequence of events with a steady core of protagonists.

More recently—if Scotch satin tape, Scotchprint graphics, or the HFE example (see chapter one) are anything to go by—this sequence has been compressed into a tight whirl of events, with the number of key players multiplied across a global stage. Vagaries of chance are either quickly leveraged or neutralized by the deliberate application of corporate muscle. While quieter research backwaters still exist, the pace has picked up. Simultaneous input from a whole range of sources is fused to push innovations forward on a broad front; technical innovation becomes one integral part of a larger thrust. And pressure from every side goads established businesses into novel patterns of action.

This increasingly rapid and complex innovation process, with its megaprojects and breathtaking financial stakes, demands astute planning,

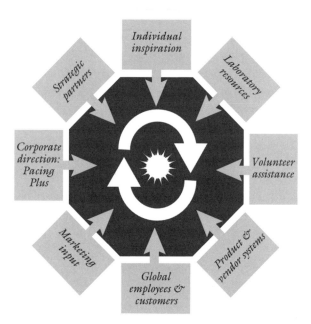

Technical Innovation Today

coordination, and strategy. Management has grown more eager to exploit ideas with strong commercial potential at ever-earlier stages. Yet many of the best ideas still emerge through a tedious, unpredictable "noodling" process that is allergic to tight management controls, flourishing instead where there is the freedom to exercise curiosity and follow up on intriguing accidents.

How can the powerful simultaneous innovation process that has emerged in recent years capitalize on breakthrough opportunities without muddying the headwaters of individual inspiration, or trampling on the flowers of initiative and volunteerism? 3M tries to preserve and encourage spontaneous innovative activity through its

- Management philosophy
- Process-focused technology centers that can transform new product ideas into commercial products
- The Tech Forum and other company-sponsored volunteer activities
- Employee recognition programs

■ Management Philosophy

A closer examination of the management style of long-time 3Mers reveals constant attention to the evolutionary development of new products, with this sometimes taking precedence over strategic planning activities. Bill Coyne, the respected leader of 3M's research efforts, calls his management philosophy a "reverse strategic planning approach." Instead of focusing on a particular industry, market segment, or application and then developing the enabling technologies, 3M is more likely to do the reverse. That is, it is more common to start with an offshoot of a core technology, find a market segment or application where it can be used, and thereby develop a new industry.[10] This is another way of describing what was referred to in chapter one as "solutions in search of problems." The technological solution is often available before the company's researchers can figure out what to do with it—only after the technology and its economic environment evolve further does its purpose become apparent.

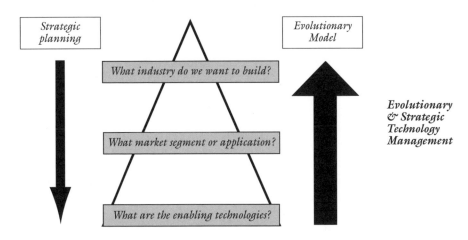

Such an evolutionary model—in which the enabling technology tends to come first—has a logic of its own. L. D. DeSimone, 3M's CEO, claims: "Innovation tells us where to go; we don't tell innovation where to go."[11] 3M tries to nurture evolutionary research activities through a hothouse-like organizational culture that allows the natural mutation process of offshoot and divide to flourish. The company is sometimes very patient in letting this natural evolution take its course, recognizing that it may take many years for a new type of research to reach fruition—if it ever does. Even microreplication, the wildly successful technology platform set in motion by Appledorn more than forty years ago, has stumbled into blind alleys and dead ends on the way to unforeseen commercial applications.[12]

Evolutionary technologies are constantly being weeded out for various reasons. Some perish for want of money, equipment, and volunteers; some are terminated without energetic champions to defend them; certain projects vanish for a time like an underground stream, only to reemerge later on. (Appledorn's skill in concealing projects from management earned him the nickname "the Al Capone of 3M bootleggers."[13]) Only the fittest survive—evolution, it is worth remembering, is a two-part process, with both variation and natural selection.[14]

It is perhaps most accurate to think of top-down strategic planning and 3M's more organic, evolutionary innovation process as complementary rather than contradictory. There is plenty of strategy at 3M. Every Pacing Plus designation represents a strategic choice and sets in motion a whirl of activity. Strategic corporate decisions are also regularly made, for instance, to build the company's strengths in growth industries such as telecommunications, electronics, health care, or software.

Technical innovation at 3M ideally proceeds according to the one-two punch of natural evolution plus deliberate strategic choice. In addition to the company's research labs and technology platforms, numerous other management devices help to bring new product ideas to the stage where they merit corporate-level focus, and ensure that they get a wide hearing beyond their point of origin. Among these are the Genesis Grants for small but promising research projects, and technical audit panels composed of a cross-section of 3Mers from outside of the sponsoring organizations who review new ideas for their commercial potential. Executives generally make strategic decisions after surveying what has popped up inside of the company through the evolutionary process—Pacing Plus programs are "recognized" after reaching a certain level of achievement rather than begotten by management fiat.

An important part of Bill Coyne's job is allocating resources to product development projects that promise to yield the best return for the company. He doesn't put a lot of faith in fashionable analytical methods such as present value analysis, nor will he invest in bright but impractical concepts.

I look at the passion of the inventors and the people around them. I want to see an innovator with a creative idea who is participating in the development process. We don't reward people who just throw out creative ideas without bringing them to market. I look for people like Appledorn who have enough sense of what's commercially viable.[15]

3M management style thus cultivates and melds together multiple approaches to innovation. Coyne has distilled what he calls the three paradoxes of managing technical innovation. Either side of each paradox may come first.[16]

Strategic Planning		Evolutionary Approach	
Manage technology	AND	Let it show us where to go	*Innovation Management Paradoxes*
Search out customer needs	AND	Concentrate on our abilities	
Prioritize development	AND	Encourage individual initiative	

The current trend at 3M is to make room in the same project team for both ends of this type of paradox. Sometimes an inventorpreneur possesses both the technical and entrepreneurial ability to bring a project to fruition single-handedly, but the growing complexity of projects makes this increasingly difficult. Pat Hager, the creator of Scotch satin tape, describes the inventor as akin to a comedian—someone with a slightly skewed view of the world: "I'm blessed with a half-dysfunctional brain. I'm always unfocused, fuzzy. At 3M, you build up a network, talk to other people, and then one day it clicks while you're thinking about another project." But few projects can benefit for long from having an unfocused comedian as their manager. It took the tactful head-banging efforts of Amy Krohn, Hager's no-nonsense counterpart, to push his discovery forward. Today, any team is likely to recruit global representatives from all of the major company disciplines: marketing, manufacturing, finance, law, and human resources—and do it at an earlier stage.

■ Process Innovation Technical Centers

Along with a management philosophy that continues to nurture evolutionary forms of innovation, 3M offers powerful technical assistance to individuals with a new product idea. The company's production processes are closely guarded trade secrets, with about 75 percent of its manufacturing done internally, and there are two in-house Tech Centers devoted to nothing but process innovation.

The Corporate Process Technical Center (CPTC), staffed mainly by chemical engineers and materials scientists, helps researchers scale up a new idea from the lab bench to production. The focus is on process and development for core technologies. 3M's Engineering Systems Technical Center (ESTC) handles the development and scale-up of key manufacturing process technologies such as coating, drying, and inspection and measurement. Staffed primarily with chemical and mechanical engineers and software development personnel, this group works closely with the company's product development, equipment design, and engineering communities to ensure a successful transition to commercial manufacturing.

Together, these Tech Centers provide a broad pipeline from the laboratory scientist to large-scale manufacturing. They also lend a distinctive competitive edge, as 3M's in-house experts can often suggest ways to improve features, raise quality, and lower costs. Many companies go commercial when a technology is defined and only then buy equipment for their factory operation, or else use suppliers to build a turn-key manufacturing plant. 3M tries to add value throughout this triangular process of innovation by leveraging the lab scientist's new product idea with scale-up and engineering systems expertise.[17]

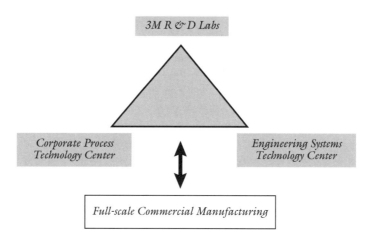

The Process Innovation Triangle

■ The Tech Forum

The Tech Forum provides perhaps the most fertile common ground within 3M for grassroots innovative activity. It is a massive volunteer organization with an administrative framework, thousands of members, and events almost every day of the year. Officially established in 1951 to "encourage free and active interchange of information and the cross-fertilization of ideas,"[18] the Tech Forum creates opportunities for 3M's technical employees to interact, share ideas and discoveries, ask questions, and find answers from unexpected places. Simon Fung, the 1998 chair of the Tech Forum, says about the organization's purpose: "Technology is there to be shared. . . . This is a way for individuals in 3M to 'network,' although that's not a good word for it. People need to appreciate that the Tech Forum is much more than that."[19]

Pat Hager, the inventor of Scotch satin tape and a Tech Forum regular, talks about the organization's influence on his work:

> Being at 3M, you get cross-fertilized. What you see out there are a lot of seminars and talks. It's great to have problems. You can seek out other people to help you and nine out of ten of them are no use, yet they have other ideas and perspectives. That community aspect is key. But you also need to have the individual desire to go look for answers. Ten out of ten of them will be willing to help you even though they're all busy. It's part of the culture, the atmosphere here.[20]

The Tech Forum is organized into chapters and committees. Chapters are focused around technology and include, for example, the Physics Chapter, the Life Sciences Chapter, and the Product Design Chapter. Any 3M employee can form his or her own ad hoc chapter with just $500. The chapters hold seminars on topics relating to their own areas of technology, addressed by outside speakers or 3M employees. In general, these are scientific talks designed for a technical audience. Where confidential matters are discussed, attendance may be limited to Tech Forum members only; otherwise seminars are open to the entire organization.

While the initial goal of the Tech Forum was to encourage technical exchange, not all chapters have a technical focus. Today, Tech Forum leaders encourage chapters that cut across business needs, management issues, and technical areas. For instance, the Intellectual Property Chapter is primarily targeted at patent attorneys.

Tech Forum committees organize specific events, education, and communications. The Corporate Outreach Committee hosts joint events for 3M technical employees and personnel from other companies. The Orientation Committee conducts a one-day introduction program for new technical employees in St. Paul. This group has recently begun broadcasting its sessions to other 3M sites around the country via 3M TV (see chapter four). The Communications Committee publishes a newsletter for Tech Forum members.

- Interface Science/Analytical Chapters: "Spectroscopic Characterization of Solid/Solid Interfaces: Challenges and Solutions"

- Modeling and Simulation/Polymer Chapters: "Molecular Constitutive Models for Mono and Poly-disperse Systems of Entangled Linear Flexible Polymer," by Prof. David Mead, University of Michigan

- Adhesives/Adhesion/Polymer Chapters: "Flame Retardant and Smoke Suppressant Additives to Plastics and Polymer Stabilizer Products," by Mary Harscher and Brent Sanders, Great Lakes Chemical Corp.

- Processes Chapter: "Fundamentals of Retroreflection."

- Inorganic/Organic Chapters: "Functional, Nanostructured Materials via Polymerizable Liquid Crystals," by Prof. Doug Gin, University of California at Berkeley.

A Tech Forum initiative, the Science Encouragement Program, brings science into the community with programs such as the "Visiting Wizards." These are 3M employees who have taken a special in-house course to become certified Wizards; they go out to local schools to demonstrate technology and encourage children to pursue careers in science. Giving a lesson in subjects like Bubblology, Cryogenic Freezing, or Magnetics, the Wizards begin by explaining scientific principles, then involve the children in experiments. In the Bubblology workshop, the school kids play with all sizes and shapes of bubble machines, including a giant bubble-blower that can produce bubbles bigger than the kids! The Visiting Wizards host an annual science fair at 3M's campus in St. Paul. Children and their parents are encouraged to stop by the booths and play with all the different kinds of technology demonstrated. At the Cryogenic Freezing booth, children watch with rapt attention as a Wizard dips a rose into the freezing chemicals, then shatters it into a million pieces with a mere flick of his finger.

The Visiting Wizards program was founded by 3M scientist Bob Barton, and has demonstrated the positive results of community outreach programs. Participants say that the program makes them feel better about themselves and the company, and gives them an opportunity to interact with other 3Mers whom they wouldn't ordinarily meet.

Although the Tech Forum is made up of volunteers, 3M management provides it with administrative assistants and limited funding. "We have a modest but significant budget," Simon Fung says. "How many companies would give their employees this kind of resource and let them run with it? Perhaps it has to do with Midwestern culture; it's a lot like church groups."

With so many people and events, an organizational structure had to be put in place to oversee the Tech Forum volunteers and manage the budget. The Governing Board of the Tech Forum plays this role in St. Paul and in Austin. Board members have access to and receive full support from senior management. They are selected in a yearly election and meet once a month. In addition, each laboratory elects one senator to serve as a representative to the Tech Forum Senate. The senate meets once a month to plan events and provide "a cohesive voice to 3M on behalf of the technical community."[21] Also, the board must receive a certain number of votes from the senate in order to make significant changes to the Tech Forum.

The biggest gathering hosted by the Tech Forum is the two-day "Annual Event," held in September at the St. Paul headquarters. Each of the 3M labs is invited to put up a booth. Since the company rewards labs when their technology is put to use by other divisions, employees have an incentive to join in on the activity. Moreover, the scientists enjoy the chance to show off their latest technical innovations. "It's like an internal trade show to showcase their products," says Fung. "People can get an idea of what the other divisions and other technology centers are doing, and develop interactions with other people."

Recently, thanks to the efforts of Fung and some of his colleagues, the Tech Forum has taken on more international functions. The first thought was to involve overseas colleagues in the Annual Event in St. Paul, but soon a different idea emerged:

I wanted to bring in overseas people to the U.S. event in the fall. We need them to be here—international makes up more than 50 percent of our total revenue. But most people from overseas already travel to the U.S. in the spring for other meetings, and it would be inappropriate from a resource standpoint for them to come again later. Since they come in the spring anyway, I thought, why not get them to show us what they have while they're here? So I organized a Global Technical Exchange in the spring of 1998. Geoff Nicholson (head of corporate Technical Planning) was a strong supporter. Even though business in Asia was not going well, we encouraged people from that region to come anyway. We asked the regional technical directors to talk about challenges in their areas in the morning. In the afternoon, labs from different countries showed us their new ideas.

This event, by switching the focus from exhibits by U.S.-based research groups to the accomplishments of overseas scientists, constituted a milestone in the globalization of 3M's technical community. It also bore several substantive fruits that would otherwise have been implausible. For example, 3M's Australian subsidiary had developed a new antibacterial cloth for its domestic market. 3M China was trying to obtain a technology like this from the United States, and would never have thought to ask for it from Australia. Because of the interactions at the Global Technical Exchange, the Chinese are working with the Australian laboratory on the product.

In addition to the Global Technical Exchange, 3M's U.S. employees have now organized a Global Technical Chapter. Its expressed goal is to "strengthen global technical capabilities by bridging the national technical communities in support of 3M growth."[22] As 3M's international business grows, this Tech Forum globalization effort will undoubtedly expand. Fung comments: "We're all so busy with our jobs, people wonder, 'Where do you find the time to do this?' It's amazing. People are dedicated. They believe they're doing what's best for the company."[23]

■ Recognizing Innovation

New product inventions are considered to be part of the job at 3M, and no bonuses are paid for innovations. But that doesn't mean technical innovations go unrecognized. The company's dual-ladder system holds not only the customary management track, but also a series of positions that reflect technical contributions. Rungs in the ladder progress from entry level technician to corporate scientist, with opportunities for salary, benefits, and other privileges that are similar to those available at the corresponding management positions. Promotion is influenced by the progress of one's technology from "emerging" to "enabling" to "core" status.[24]

Visitors to 3M's St. Paul headquarters building can walk down a long hallway lined with glass cases that house trophies for some of the more than twenty company awards. The most prestigious is election into the Carlton Society, named after the company's first head of R&D and later president. Just a few such awards are given annually. Induction into the Carlton Society is the highest form of peer recognition at 3M. Award winners are selected not only for technical excellence, but for sharing knowledge and insights with others. This elite group includes Roger Appledorn, Geoff Nicholson, and Art Fry, the co-inventor of Post-it notes.

Other 3M awards recognize areas such as technical excellence, engineering achievement, and process technology. The Golden Step Award recognizes the practical side of technical innovation—growth of a new business beyond $10 million in profitable sales. The Alpha Program supplements 3M's Genesis Grants as a way to distribute seed money for an idea to generate new business or to improve efficiency.

Carlton Society Bust   Golden Step Award   Innovator Award

Until 1997, however, Bill Coyne, 3M's restless R&D leader, felt that something crucial was still missing. So he introduced the 3M Innovator Award, specifically aimed at individuals who generated product and business breakthroughs during their Fifteen Percent Time. Up to ten employees from around the world are now selected each year, including those like Richard Miller, the inventor of Aldara cream (see chapter one), whose ideas were once thought to be borderline or impossible. Coyne is seeking to preserve and foster passionate belief in an idea, along with the willingness to pursue it in the face of all odds. A nomination package for the Innovator Award is distributed throughout the company each year. Its language provides evidence of Coyne's own deepest convictions:

> Individual inspiration and effort are the heart and soul of 3M innovation. The power of the individual to dream, conceive, and breathe profitable life into new ideas and products is a great 3M tradition and a fundamental asset to our global business growth. . . .
>
> Thanks to a tradition established more than a half-century ago by then-president William McKnight, time is set aside at 3M for the pursuit of individual projects. Nondirected employee time has taken 3M in bold new directions. . . . The award is designed to honor McKnight's keen insight by reemphasizing individual innovation as a driving force within the company.[25]

Key Questions To Ask About Innovation

Technical Innovation

1. What are your technology platforms?

2. Are long-term research groups in touch with customers and flexible enough to support short-term development when necessary? Do research projects with a short-term focus leave room for longer-term efforts?

3. Can you implement the radical innovation practices necessary for Type A Innovation—that is, Creation of a New Market or Industry: intelligent accident, direct customer contact, resource bootlegging, volunteer recruitment, market creation, and staff contributions?

4. Are you familiar with Appledorn's prescriptions for organizational culture (freedom, never give up), communication (opening doors, interface with customers), and management style (being a servant, breaking the rules)?

5. Does your style of technical innovation simultaneously integrate individual research efforts with laboratory resources, marketing ideas, global employees and customer input, product and vendor systems, and strategic partners?

6. Is your approach to innovation dominated by strategic planning or a more evolutionary model? What is the proper balance between the two ("manage technology" vs. "let it show us where to go")?

7. Do you have process innovation to better enable product innovation?

8. What volunteer employee activities foster innovation, and how can these be encouraged without being suffocated?

9. Does the company recognize innovative achievements in a meaningful way?

4

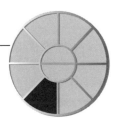

Innovative Staff, Innovative Company

Innovation applies in every discipline.
—L. D. DeSimone, CEO

Each staff function has an important role in building an innovative climate at 3M. Human Resources recruits would-be innovators and helps to determine how they are evaluated and rewarded. Information Technology (IT) equips them with the tools to communicate ideas and discoveries rapidly and across great distances. Finance measures the results of innovative efforts and gauges what investments are possible to support capital investments. Overall, when staff employees work skillfully, their counterparts in the research labs and divisions who conceive and commercialize new products become freer to focus on their work.

While the basic mission of 3M staff functions is supportive in nature, there is plenty of room for innovation in staff jobs as well. 3M's definition of innovation ("New ideas + action or implementation which results in an improvement, gain, or profit") is purposefully broad. Employees in any staff discipline can aspire to be innovators. This egalitarian readiness to allow staff in any department to let their creative juices flow is good for morale: the factory worker or administrative assistant can claim a share of the spotlight. It is surprising to find just how many 3Mers take to heart the corporate vision to become the "most innovative enterprise in the world," asking themselves what they can do to support product innovation and reinvent their own jobs.

Given the general prestige and enthusiasm attached to innovation, there is a tendency to label certain things as innovative that look a bit mundane or which are perhaps not particularly unique to 3M. But it is important to the company for employees to approach what they do in a fresh way and to be open to change, as these efforts often produce valuable results.

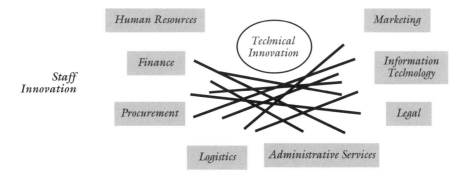

Human Resources

Kay Grenz, vice president of Human Resources, underlines 3M's philosophy of steady staff support:

> Human Resources at 3M doesn't jump into the latest fad in the marketplace. We wait and see what the consequences are rather than immediately suggest a lot of trendy plans and proposals. We're trying to do fewer things better. . . . Our job is to provide stability so employees can concentrate on their jobs.[1]

Human Resources defines its mission as increasing the contribution and growth of individuals, teams, and organizations, while maintaining an environment where 3Mers take pride in their company. Pride, satisfaction, and innovation in both products and processes are constant themes.[2]

3M still unofficially practices lifetime employment. It is possible to get fired, but normally only for a serious ethical breach, gross incompetence, lack of motivation, or negligence. This job stability nurtures risk-taking and allows the lessons of a career to be put to work for the company's benefit. Dick Lidstad, Grenz's recently retired predecessor, tells a story about how he once had to face his manager to discuss a failed project that had cost somewhere between $5 and $10 million. His boss's comment was: "So, tell me what you learned." In a similar vein, the spirit of cooperation and volunteerism within the organization owes a lot to the fact that employees don't have to worry about sprucing up their résumés or looking for another job. 3M is as much of a community as one can find anywhere in big corporate America.

The company is attempting to preserve this "community" approach in the face of pressures on its work force. A reduction of 4,500 employees, announced in late summer 1998, is to be accomplished by early 2000 primarily through early retirement and attrition, although some layoffs are being made on the basis of performance. At the same time, 3M's employee turnover in the United States has doubled from 3 to 6 percent since 1994. This is still quite healthy by American corporate standards, but has raised concerns within Human Resources about how to preserve the experience and sense of dedication that will ensure continued innovation.

In the mid-1990s, turnover of personnel was a far greater concern overseas, with the retention of high-potential employees being a vital HR issue, for instance, in much of Asia outside of Japan. In a few hot markets in Asia turnover exceeded 20 percent annually, although more unsettled economic times have since dampened employees' eagerness to leave behind a secure position. 3M is still on the lower end of the turnover spectrum among foreign capital companies.

Top priorities for 3M Human Resources worldwide now include

- Hiring innovators
- Identifying, developing, and retaining high-potential employees
- Performance management
- Implementing change management skills
- Accelerated knowledge transfer
- Leadership development

All of these priority areas have vital links with innovation; several will be taken up here as examples.

■ Hiring Innovators

What things did you make as a child? How do you think this product sample is made? What was a "dead end" you encountered while working on a problem? How did you handle it?

If you are applying for a job at 3M, you could be asked these questions. 3M puts a great deal of effort into hiring prospective innovators. During its early history, the company recruited individuals who had grown up on farms doing a little bit of everything, including fixing machinery. The rural upbringing of William McKnight and other influential management figures shaped an approach to recruiting that is still alive now that the company is brimming with Ph.Ds.

A few years back a team of 3Mers composed of recruiters and leading members of the technical community interviewed twenty-five of the most prolific inventors within the company. They were looking for signs of innovative potential to use in screening job applicants. The innovators whom they met, including people like Roger Appledorn, exhibited common characteristics that have become the basis for current hiring practices.[3] (TABLE)

One of the researchers involved in the study, George Kiperts, subsequently wrote a pamphlet for 3M recruiters called "Hiring Innovators." Kiperts explains that the team's findings are not intended to be the final word, but they have been useful as the basis for job interviews: "It does help recruiters to look for certain qualities," he observes, noting that interview teams expressed surprise that such traits as "broad interests outside the job" and "work cycles" with changing levels of productivity could prove to be key indicators of innovative potential.

College graduates with either four-year or advanced degrees make up seventy-five percent of the new employees 3M hires each year. Recruiters go to seventy campuses a year, make a concerted effort at thirty, and derive most recruits from among the Big Ten universities in the Midwest. Hiring for college graduates begins with a number of annual requisitions determined by top management. The idea behind this system is to keep hiring counts steady even as 3M's business fluctuates—once the requisitions are set for the year, they are not rescindable.

Beyond this framework set by management, 3M's recruiting is primarily done by thirty independent volunteer teams. These recruiting teams have grown from an ad hoc process into what Kiperts calls a "semi-organized" effort. The Staffing Resource Center provides inter-

viewer training, an on-campus interview schedule, and company litera-
ture, including copies of Kiperts's pamphlet for recruiters. The rest is
up to the volunteers, some of whom are alumni of the schools they
visit. The teams generally recruit not for specific positions but for people who will make good 3Mers. Team members keep their eyes open
for what they call "water-walkers," or people who are so extraordinary
that the interviewers might wind up working for them in a few years.
The volunteer teams recommend job candidates to division or lab
managers, who make the final hiring decisions.

3M Innovators: The Characteristics	
• *Are Creative*	Inquisitive/Ask questions Explorative Look for solutions Insightful/Intuitive thinkers Ideas flow easily Visionary
• *Have Broad Interests*	Eager to learn Explore ideas with others Hobbies Multidisciplinary
• *Are Problem Solvers*	Experimental style (do it first, explain later) Tinker with things (hands-on) Not afraid to make mistakes Willing to do the unobvious Practical Take multiple approaches to a problem
• *Are Self-Motivated/Energized*	Self-starters/Driven Results oriented (doers) Have a passion about what they do Accomplishment—urge to succeed Sense of humor Sense of contribution, value, and purpose Take initiatives
• *Have a Strong Work Ethic*	Committed Work in cycles Flexible work habits (not structured) Drive toward work completion Tenacious
• *Are Resourceful*	Network Get things done through others

In maintaining 3M's links to universities, volunteer teams are the main conduit. They distribute scholarships between different departments, with the number of scholarships to each university depending upon such factors as graduates hired in the past. Many scholarship winners are eventually hired. Volunteers also take part in alumni associations, industry/academic banquets, and guest presentations for classes. Research tie-ins with professors work well; fifty percent of the candidates with advanced technical degrees are recommendations from faculty or recent graduates. Some schools regard the company as sufficiently important to their students' futures that they consult it in the development of curricula. For its part, 3M is not shy about leveraging its presence on campuses to recruit strong candidates.

Wanting to make sure that 3M attracted the best Ph.D. talent, Kiperts and his colleagues began a fast-track recruiting process in 1996. Volunteer teams for six key campuses were asked for their top two or three candidates, a fast-track team member held a second round of interviews, then all the top candidates were invited in for group activities. Bill Coyne, 3M's senior vice president of research and development, spoke to them, and further interviews were conducted. After the in-house session, 3M responded with quick job offers, and got a strong seventy percent acceptance rate in return. "These are the best of the best," says Kiperts.[4]

■ 3M Live

Change always looked likely after Leon Royer, a crusty iconoclast and hero of several 3M business triumphs, became head of Organizational Learning Services. This group had traditionally assumed responsibility for knowledge transfer and change management; its new head brought with him a radically different perspective. Royer had been head of the Commercial Tape Division labs when Post-it notes were first commercialized, and was later instrumental in rescuing a failing electronic components packaging business. He felt that too much employee time and corporate resources were being invested in activities of dubious value such as classroom instruction.

Royer soon sent a tart form letter to long-time external training vendors, informing them that Organizational Learning Services would no longer support their efforts by recruiting participants, furnishing classrooms, or providing refreshments. Vendors were instructed to arrange their own off-site facilities for training events, and to recruit trainees through paid advertisements in *3M Stemwinder*, the company's weekly employee newspaper. Some vendors, particularly local ones, survived this tough new regime; others that were physically removed from St. Paul and already had slim profit margins stopped working with 3M. Ironically, 3Mers from other staff departments and divisions soon began to seek out alternative training opportunities and to bootleg them around Royer's increasingly businesslike organization.

While Royer is now retired, his organization continues its struggle to reinvent itself. Before Royer it had variously been known as "Sales Training," "Education and Training," "Education, Training, and Development," and "Human Resources Development." After the "Organizational Learning Services" title that Royer inherited, it has undergone further identity shifts, including "Leadership Development Center" and the present "Development and Measurement."

One success born during Royer's tenure was 3M TV. Arlan Tietel, 3M TV's chief administrator, is one of those 3Mers whose enthusiasm for his job seems wildly implausible—until you've met thirty or forty of them. With Royer's support, Tietel managed to obtain the funding necessary to get 3M TV off the ground. "Leon was an inventor who believed that every business should have its R&D department," Tietel says. "3M TV creates a new way to do training. . . . He felt that this was bigger than Post-it notes."

Now Tietel is quick to position 3M TV as a tool to generate new business rather than as a training instrument—and thus as more than just a drain on resources. Its use, he says, can "drive sales growth, costs, and profits, while changing the way 3M does business." At the same time, Tietel's loopy grin reveals a bit of the human resources coyote in wolf's clothing—he seems to enjoy the heck out of what he is doing.

The first 3M TV broadcast took place on April 29, 1996: a national conference for 325 sales managers broadcast for two hours over the airways. The cost for a face-to-face sales meeting would have been $325,000 for travel alone, not to mention the time several hundred sales managers could be spending with customers; the inaugural broadcast cost less than a tenth of that. Tietel sat and sat and watched with tears in his eyes: "The first day out of the box we easily saved money for the company."

Such broadcasts can be alternated with direct face-to-face meetings, Tietel notes, and are not intended to supplant them completely. He bristles at questions about 3M TV's ability to match the interactive environment of a live meeting. "To what extent are presenters interactive when they do see their audience?" he asks. "We make sure that there is some sort of interaction within five minutes of the start of a broadcast, and every ten minutes thereafter." Previously, he adds, an individual instructor could serve only thirty trainees, but now three hundred or three thousand can be served—3M TV can get the message out to larger masses of people in the same period of time.

3M TV has expanded to 50 hours a month of broadcast time, with a goal of reaching 100 hours. Today there are 80 3M TV sites in North America, 20 in Europe, and 13 in Asia, with a further 9 sites soon coming on-line in Latin America. On a typical day, a broadcast on the subject of basic supervisory skills will run twice with a total audience of over 500 people.

3M is one of about two hundred companies that support an internal TV network worldwide. It is also part of a group that has its own satellite transponder available twenty-four hours a day, seven days a week. The company's efforts are still small compared with those of giants like Ford, which broadcasts a host of offerings to its six thousand dealers, but, concludes Tietel, "We're among the leading pack."

Tietel's goal is to be able to conduct a new product introduction to a global 3M sales force in a single day, so that the salespeople can be on the street selling the very next day. He cites the recent example of a new product introduction to an American divisional sales force that took place in four hours at a cost of $5,000. This resulted in major savings over the costs of a traditional road show or national meeting, and provided the division with more sales days. Tietel's dream is to have 3M TV available on the personal computer of every company employee; he is currently overseeing a beta test run by a firm that is developing video-streaming technology to enable two-way audio and video interaction.[5]

■ Leadership Development

Executives in the upper reaches of 3M have sponsored an intriguing internal study to identify the qualities of the company's best leaders. Its purpose is to generate a tool to assist in assessing and developing the next generation of 3M leadership. The driving force behind the new "Leadership Competence Profile" has been Margaret Alldredge, the energetic executive director of the Selection, Assessment, and Leadership Development organization within Human Resources. Together with her colleague Kevin Nilan, an industrial psychologist who has a background in research and assessment, Alldredge has developed executive competence profiles that uniquely reflect 3M's own corporate culture.

The Leadership Competence Profile was born partly from 3M's desire to focus on developing world-class leaders who are equipped to support innovation and to raise innovators. After examining external sources of information, Human Resources proposed an extensive interview process with 3M leaders. Concerns about commitments of time and resources led management to turn down the proposal, but the team asked for a deadline and, with the help of volunteers, carried out seventy interviews anyway. "We have a tradition of doing what you think is right, of following your nose, head, and heart," says Alldredge. Interviewers asked for illustrations, critical incidents, or stories of leaders who modeled the following twelve corporate competencies:

- Vision & strategy
- Intellectual capacity
- Maturity & judgment
- Developing people
- Customer orientation
- Inspiring others
- Global perspective
- Business health & results
- Ethics & integrity
- Building alliances
- Nurturing innovation
- Organizational agility

L. D. DeSimone, 3M's CEO, was skeptical—his aversion to any sort of leadership cult or personality typing is well known. But Alldredge and Nilan enticed him into dialogue about people and situations that he knew about and enjoyed commenting on. "This is a company of stories; we teach through myths," asserts Alldredge.

She and Nilan established a set of behaviors for each competency area and then reviewed their findings with other executives, eliciting more interest as the project gathered steam. Notes Alldredge, "As a group of executives, they are passionate about leadership and developing people." The sample behaviors cited below for the "Nurturing Innovation" category emphasize the need for leaders to foster creative activity, tolerate mistakes, champion risk-taking, and usher projects through to commercialization.

Nurturing Innovation: Behaviors

- Creates a climate that supports individual and organizational creativity, challenges employees to take initiatives outside their comfort zones, and tolerates setbacks to maximize individual and organizational learning.

- Champions those who take reasonable and informed risks in the service of business generation.

- Coaches and works with employees to fully develop, document, sell, and then commercialize their ideas and products.

The finished profile will become a coaching tool for approximately five hundred 3M employees at the director level or above. Alldredge and Nilan are not seeking to build a complex quantitative device—the company already has another tool for multisource feedback based on leadership attributes. Instead, they are providing a framework for structured discussion between leaders and their immediate subordinates.

We want to have Executive Conference members use it to talk to their directors, to set expectations and prompt open dialogue. We'd rather let it evolve and not dictate its usages too soon. This way everybody is able to have a hand in developing it. The profile is meant to be a discussion and development tool, with some structure but not too much—not overengineered. We prefer to use simple tools in sophisticated ways rather than using complex tools simplistically. There is something in our process of innovation which allows that.[6]

This approach is reminiscent of the way that other projects at 3M are managed—patient guidance of the evolutionary process to allow the work to acquire a life of its own.

Finance: Beyond Profit and Loss

For Giulio Agostini, 3M's chief financial officer, innovation means changing 3M's culture of financial management. One of several senior executives who came out of 3M Italy, the silver-haired, urbane Agostini seems a bit out of place in the suburbs of St. Paul. Perhaps for this reason, he has done much to shake up a conservative financial culture since being transferred to the head office.

According to Agostini, most of 3M's managers are already good at cost control and generating profits. However, financial innovation means not only to run on a profit and loss basis but also to manage a unit's balance sheet. He states, "You don't stop at the operating level. If you use ten billion dollars to run the company, there is a one billion dollar cost to use that money that can be reduced." Agostini speaks of maximizing shareholder value, which for him sets a higher standard of performance: "It focuses the organization to find the best possible way to run the company."[7]

One area in which Agostini has applied his views has been leveraging 3M's balance sheet to reduce the cost of capital. The company took pride in not joining in the financial leveraging frenzy of the 1980s, but now Agostini is steering it in a different direction. He has deliberately foregone 3M's cherished Triple A financial rating for long-term debt because he considered it a detriment to shareholders. "Leveraging a balance sheet is the modern way to reduce the cost of capital," he says. "We can use someone else's money at a lower interest rate."

Rethinking outsourcing practices has been another Agostini theme. He has pushed the company to outsource activities and use external services that are not part of its core business. "We have traditionally done everything inside of the company, even cooking the food. You don't create value this way. Let's concentrate on what we do well."

3M has normally paid suppliers more quickly than it was paid by customers. This fifteen- to twenty-day difference, Agostini observes, may be a further unnecessary cost: "Why do we pay our suppliers in 28 days? There are suppliers who would be proud and happy to work for 3M and get paid in 60 days." He is working with purchasing and procurement to establish comprehensive discipline in finance. "Every stream of cash flow has to be dominated," he asserts.

Taxes represent another opportunity. Because the company pays 40 percent of its income in tax, and has sixty-five subsidiaries across the world, all subject to different forms of taxation and regulation, there is lots of room for creativity within the rules. "The tax area is not so rigid as you would imagine," Agostini says. 3M has managed to reduce its tax burden by several percentage points over the last seven years.

A new approach to auditing practices has brought more change. Under Agostini, corporate auditors have adopted a proactive, partnership approach to the various business units. Rather than being seen as corporate watchdogs who check up on the businesses to protect 3M from mistakes, Agostini wants the auditors to be seen as friends: "I don't want a spy, someone people are afraid of."

Investor relations have benefited from a similar proactive policy. Agostini has increased the number of meetings with outside investors, and placed attention on psychological as well as technical aspects of working with them. His point is that creating value for shareholders creates value for everyone. 3M employees own 10 percent of the company—ten million shares, with options for twenty-six million more. A $10 increase in the share price creates almost $400 million in new wealth for employees. Establishing a portfolio of employee compensation that includes a 401(k) plan, stock options, performance bonuses, and growth sharing has encouraged 3Mers to look beyond their own salary increases to the general financial health of the company. This works well for 3M, for employee motivation, and for customers, who benefit from savings that are passed on to them.

Gazing fondly at the baton on the windowsill of his office, Agostini tells a story that embodies 3M's general financial philosophy. When the Minnesota Orchestra sought money for its 1998 tour of Europe, 3M, a longtime supporter, offered a generous donation of $100,000. Rather than leave it at that, however, Agostini called his old Italian friend Edoardo Pieruzzi, now head of 3M Europe, and informed him that he would have to put up half of the donation money. Pieruzzi, somewhat pained at this $50,000 dent in his budget, asked, "Giulio, why do you make me pay for a symphony from Minnesota?" Agostini's response was that the *Minnesota* Orchestra afforded an opportunity for *Minnesota* Mining and Manufacturing to provide value for its customers. Taking the hint and determined to get his money's worth, Pieruzzi created a series of highly successful customer events around the orchestra concerts in the United Kingdom, France, Germany, and elsewhere.

Not everything goes as smoothly as Agostini and 3M would like. 3M's stock price is susceptible to fluctuations in global markets.[8]

Increased pressure to reduce expenditures on top of 3M's already "Scotch" approach to cost control can have unintended side effects: less travel and hence less global interaction among 3M employees, or small but cumulatively critical cutbacks on projects with long-term promise but slim prospects for immediate payback. The perceived quality of outsourced cafeteria food, incidentally, has declined enough for it to be a source of employee dissatisfaction. Sorting through his question cards prior to a managerial meeting, Agostini grumbled about such trivial complaints: "Don't they have anything better to ask about than the food?" Yet there may well be a cost to the corporate community, however unquantifiable, of dining rooms that are a bit less crowded and convivial, not to mention the lab manager who is more inclined to turn down an expensive new idea. Leverage can be a double-edged sword.[9]

■ *3M Mexico*

Financial innovation is sometimes required on the fly to protect the health of a subsidiary. That's what happened with 3M Mexico in the mid-1990s.

At the start of the decade, the Mexican economy was in great shape, with steady growth and low inflation. The ratification of NAFTA (the North American Free Trade Agreement) made future prospects look even brighter. Then, in December of 1994, the peso suddenly began a steep plunge, exacerbated by instability in the Mexican government, and dragged the economy into recession with high rates of inflation and unemployment.

3M Mexico was thrown into crisis. Under the subsidiary's managing director, Bill Allen, its management committee worked intensively on an operating plan to deal with the peso's collapse. Their first step was to send a letter to every 3M Mexico employee, explaining in very direct terms the challenge facing the company and the need to redouble efforts for customer satisfaction and service. Next came a series of tough measures:

- Aggressive price increases to offset the effects of devaluation for imported goods and, equally, of local inflation and devaluation on goods manufactured in Mexico. This was done across the board, with only a few exceptions made for strategic reasons or because the products were under governmental price controls

- Tracking of price changes versus currency changes on a weekly basis for all commodities to be sure that prices were staying current with devaluation

- Pricing in U.S. dollars wherever possible because of continued daily fluctuation in floating exchange rates. Widespread dollar pricing appeared to be impossible at the start, but after one year 70 percent of sales were priced in dollars and converted into local currency at the daily exchange rate

- Close surveillance of competitors' pricing

- Offers of attractive cash discounts for timely payments and penalties for overdue accounts receivable

- An 8-percent reduction in employee numbers accompanied by cost reductions in other areas

These were difficult steps to take. Prices for some imported products increased by more than 100 percent, with the prices of locally manufactured goods going up almost as quickly. In certain instances the Mexican Commerce Department required the company to justify increases. But what 3M discovered through this process was that competitors were happy to follow its lead, and were not likely to use the devaluation to grasp market share. Everyone was just trying to survive, and 3M Mexico did a better job than most.

3M Mexico also developed an innovative accounting and measurement tool, a "replacement cost, real terms commodity Profit and Loss statement format that enabled management to project ahead of the currency inventory situation." In other words, managers could forecast the effects of currency changes on their business results, factoring in key variables such as the high cost of money. "Another measurement tool developed by the financial department allowed us to monitor price versus devaluation, which meant that we could accurately gauge the price increases we needed."

3M Mexico's performance held up remarkably well through the crisis. A mid-1995 survey by the American Chamber of Commerce in Mexico City showed that 3M Mexico was performing in the top tier of sixty-two member companies in terms of both sales and profit. Long-term investment in Mexico continued throughout this period, with major upgrades of factory equipment and the purchase of land for a new

Mexico City headquarters. Lasting benefits which accrued as the economy improved were dollar pricing to protect against further devaluations, low inventory levels, and very healthy accounts receivable.

Nor does the story end here. 3M drew on this experience when the next major currency crisis hit—in Asia. Bill Allen, the managing director in Mexico, was an acquaintance of Ron Harber, the executive in charge of 3M's Southeast Asia Region, thanks to a previous expatriate stint by Allen in Hong Kong. When the currency crisis hit Asia in 1997, Allen fired off a message to Harber summarizing the measures instituted in Mexico "to reinforce what you're probably doing already or maybe even give you a new idea or two." Allen was subsequently transferred from Mexico to Japan, where he became 3M's top executive in the midst of that country's worst postwar economic crisis.[10]

■ Reengineering Procurement

3M's procurement operations are enormous. In 1996, just after the current program to reengineer its procurement function began, the company spent $5.9 billion a year on goods and services in the United States alone. Costs for processing these transactions were $56 million. Three organizations—Purchasing, Disbursements, and Corporate Receiving—were struggling to administer 55,000 American suppliers, with 250 new ones being added each month. Another 60,000 suppliers were being used by 3M outside of the United States.

Since October 1995, the Procurement Reengineering Project has examined and restructured a process that had become complex and expensive. The cross-functional team assigned to this job, which took place under the auspices of 3M's Supply Chain Excellence initiative, made further disconcerting discoveries in their early research phase. They found forty-five different ways to initiate a purchase, involving twenty-five different corporate systems. Some 25 percent of employee time in this area, worth $14 million, was spent on correcting errors. Even worse, the procurement process was so complicated that 3M employees were applying their creativity to bootleg around official channels: three billion procurement dollars were being spent with little or no participation of purchasing professionals. Some businesses had actually hired their own purchasing people and set up their own stockrooms, while non-purchasing employees were spending much of their time handling procurement issues.

The reengineering team defined its mission as designing and implementing a procurement process that is simple, provides accurate and readily available information, leverages opportunities for global sourcing, and minimizes costs. They became serious students of reengineering guru Michael Hammer, attending conferences and eventually inviting his organization in to conduct customized training. Eighteen procurement employees have become certified reengineering coaches.

But Wendy Stanton, a core team member from the beginning, notes: "We took the reengineering methodologies with a grain of salt. You have to apply them to your own environment and do what works." The 3M team found that before focusing on process redesign, which is the *sine qua non* of reengineering, they had to look at what was being bought. ("You can't cram it all into one process.") Rather than first analyzing the payment process or the ordering process, they segmented their approach into three distinct types of procurement profiles based upon the needs of internal clients:

1. *Repetitive Buys by Many People*—goods or services purchased frequently by almost any staff member

2. *Repetitive Buys by Few People*—goods or services purchased on a regular basis by certain groups

3. *Special Needs*—unique goods or services that may either be purchased once only or will later become a repetitive purchase

The procurement efforts and criteria for decision making are very different for each type of purchase, Stanton notes:

For example, goods and services that typically fall in the "Repetitive Buys by Many People" profile are low-dollar and require fast turnaround. Clients typically do not care who the supplier is and want the good or service at the lowest possible cost in the most efficient manner. For goods or services that typically fall in the "Special Needs" profile, developing strong supplier relationships and quality is important.

The reengineered procurement function now has a matrix of activities that integrates primary process steps with the three different procurement profiles:

	Source & Price	Order Goods & Services	Supply of Goods & Services	Receive Goods & Services	Pay Supplier	Report & Measure
Everyday Needs						
Replenishment Orders						
Special Needs						

3M Procurement: Current Activity Matrix

These activities are carried out by three subgroups in a new organization called Procurement Operations. The Business Unit group works with internal clients to initiate purchases, the Commodity Group negotiates contracts with suppliers, and the Process Group supervises the ongoing reengineering effort. (The previous functions of Purchasing, Disbursements Services, and Corporate Receiving were abolished in 1997.)

Successful pilot programs were carried out with three internal customers—a factory, a research laboratory, and the corporate library. These have introduced new methods for everyday purchases, including an electronic catalog and procurement cards; using the latter, transactions with suppliers are handled by GE Capital, simplifying vendor relationships considerably. The reengineering team has also broken with precedent by looking outside of the company for software. Its new procurement structure is supposed to be in place for all of 3M's U.S. operations by the end of 1999.[11]

Marketing for Better Customer Relations

3M's Corporate Marketing Division has come a long way since the days when it rejected Appledorn's overhead projector idea. Now it casts itself as the guardian of customer relationships and the steward of efforts to be the "preferred supplier" to its customers. Corporate Marketing promotes skillful management of relationships with customers so that 3M pays attention to their needs—both articulated and unarticulated—and acts with one voice. Over the last decade or more, the marketing function has contributed greatly to 3M's ability to balance the product-out momentum of internal innovation with real customer needs.

The company's divisional structure creates a natural tendency for each business within it to act like a group of independent entrepreneurs. CEO DeSimone stresses the imperative to beat the "big company, big numbers trap"; he wants each pocket of entrepreneurship to perform as a small firm would, yet have access to the capabilities of a large organization. However, practical issues arise when sales representatives from five different divisions come to call on the same customer in the same week, without coordinating their efforts or even knowing each other.

Corporate Marketing has therefore undertaken initiatives to unify 3M's customer relationships:

- *Strategic Accounts Management*, designed to coordinate a team-selling approach across divisional and functional lines, while streamlining communication with key customer contacts

- *Industry Centers*, created for the automotive, construction, electronics, office, and home markets to coordinate divisions that deal with the same industry

- *Customer-Focused Marketing* (CFM), which rewards one division for selling the products of another, granting the various divisions access to different customers and distribution channels

- *Integrated Solutions Initiative*, which sets up cross-divisional teams that work together to serve a range of customer needs in a comprehensive way

Under the corporate banner of "Earning Customer Loyalty," Corporate Marketing is refining 3M's business processes to focus more closely on the customer. This approach includes market segmentation, brand promise and customer relationship management, and new methods for measuring customer satisfaction. 3M is also working to digitize all of its most important data to be available to customers and employees around the globe, twenty-four hours a day. Modern telecommunications, information technology, and a global data warehouse will deliver that data to any salesperson in the field, anywhere in the world. This puts the accumulated resources of seventy thousand people into the laptop of even a junior sales rep in territories like Brazil, Poland, or

Malaysia—providing, of course, that the rep takes advantage of what is available. Corporate Marketing uses the following diagram to illustrate the concept.[12]

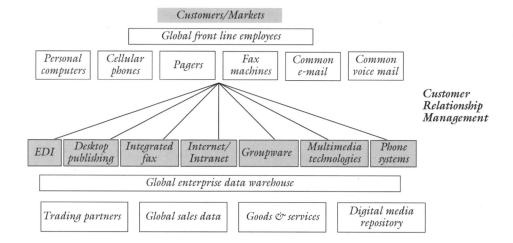

■ *Kmart Financial Analysis Modeling Tool*

Michael Linnerooth is a young sales and marketing analyst in the Construction and Home Improvement Markets Division. This is the part of 3M that sells such items for those major weekend projects as tapes, power-tool accessories, sandpaper, face masks, and items for wood refinishing. At the start of 1997, Linnerooth found himself worrying about how to meet an ambitious sales growth target for the Kmart account, one of the division's top ten accounts. Already, between 1993 and 1996, 3M had nearly tripled its Kmart sales by converting the customer to 3M product lines for abrasives, filters, and tape. With minimal opportunity for any further line conversions in 1997, he pondered how to achieve further sales growth through more mundane devices such as promotional campaigns and changes in product mix. "My problem was how to stand out among a hundred vendors," he recalls.

Linnerooth looked to Kmart's Partners Information Network (PIN), which provides information to vendors, to help give 3M the edge. A finance major, he claims that "Excel was my best friend in college." In this spirit he began to take the Kmart data, plus his own knowledge of Excel, and recast the information for 3M's ten main product categories into a format that could be easily displayed to Kmart's buyers. He started in February, working in the evening and on weekends. By summer he was adding 3M factory and inventory data to his spreadsheets. Linnerooth eventually created a modeling tool that could

- Track monthly point-of-sales data at Kmart for 3M products
- Monitor Kmart's gross margin, sales dollars and units, and profit dollars—all by item, category, and total business
- Monitor 3M's sales and profit by item, category, and total business
- Monitor inventory for all products

Linnerooth's innocuous-looking set of spreadsheets had a striking effect. He was able to identify the items that would help to increase 3M sales, profits, or margins. This information could be used with his own divisional management to justify promotional activities, category adjustments in favor of one product over another, and further changes that would appeal to Kmart's retail strategy. Linnerooth could then sit down with a Kmart buyer, recommend a promotion, predict its results based on historical data, and allow the retailer to stock the right amount of inventory in advance. When a 3M price increase was necessary, he demonstrated to the buyer what Kmart's share of the increase would be. (A little competitive research at other stores enabled him to show how the raised price would still be the lowest in its category.) He could also suggest changes in the product mix to feature profitable items: "This is a way to sell the customer higher-margin products and have them feel the benefits."

As the reputation of Linnerooth's modeling tool grew, buyers began to call him, asking, "We have space in an upcoming advertisement—what do you recommend?" His format could even be used to discover a win-win solution in cases where the interests of Kmart and 3M were not necessarily in alignment. "Bottom line, we are looking to increase each other's business," Linnerooth says. When a competitive threat emerged and there was a danger that 3M's line of filters would be replaced by a competitor's lower-priced products, Linnerooth again consulted his analytical model. "We were able to show Kmart that while 3M filters represented only 18 percent of retail sales and 26 percent of unit sales, 3M was 90 percent of the total profit in this category." Needless to say, after some follow-up meetings on merchandising and promotional programs, 3M retained and expanded its business with the Kmart account.

The account's 1997 results were outstanding. Without any major line conversions, 3M increased its business with Kmart 10 percent in point-of-sales numbers, grew margins on key categories, and significantly improved lead time for promotional activities. Total profitability for Kmart increased by over a million dollars.

Linnerooth's job portfolio has now been broadened so that he can roll out this financial analysis model for other key account salespeople. 3M is also trying to take his improvised Excel spreadsheets and tie them into its information technology systems such as the Super User Network (SUN). In the terminology of 3M marketers, Linnerooth and his laptop have added a valuable custom software solution to the toolkit of frontline employees, and expanded the company's global enterprise data warehouse.[13]

3M Staff Functions: Developmental Areas

Notwithstanding these examples of innovation, 3M's staff functions sometimes appear to be less nimble than their business cousins. Like staff departments elsewhere, they have been criticized for having their own agendas and being unresponsive to the needs of the Business Units. Efforts to increase the responsiveness of staff units have achieved results; however, 3M's admirable caution against embracing new fads too quickly may also work against the company. Staff functions may not take enough risks to be at the leading edge with their policies and programs.

Another issue is the performance of staff personnel, particularly outside of the United States. In some of the larger 3M subsidiary organizations around the world, it is not uncommon for the staff departments to be saddled with mediocre employees for whom the businesses have little use. In Europe this problem was compounded by an organizational change that allowed heads of the new European Business Units to select key players for their more centralized operations, leaving lesser performers behind in the subsidiaries. Company-wide hiring practices, too, have long prioritized the acquisition of technical skills over administrative excellence. Only since the early nineties have there been systematic global exchanges of staff personnel for developmental purposes.[14]

At the same time, there are subsidiaries, particularly smaller ones, that do a better job than the U.S. home office of rotating strong performers between line and staff functions. Some of the individuals who are reassigned in this manner become excellent managers. In recent years, 3M has begun to take more decisive steps to improve the overall quality of subsidiary staff operations. Housecleaning has taken place in Europe and elsewhere through early retirements and reductions in the size of certain staff departments.

A specific structural weakness for 3M is the relative lack of technical capabilities among marketers. One typical pattern in a subsidiary is for salespeople to move into more strategic marketing roles, which is fine except when marketing lacks sufficient technical depth to grasp unarticulated customer needs. In the absence of a technical marketing function, subsidiary sales groups are limited to selling what they receive from headquarters and what customers say they want, without inventing local solutions that might make customers much happier.

Staff training and development outside of the United States could be reinforced to better reflect 3M's global priorities. There is a myriad of developmental options available to mature employees in St. Paul, but out where the rubber meets the road in Latin America, Asia, or Africa, sales supervisors are hard pressed even to take subordinates along on customer calls, let alone provide systematic coaching and training opportunities. Fast-growing subsidiaries, particularly in Asia, have encountered employee retention issues due to perceived career limits or a lack of attachment to the global organization. This generally relates to the quality of supervision: in countries where supervisors are relatively new and inexperienced, without adequate training and development opportunities themselves, they may either neglect the career development of subordinates or become overly autocratic.

3M is seeking to address these issues. Greater quantities of information are becoming available to employees worldwide through 3M TV, albeit in a somewhat impersonal format. Mentor programs are underway, sending experienced salespeople or corporate scientists from the United States to work with overseas subsidiary employees. A fresh look at the changing demographic profile and developmental needs of the company's global employee base might lead executives to empty more offices in St. Paul and put increased training and development opportunities, as well as other staff resources, out where the most urgent needs reside. The large number of early retirements at headquarters in response to generous 3M packages over the last few years offers the chance for a shift in priorities. The more that staff functions around the world can both support innovation and become innovators themselves, the more innovative 3M as a whole will become.

Key Questions To Ask About Innovation

Staff Innovation

1. How can staff functions best support innovation? Areas to explore include:
   - For human resources: recruiting; corporate TV; leadership competencies.
   - For finance: balance sheet management to reduce capital costs; rapid response to international crises; procurement reengineering.
   - For marketing: coordinated approaches to customers; global data warehouse; analysis of customer data.

2. Are staff functions innovative themselves in their support for innovation? Do they successfully balance steady support for new product invention and commercialization with calculated risk-taking?

3. Are staff departments in subsidiary operations able to contribute significantly to global business expansion? How can headquarters staff resources be leveraged to augment subsidiary performance?

5

Global Innovation

Pratib Kumar is at the frontline of 3M's global sales operations. His territory is the southern Indian city of Bangalore—about as far away from St. Paul as you can get. There is no direct flight to Bangalore from North America. You fly through day and night almost as far as a commercial jet will go, wait numbly for a few hours to change planes, and then board another long flight for Mumbai, formerly known as Bombay. In Mumbai, on the coast of the Arabian Sea, there is another bleary wait through a second night and another plane change. Then, after a ninety-minute flight southeast into the interior of the Indian subcontinent, you finally arrive in Bangalore. It is eight in the morning, thirty-one hours and two calendar days after the start of the journey.

By Indian standards, Bangalore is an urban paradise, sometimes called the "Garden City" for its greenery. Located on the Deccan Plateau, it is relatively cool, although this could still mean that the temperature approaches 80° F in the early part of the morning. A jumble of motorcycles, small cars, motorized rickshaws, and taxis fills the city streets. Over the last decade, the population of Bangalore has grown more than tenfold, with an accompanying boom in both traffic congestion and air pollution. Driving much of this growth has been Bangalore's role as a center for India's high-tech industry. The industrial district in Bangalore's suburbs houses the offices and factories of American, Japanese, and European multinationals, including 3M's subsidiary headquarters. Birla 3M, as 3M's Indian operations are called, is a joint venture between 3M and the large Birla conglomerate.

Already sweating in the bright morning sunshine, young Kumar strides purposefully around to the retail shops in the southern half of the city. He has about fifteen hundred customers, not unusual in a country where retailing is dominated by millions of small mom-and-pop stores. There are still only four supermarkets in Bangalore. To serve all fifteen hundred of his customers each month, Kumar must visit sixty stores a day, taking just enough time for pleasant banter with each customer. He continues his rounds from morning until evening, doing his best to economize on bus fares by traveling on foot. It's tough work, especially in the blazing heat of midday.

Scotch-Brite, the household scouring pads from the 3M nonwovens product family, is Kumar's main item. A single Scotch-Brite pad retails for 5 rupees, or about 12 cents—not inexpensive in a country where monthly incomes are often less than $100. Kumar says that he manages to sell it "by explaining that it's more convenient to use and does a better job of getting things clean than coconut husks, and it lasts longer than other products." Brand awareness helps. "Most consumers have not heard of 3M yet. But they know Scotch-Brite. They come in to buy the product by its brand name."

As Kumar negotiates with a smile for a little better display location that will draw the eyes of buyers, he also writes down the day's sales into his order book. Kumar's modest monthly salary is supplemented with a substantial bonus if he sells more than thirteen thousand pads in a month. It is a source of pride for him to work at 3M. Particularly in Bangalore, a place known as the Silicon Valley of India, foreign capital companies are popular employers, and 3M's Bangalore operations, including a factory, are substantial and growing. Around eleven o'clock on this particular morning, Kumar emerges with a broad smile from a shop that stocks hardware goods. He's just obtained an order for 150 pads, another solid step toward his monthly quota. "This is a good omen," he beams.

Innovation across Borders

Around the world, 3M has thousands of salespeople like Kumar. How does the stylish notion of innovation apply to their work and help them make their sales quotas?

Innovation on the geographical frontiers of 3M's operations has a far different look than in St. Paul, Minnesota, where the core of its research community resides. In many of 3M's newer markets, the focus is less on inventing new technologies than on bringing the company's existing resources to bear on local customer needs. More specifically, there are seven distinct but interrelated areas of innovative activity that can be found in 3M's global operations:

- Sales and marketing techniques
- Product packaging
- Product adaptation
- Commercialization of new technologies
- Acquisition of technical information
- Co-design
- Original inventions

■ Sales and Marketing Techniques

Many 3M subsidiaries are primarily sales offices and lack the personnel or technical capabilities to invent products. However, there is still plenty of room for innovation in sales and marketing. In the words of H. C. Shin, who spent eleven years working for 3M Korea before serving a three-year stint as managing director of 3M Philippines:

> Asian subsidiaries don't have to reinvent the wheel; most of the development is done in the U.S. Our duty is to figure out how to transfer products to different customers—to deal with the implementation and execution. But there are still many ways to innovate—for example, in the area of marketing strategy. A program is developed in the U.S.; we can modify that but maintain core elements.

3M Philippines created an event called "Customer Salute." Thirty to forty employees run a day-long show at a key customer site, including product booths, presentations, and technical seminars along with live music, Filipino snacks, and a raffle. A similar type of event occurs in the United States, Shin notes, with one crucial difference: the customer is usually invited to the 3M campus. In the Philippines, 3M took the event to the customer. The intent is the same—to demonstrate in a single location 3M's ability to provide integrated customer solutions—but the mode of execution in the Philippines emphasizes 3M's readiness to fit in with the local culture and business practices.[1]

At 3M Korea, Shin's colleague H. D. Ryoo, a sales director for the Commercial Graphics Division, has developed an intriguing way to convince big corporate customers to purchase advanced products: inviting them to Japan to view applications not yet common in Korea. This draws on many customers' sense of rivalry with their Japanese neighbors. "For them, seeing is believing. To let them see with their own eyes is a really good way to sell customers."[2] Shin himself developed a permutation of this approach by occasionally taking important Filipino customers to view new product applications in the United States.

In Europe, where 3M subsidiaries have built up sizable local operations over several decades of hard work, the cost and extra workload of keeping web sites up to date in a host of languages was proving too much for some subsidiaries. Enter 3M Europe's "Webmaster" Ronald Faas (his official title is Interactive Marketing and Communications Manager). He pioneered a dynamic web publishing application that allows 3M employees to put country-specific information into databases in their local languages. These databases are then drawn upon "real-time" to generate web pages as customers post inquiries—avoiding the need to reprogram when presenting the latest information. The program, tailor-made for 3M's European and Middle Eastern operations, provides templates so that employees across these regions can share content created in different languages. It also extends web site development workflow into other systems to facilitate quick management approval and publication of new materials. States Faas:

> A year ago when we started, there were a couple of hundred static European web pages. One year later we had over two thousand pages. If you were to translate what we had at the end of the year into static pages, it would mean eight thousand HTML pages, an impossible number to have developed in such a short time frame and at such low cost [without the new interconnectivity]. We earned back the cost of putting the system in place in less than six months.[3]

Web site development now falls directly into the hands of local employees, giving them the ability to update the web content to fit country-specific needs with ease and at minimal cost. "This is about making the actual implementation as easy as possible for people at the country level," says Jean Waller, manager of Communications Technology and Resources for 3M Europe.[4] Customers are drawn to continuously updated information and visit such web sites repeatedly. In fact, dynamic web publishing has proved to be such a success in Europe that there have been calls to implement it throughout the company.

■ Product Packaging

There is more to maximizing packaging use than just translating product information into local languages. Sizes and colors with local appeal, or the inclusion of a brand mark from a joint venture partner with a strong local image—for instance, the Sumitomo logo for products of Sumitomo 3M in Japan—can all enhance marketing. In some countries, modified packaging may be necessary simply to make sure that the product arrives safely. An employee of 3M China observes:

> The way overhead projectors are packaged in the U.S. assumes a good road and highway system. But in China we have to change the packaging. . . . I was very upset when two-thirds of a shipment of projectors was broken in transit. Or, to give another example, there were cans of cleaner that arrived in the customer's warehouse with scratches on the cans because they were bouncing up and down in the truck.[5]

Packaging several products together in a kit can also enhance both sales and profits. Sumitomo 3M's tireless marketers have created a "Sleep Kit" for Japan. It includes mattress covers made with a 3M porous fabric along with the BreatheRight strip that some people wear across their noses at night to prevent snoring. The combination of occupational health and safety respirators with extensive user training (see chapter one) is a different kind of package that incorporates a 3M service; it has been successful in various world markets.

■ Product Adaptation

Modifying existing 3M products enables subsidiaries to tailor their offerings to local preferences. Geoff Nicholson, 3M's head of Corporate Technical Planning and chief of International Technical Operations, likes to give an example that begins with a problem: 3M's scouring pads, an offshoot of its nonwovens technology platform, weren't selling well in the Philippines. So local company employees studied consumer behavior and observed that many people used coconut husks for cleaning (a common practice across southern Asia). So they changed the color of 3M's scouring pads from green to yellow, the color of the husks. Sales took off.

3M Mexico has a similar story. A local employee noticed that the scouring pads on the market did not stand up well to caustic detergents used to clean away the spicy cuisine. A cross-functional team from 3M Mexico decided to develop a more resistant cleaning pad, with a sponge and web fiber scouring pad laminated together by a solventless adhesive. This product also gave a lift to sales. In both cases, alert observation of local customs, combined with relatively minor product modifications, resulted in significantly increased business.[6]

At Birla's 3M facility outside Bangalore, India, researcher Abhijeet Saungikar adapted another standard 3M product, Scotchgard fabric protector, to meet a local need. Noting that an Indian woman's most prized garment is her silk sari, worn only on special occasions, he proposed a new product called Silkgard to protect the expensive silk material from spots and stains. His idea drew little support, but Saungikar persisted, actually investing his own pocket money in product development (for which he was eventually reimbursed). Silkgard is now on the market and has met with a positive reception from retail customers and consumers, while the sales associates of Mr. Kumar who represent Scotchgard products have added a promising new item to their portfolio —one that Indian customers are willing to pay for.[7]

Throwing Light on Italy's Great Art

An engaging European story of product adaptation comes from Italy, where the 3M organization in Milan has come up with dozens of new applications for light management technology. Originally developed in the United States, the technology distributes light from a single source over a large physical space; an early application was lighted road guardrails in North America and Europe.

Even with only one bulb every thirty meters, the guardrails give out a bright, fluorescent glow clearly visible on the darkest nights. The 3M barriers have helped to reduce accidents along dangerous roadways.

Antonio Pinna Berchet, general counsel of 3M Italy, felt strongly

Illuminated
Guardrail

that this technology could be put to other uses. Because of its low energy requirement and its ability to illuminate without generating heat or dust, Pinna Berchet believed that the technology could be transformed into a new lighting system with many advantages over conventional lighting. He was not limited by his official position as the subsidiary's chief lawyer. "I consider 3M a very innovative company, foremost because they give you the freedom to invent your role in the company every day," he says.

Pinna Berchet's position also involved public relations work. From his close ties with the Milan municipal government, he knew that the Central Institute of Restoration of Rome had undertaken the large project of restoring Leonardo Da Vinci's masterpiece, *The Last Supper*. Unfortunately, once the fresco was restored, the institute's best efforts would be damaged by conventional lighting. Pinna Berchet saw the opportunity: 3M Italy could adapt the light management technology in order to create a system that would allow admirers to view the masterpiece while also protecting it from the impact of dust, radiation, and direct light.

Pinna Berchet proposed this project to his colleagues and the organization mobilized at once, creating a film that could be placed inside the tube to amplify the light. Experiments using this Optical Lighting

Film (OLF) to light rooms proved successful, and with proposal and prototype in hand, Pinna Berchet presented his company's solution to the institute's Restoration Committee and offered to cover all the installation costs. After two years of study, the committee accepted.

"Today, *The Last Supper* is lit through our system," says Pinna Berchet with pride. "With our system, it is possible to keep the lighting source remote and to light just the piece of art with a tube. The system was put in place three years ago, and it is working perfectly." Not only has 3M Italy solved a problem which had plagued the art world for years, but it has also generated a tremendous amount of positive press for the company.

The Last Supper with OLF

Since their success with *The Last Supper*, Pinna Berchet and his colleagues have sought new applications for OLF technology. It has proved effective at lighting large screens in multiplex cinemas, for instance. Instead of lighting the screen from the ceiling, 3M's system allows the screen to be lit from the floor with a single tube. The tube generates no heat, uses less energy than do conventional lighting systems, and offers major savings in maintenance costs. Maintenance people used to require an entire day to change ceiling light bulbs; they can replace the floor tubes in a matter of minutes.

3M Italy is also experimenting with the use of OLF to "transport sunlight underground," creating the illusion of daylight. Pinna Berchet explains: "The first prototype of this system will be put in Pompeii in order to light the old theater that was completely covered by volcanic dust two thousand years ago. This theater is buried under nine meters of volcanic ash. There will be a large celebration next year. Our system will be used to transport sunlight into the theater. It effectively transports 92 percent of the daylight from above ground." 3M Italy envisions this technology to have enormous potential as natural lighting for subway systems, garages, and underground buildings.

In order to generate more applications for its light management technology, 3M Italy has developed a close alliance with the local designer community. "We have a lot of contacts at the most important designer school in Italy, in Europe, and probably in the world—the Domus Academy in Milan," effuses Pinna Berchet. "It is full of talented architects and designers, so every time you present new technology they have lots of new ideas. This is part of our innovative approach, a way of cross-fertilizing ideas." Not that 3Mers in Italy lack ideas themselves. They are developing prototypes for more applications that will be available to 3M worldwide. "Now," he says, "the problem is not [lack of] ideas. The problem is time."[8]

■ Commercialization of a New Technology

Japan has proved to be a fertile ground for the commercialization of new technologies. Sumitomo 3M, with its advanced technology base and demanding customers, has both the capability and the motivation to scan the company's technological resources for potential new products. This applies even to an area like porous film that 3M has developed over many years in the United States. Current porous film projects at St. Paul include transdermal patches, components for electric vehicle batteries, and drug purification. It is Sumitomo 3M, however, that has scored a modest early success with agricultural garments.

Fastidious Japanese farmers expressed interest in a protective uniform for daily wear that would keep out dust, particles, and chemicals while remaining comfortable and easy to wear. Sumitomo 3M utilized porous film to create just such a uniform, and has established an expanding customer base of agricultural users. Reaching this market is easier than in the United States because Japan has one giant farmers' cooperative that serves as a distribution channel.

Gene Shipman, a corporate research scientist in 3M's Process Technologies Laboratory, comments on some advantages of working with Japanese colleagues and customers:

> They are less concerned about getting the business going immediately. Westerners always rush for business and commitments, but the Japanese take longer and make better arrangements. If you become a good partner they will come back time after time. . . .
>
> We send them the rollout material and they make the finished goods themselves. We've learned that they're better at making them. The material has to look perfect and be perfect even before it goes into the final product. They have challenged us to shoot for the highest possible level of quality.

The design and quality of a product introduced in Japan constitute strengths that can ultimately be put to use for 3M as a whole. Japanese-style innovation—grounded in close, cooperative, long-term relationships with customers—provides substantial advantages to product developers.

Sumitomo 3M is now working with Shipman's laboratory on another innovation: facial wipes. Japan's hot and muggy summer climate, along with high standards of personal hygiene, make the country a natural market for products that will quickly remove sweat and grime. Facial blotters made with porous films remove oils better and have more capacity than alternative materials. Shipman admits that the perfectionism of his Japanese counterparts can be frustrating, with continual demands for more colors, greater sweat absorbency, fragrances, and easy-use dispensers. Yet they have gained entry into a new cosmetics market that was not on the St. Paul radar screen:

> This was all driven by Sumitomo 3M. They know that the Japanese oil-blotting-paper business was $300 million last year, and they're trying to capture 10 percent of that market. . . . Now the U.S. people are looking at importing this Sumitomo 3M idea.[9]

■ Acquisition of Technical Information

The fires of innovation can be stoked by bringing in fresh technology from outside of the company, a point pondered back in 1990 by Jan Alboszta, a 3M Process Instrumentation and Control Systems engineer. Alboszta observed the tremendous changes occurring with the collapse of the Soviet Union. As he points out: "One-third of the world's Ph.D. population was in the former Soviet Union countries. . . . Much of this vast knowledge base was in danger of never being used."

Alboszta, a native of Poland who is fluent in five languages, felt that it was "just common sense" for 3M to make use of the technical resources in Russia and the other parts of the former Soviet Union. Taking advantage of 3M's Fifteen Percent Rule, he began exploring the viability of a systematic technology transfer program. He reviewed international science journals, visited institutes, and talked with prospective participants. 3Mers he spoke to were initially interested but noncommittal. On the other hand, scientists in the former Soviet Union had a strong economic motivation to establish contacts: many of them were working without pay or taking menial jobs to supplement their incomes.

Enthused by the results of his preliminary investigations, in 1992 Alboszta fired off a message to a 3M executive and a few days later found himself in Geoff Nicholson's office. The executive, Chuck Kiester—senior vice president of Engineering, Quality and Manufacturing Services—was so supportive of the plans put forward by Albozsta that he offered to fund a position for him on Nicholson's staff out of his own budget. Within six months the first agreement had been signed between 3M and a Russian research organization; by the end of 1997 Albozsta was involved with twenty-eight active projects. He now works for 3M International Operations.[10]

Al Pocius, group leader at the 3M Adhesive Technologies Center, describes one example of a technology imported from the former Soviet Union that contributed to a research breakthrough. 3M scientists in St. Paul had identified two key challenges for adhesive product development: creating products that would either adhere to oily metal or bind low-surface-energy plastics like Teflon and polypropylene. Thanks in part to work by a 3M France scientist, Alain Lamon, the first problem was successfully addressed, resulting in a product now sold to the automotive industry. But solutions for the second remained stubbornly elusive, and the 3M researchers knew that a major technical leap was necessary in order for real progress to be made. Some researchers, including the bulk of the adhesives industry, even felt that a solution was impossible.

In 1991, as the Soviet Union was breaking up, 3M France heard from some Soviet scientists who claimed to have discovered a method by which direct bonding of polyolefins and Teflon could be accomplished. Their initial response was extremely skeptical, but in 1992, Alain Lamon and Marcel Simonnet of 3M France traveled to the former Soviet Union, bringing test specimens for bonding with the adhesive technology. The results obtained in the tests led them to believe that astounding breakthroughs in adhesive technology could be made. In 1993, a team comprised of Jan Albozsta, Al Pocius, and Dave Cleveland (patent counsel) traveled to Russia, and eventually worked out a technology purchase agreement.

Considerable modifications still needed to be made to what the Russians considered to be a commercially finished product; the original work purchased from the Russians was used only as a starting point. The technology that 3M purchased has already led to a flurry of innovative activity, with many patents obtained and others pending. A first version of a new adhesive, DP-4000, is in test sale and an improved version is in scale-up. Applications are being found in the general industrial market, the automotive after-market, and marine trades.

Pocius identifies three critical ingredients to this success. First, he says, "We were ready"—having identified a critical new application area and begun the search for solutions. Second, of course, was the overseas connection provided through Lamon and Albozsta to the Russian scientists who held the missing pieces to the puzzle. The final ingredient to cement the puzzle together was support and buy-in from the Adhesives Division, which was not only open to obtaining information from a nontraditional source, but also took on the risk of financing the project.[11]

■ Co-Design

3M is moving increasingly toward product design strategies that incorporate global input and multicultural teamwork from the start. Sumitomo 3M researchers, because of their advanced technical skills, mature lab operations, and large domestic market, are again at the forefront of this trend. Japanese scientists were involved in the early design of the HFEs that replace ozone-depleting chemicals (see chapter one) and in the development of 3M's Brightness Enhancement Film, both products for which there is a large Japanese market.

Ikuko Ebihara, a Japanese scientist on assignment in St. Paul, provides an example of co-design in progress. She is helping to develop structural adhesives, another promising field. An intensely bright and serious young researcher, Ebihara is one of the twenty to thirty Sumitomo 3M employees who reside in St. Paul at any one time. Her work also includes modifying product formulations for the Japanese market, working to improve manufacturing processes, filing for Japanese regulatory approval, and troubleshooting activities with Japanese customers. Thus, co-design can be a multifaceted activity that flows naturally into manufacturing, regulatory, and technical service issues. She has gone beyond her official duties by participating in the 3M Tech Forum and other networking activities that may lead to future co-design projects with Sumitomo 3M. Ebihara has been deeply impressed by the regular St. Paul sessions held to exhibit new technologies to others from around the company:

> At poster sessions here in the U.S., we sell our own technology to different divisions. This is very unusual for Japanese. We started it in Japan several years ago but it is still not too popular. Here the strength of the 3M organization is cooperation, networking. You know who is working on what.[12]

■ Original Inventions

Aside from earthshaking technological breakthroughs, which are rare in 3M's subsidiaries, many inventions build upon established products. But there is a point at which the innovative contributions of the inventors cause a product to take on a qualitative difference—something more than a mere incremental line extension.

3M Canada, for example, has been working on a Biorational Insecticide Replacement (BIR) program intended as an environmentally safe substitute for pesticides. This program combines 3M's encapsulation techniques with the latest in synthetic pheromone technology, creating a product which disrupts the mating cycles of insects that damage crops and forests. Synthetic pheromones replicate the natural odor of chemicals released by female insects at mating time, disrupting mating patterns by confusing the males and hence reducing the numbers of pests in the next generation. The encapsulation technology used by 3M enables a slow release of these chemicals, providing significant advantages over frequent spraying or hand-tying of products onto each plant.

BIR tests have been conducted in Canada, South Africa, and the Czech Republic and have been extended to the homes of international pests such as borers damaging pine trees in Chile and oriental fruit moths in Michigan. An intensive analysis of European markets is now under way. Providing that regional regulatory hurdles can be overcome, BIR represents a highly original application of a 3M technology in a new market.[13]

Back at Sumitomo 3M, a team was put to work on a different but equally pressing problem: outbreaks of hospital infections caused by staphylococcus bacteria that are resistant to antibiotics. Sumitomo 3M already manufactured a decorative wall covering used in elevators and other facilities that require fireproof surfaces resistant to scratches, stains, and solvents. The Japanese team had the idea of combining this so-called Di-Noc technology—abandoned years ago in the United States but successfully maintained in Japan—with antibacterial properties.

Sumitomo 3M researchers examined various antibacterial agents for plastics and finally selected an organic agent that resists both bacteria and fungi. This agent was compounded into the top surface and acrylic layers of the decorative wall covering and became Antibacterial Di-Noc film, the 3M award-winning product now used in operating rooms, hallways, reception areas, and other interior surfaces in medical facilities.[14]

■ Changing the Mix

In 3M subsidiaries around the world, innovative activity in areas such as sales and marketing or product adaptation is still far easier to find than the more complex and demanding processes of co-design or original invention. Up until the last decade, the standard pattern was for new products to be hatched in St. Paul, introduced into the American market, and then gradually rolled out to subsidiary customers. A different pattern, now taking shape with high-priority projects like the Pacing Plus programs, calls for co-design and simultaneous introduction into key global markets. As the company continues to grow its overseas business, it will be necessary to transform innovation in major subsidiaries toward closer and more intensive cooperation in every type of innovation.

Support for Innovation: Formal Methods

3M cultivates innovation on a global scale through a number of formal organizational mechanisms. The most venerable of these are its *organizational structure* and corresponding *expatriate assignments*. 3M's International Operations are overseen by Ron Baukol, an executive vice president who is one of the top handful of company leaders and a member of 3M's board of directors. His high profile within the company brings prominence and attention to its non-U.S. business. Reporting to him are the executives for the different geographical regions as well as the managing directors of each country's operations. Each region and major subsidiary also have a technical director, a manufacturing director, and a marketing director. This structure intersects with and is balanced by 3M's forty-plus business divisions, which have their own reporting lines.

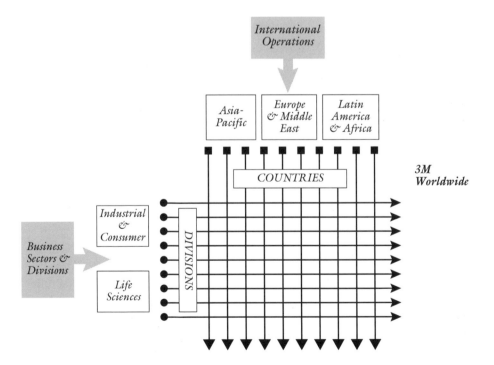

3M runs its overseas subsidiaries with a comparatively small number of people from the home office. Only 180 Americans are on assignment in other countries, a small number for a company of 3M's size, especially with half of total sales (nearly $8 billion) and over thirty thousand employees working outside of the United States. But these expatriates are in pivotal positions to facilitate technology transfer. The country managing director is traditionally an expatriate, and often the other regional- and country-level directors are as well. An expatriate technical director is likely to have spent his or her entire previous career within the St. Paul research community, and is therefore ideally positioned to be a conduit for technical information both from and back to the United States. Recently there has been a stronger trend toward expatriate assignments with no U.S. involvement to transfer technologies or staff expertise between other countries—for example, Japan to Thailand, Germany to Belgium, or the United Kingdom to South Africa.

Inbound assignments to the United States are another vital part of 3M's expatriation strategy. At present there are over sixty 3Mers in St. Paul and Austin from subsidiaries around the world, plus a steady flow of employees who come on shorter-term visits. The bulk of inbound expatriate assignments are still for researchers who come to study a particular technology and to build links with 3M's U.S. technical community. Such people may engage in product adaptation or co-design activities during their visit. More importantly, they become key contacts and coordinators for cross-border technical exchange and innovation after returning to their home countries. At major overseas research sites such as those in Japan or Germany, there is now a core of scientists who have had extended stays in the United States and are well-versed in the corporate culture. New transfers of information and ideas can happen relatively quickly with these scientists because there is already a common foundation of technical knowledge and research procedures. One veteran 3Mer notes:

There is great value in sending people on assignment to St. Paul for extended periods. This is an investment on which we reap huge dividends for years and years afterward in terms of contacts, language ability, and understanding of the way things are done. The difference before and after is almost like night and day in their ability to interact and get things done.[15]

Overseas assignments in all directions are consistently cited by 3Mers as the single most important factor in improving cross-boundary working relations. A key to the company's success in this area has been its dogged consistency in supporting such assignments over the last several decades, not only to achieve business goals but to develop future leaders. Since 3M has a relatively low turnover of employees it can build upon the experience and personal relationships developed. 3M is quite serious about the need for top management candidates to have significant overseas experience. The current CEO, L. D. DeSimone, worked in Brazil for fourteen years, eventually as the managing director. Originally a Canadian, he speaks five languages (English, French, Italian, Portuguese, and Spanish). Most of DeSimone's executive colleagues at 3M are former or current expatriates themselves, including all of the six executive vice presidents and ten out of twelve members of the company's Operations Committee (five of whom were born outside of the United States).

Cross-border teams are another formal support mechanism for global innovation. First developed in Europe, these teams are designed to bring a more intense focus, better cooperation, accelerated pace, and systematic follow-through to company efforts in markets where there are major growth opportunities. Originally known as EMATs (European Management Action Teams), they regularly bring together relevant personnel from the United States and local subsidiary operations to share information and make decisions. Such teams have been vital in encouraging U.S. members to allocate more time and energy outside of their home markets. At the same time, regular team meetings enable non-U.S. participants to present their viewpoints more forcefully and to assume greater responsibility for customer issues. The success of the European teams has led the company to extend the model to include JMATs (with Japanese and American members) and APMATs (dealing with Asia-Pacific business). 3M has studied the performance of these teams with an eye to disseminating successful cross-border teamwork practices into different parts of the company.[16]

Mentor programs for both salespeople and scientists transfer experience, insight, and innovative ideas from St. Paul to other locations around the world. In China, for example, one of the steps taken recently to reverse worrisome employee turnover in a key division was to implement a so-called 3/3/3 Program: three American sales reps travel to China to coach Chinese counterparts for three weeks, three times per year. Likewise, Geoff Nicholson, the international technical head, has created a program that sends 3M corporate scientists to overseas labs on a regular basis. These scientists hold technical seminars (often to packed houses) and remain on site long enough to interact with promising young employees. With their long records of inventions, patents, and successfully commercialized products, 3M's corporate scientists command awe among the younger researchers, and their presence has an inspirational effect.

Corporate Enterprise Development (CED) is a group formed in 1997 to nurture new businesses within 3M by offering seed money and access to other resources. Two-thirds of its efforts are being invested outside of the United States. CED is another brainchild of Bill Coyne, chief of research and development, who complains, "We weren't creating enough new businesses within the company, and I felt that we needed an organization to accelerate the process."

One goal of CED is to identify opportunities with significant export potential beyond the country of origin. A good illustration is the natural insecticide program at 3M Canada. CED also tracks startup companies in relevant markets and technologies, allowing 3M to develop early business relationships while keeping abreast of new trends. Most new business supported by CED begins with employee proposals— it has been inundated with ideas from its inception. For an idea that passes a first review, CED then funds development of a business plan, and ushers it into either an existing business unit or a new unit created and temporarily funded by CED. Besides the Canadian example, there are already eight other new programs under way in such diverse areas as reusable packaging, odor removal, toys, fuel cells, freshness indicators for consumer products, and cleanup of nuclear facilities.[17]

Support for Innovation: Informal Methods

3M's secret weapons in the global innovation race come from unexpectedly low-tech sources: friendship and volunteer activity. *Friendship* assumes particular significance at 3M. Years of expatriate exchanges and overseas travel, combined with the generally low turnover of employees, have produced a network of global contacts that crisscross the official organizational structure and supplement its functions.

Friendship as a competitive advantage originated in St. Paul's brand of Midwest hospitality—countless invitations to come over for dinner and thousands of backyard barbecues. One of 3M's top global leaders offered a surprising confession from his younger days: "I first learned the true meaning of friendship in the United States."[18] This hospitality has been reciprocated in countless ways in private homes, restaurants, and karaoke bars, and at national landmarks around the world. Today, anywhere you go in the 3M world there is somebody who knows someone else who knows you. In this era of thin company loyalties and even thinner reservoirs of social time, 3M offices everywhere maintain an uncommon personal warmth.

Personal ties can provide an indirect boost to cross-border innovation. If a would-be innovator in a 3M subsidiary environment needs information, his or her personal network becomes a powerful search engine. When a question emerges that has been answered before by one of 3M's seventy thousand employees, personal contacts save the time and trouble of long background checks, speed the exchange of news or best practices, and open backdoor channels for obtaining product samples or resources. And in the event that a conflict arises over the priority or direction of a particular project, the fact that the parties involved have known each other for a long time makes it easier to seek out a reasonable compromise. Trust, openness, mutual commitment to a common enterprise—these are intangible but incredibly valuable supports for innovative activity.

Volunteer activity complements friendship by enhancing personal ties and putting them to practical use. 3M's Language Society, for instance, is a resource that any global company would envy and which would bankrupt Berlitz if it caught on. It had its beginnings more than thirty years ago when a group of German 3Mers residing in St. Paul started getting together to speak their mother tongue. Their meetings grew and became more regular, and other people began to get interested in learning the language. The Language Society has mushroomed from these humble beginnings: today it teaches 15 languages in 66 classes per week, with nearly 70 volunteer teachers, and a total membership of close to 800. There are now some paid positions to carry out document translation, interpreting, and tutoring. The society has branched out into different activities such as festivals to celebrate various national cultures. It also helps to spread the knowledge of foreign service employees (FSEs), or expatriates, by inviting them to make noontime presentations on their countries for various audiences, videotaping these presentations for 3Mers who could not attend.

The 3M FSE Volunteer Services Program performs a related set of activities. This began as a grassroots movement among spouses of former expatriates who felt that the company could take a more proactive role in assisting employees and their families with overseas assignments. A determined group of women, led by Nancy Skaar, the wife of a 3Mer formerly posted to the Netherlands, had to swallow an initial rebuff from International Human Resources and lobby the spouses of top executives who had been expatriates themselves. Eventually their arguments were heeded. Now anyone who comes to St. Paul for more than three months is assigned a guide who helps with the logistical details of the move (be it documents, health care, schools, neighborhood orientation, or recreation). The guides, who receive a modest reimbursement that sometimes barely exceeds out-of-pocket costs, often become good friends with the families and provide very personal help such as driving them to the hospital or answering their calls in the middle of the night. Similar networks for expatriate orientation have sprung up or are planned overseas. The Volunteer Services Program publishes a newsletter, *3M Around the Globe*, which goes out to every expatriate. Expatriates newly assigned to a country are introduced to 3Mers who are either from that country or have lived there. Homecoming events are now held for returning expatriates and their families.

What is good for the adjustment of foreign service employees and their families seems to be good for 3M. There may be no greater source of support for cross-border innovation than the ability to settle family logistics, make connections with the right people in an unfamiliar environment, and have access to the hard-won knowledge of one's expatriate predecessors. FSE volunteer activities thus enhance global relationships by making sure that each individual has a productive stay and that they remain connected within 3M's invisible but vibrant human grid.

■ The Indian Connection

The powerful chemistry of friendship and volunteer activity reaches from St. Paul to Pratib Kumar and his Birla 3M colleagues. Significant assistance for technical innovation in India comes from American corporate headquarters, but not always through official channels. It turns out that a group of Indian 3Mers resident in St. Paul have interpreted the Fifteen Percent Rule as a green light to help out Birla 3M at every opportunity. Milind Sabade, a researcher with science degrees from Bombay University and a Ph.D. in polymer science earned in the United States, describes his motivation:

The Birla 3M operation is small. In the early 1900s, 3M was small, too. In India we have about three hundred employees now. There is no other joy or pleasure as great as seeing that we are helping the operation in India. I have fire in my belly to do something good. Also, I have empathy. I understand their problems not in terms of technology, but in terms of how we at headquarters can help. 3M is a tremendous library even for someone here at headquarters— an ocean of knowledge. To make use of that knowledge, you have to know how to use the library. It's very difficult for them being so far away. I take pleasure in helping them in small ways.

There are several types of assistance that he and other Indian colleagues resident in St. Paul provide to Birla 3M:

- Identifying promising new product opportunities
- Finding and recommending testing equipment suitable for colleagues in India
- Locating people in St. Paul who can assist Indian scientists with a specific issue or technical problem
- Helping to reformulate existing 3M products so that they can be manufactured in India using local materials for local markets
- Searching out raw material suppliers in the United States to meet needs that cannot be supplied in India
- Obtaining product samples that might not be readily available through regular channels

Sabade describes the Indian group in St. Paul as informally formal: "Sure enough there are a lot of Indians here at headquarters, maybe seventy-five to a hundred. We all handle different aspects of the business. So we pass questions along until we find the appropriate person to provide an answer. I know most of them." An e-mail tree and occasional social get-togethers help to keep the group linked.

Sabade's efforts had their start when Nagaraj Maskeri, Birla 3M's technical manager, came to St. Paul on a short-term trip. Sabade and Maskeri discovered that they were from the same hometown in India. As they got to know one another, they started thinking that some of the people of Indian origin in St. Paul could help to improve links with Birla 3M. Sabade has been active ever since. His activities mean a lot to colleagues in India; for them to be able to send a message from so far away and then count on a speedy, useful response has built a good deal of trust and spurred on the work of both sides.

At a first meeting Sabade appears to be deferential and concerned with protocol ("Official channels are effective; this is just a supplement"). Yet he, like Abhijeet Saungikar, the creator of Silkgard, has clearly caught some of the rebellious spirit of the 3M research pioneers. When asked what he would do if his superiors in St. Paul told him to cut back on his help to Indian colleagues, Sabade tactfully praises his managers and adds with a slight smile: "So far there has been no resistance. If there were, I would go ahead and do it anyway and just not tell them about it right away."[19]

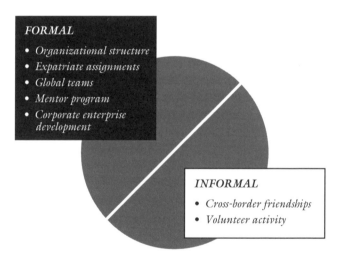

Support for Global Innovation

FORMAL
- *Organizational structure*
- *Expatriate assignments*
- *Global teams*
- *Mentor program*
- *Corporate enterprise development*

INFORMAL
- *Cross-border friendships*
- *Volunteer activity*

■ Global Innovation: 3M Advantages

A common sequence of activities enables 3M subsidiaries in developing countries to establish themselves quickly. Once the sales potential of a new location has been established, the company moves from selling through agents and distributors to hiring its own direct sales force.

Soon afterward, even in operations with only a dozen or so sales employees, 3M begins to send in jumbo-sized rolls of materials for conversion into localized products. For a small amount of capital and with minimal space requirements, this key step allows a fledgling operation to offer finished products in local packaging in the appropriate languages. Subsidiary employees are thereby encouraged to investigate and respond to local customer needs. Converting product in this way is also looked upon favorably by local governments.

The next stage is full-scale manufacturing, which holds further opportunities for customization. 3M's financial health and diverse product portfolio facilitate investment in manufacturing facilities around the world. Already, 70 percent of products sold by the company in non-U.S. markets are produced outside of the United States, and the company is continuing to make substantial investments. Strategic placement of a new factory in a rapidly developing country or region provides a tremendous boost to subsidiary innovation by making it easier to modify existing products and create customer-focused applications. Manufacturing facilities ultimately become the nucleus for a stronger engineering presence and local R&D, setting off a virtuous circle that enables local employees to add new products and grow customer demand. "Local manufacturing has been a key factor for us in gaining dominant market share," says a 3Mer from Singapore. "It gives us flexibility and the ability to make a quick response to the customer."[20]

In this way, 3M has learned how to leverage its presence in a new market while controlling costs. The systematic application of this know-how has become a powerful advantage.

Agent/distributor ⇒ Direct sales ⇒ Conversion ⇒ Manufacturing — *Subsidiary Development Sequence*

A second competitive advantage for 3M around the world is having products to serve an economy at any stage. Whether a country is still in the early developmental phase, is an established industrial force, or has become an advanced high-tech leader, 3M's enormous product portfolio holds something for everybody. And as a national economy grows in complexity, it can consume a greater variety and quantity of products. Sales in a developing economy might start out with a focus on areas like transportation safety, construction, or basic consumer goods such as Scotch-Brite pads. An advanced economy like Germany's can potentially use almost every product in 3M's portfolio.

*3M Products
for Global Markets*

ADVANCED ECONOMIES
Electronics, computers, office supplies, aerospace, health care

INDUSTRIAL ECONOMIES
Automotive, general industrial, worker safety, plastics, chemicals, consumer products

DEVELOPING ECONOMIES
Transportation safety, telecommunications, construction & building maintenance

Having a broad range of products and a global network of sub-sidiaries creates developmental precedents for any given country. A "cascade effect" can take place among subsidiaries as the experience of a nearby regional leader is often more relevant to an expanding country operation than is input from the U.S. domestic market. In Asia, for example, Japan can share with Korea, Taiwan with China, and Singapore with Malaysia. Analogous patterns of exchange are taking place in Europe, Latin America, and Africa. Subsidiary employees who are relatively new to the company do not have to reinvent the wheel because they have a whole vehicle ready to roll in the form of a product and an established procedure for getting it to customers. Even the humblest forms of innovation in areas such as sales and marketing require a baseline of infrastructure and resources, and this, plus the credibility attached to the 3M name in many markets, gives employees far away from St. Paul the latitude to start thinking for themselves.

A 3M employee in Asia describes how this learning process has worked for him:

> When we started in this country, it was tough to think about how to launch our products. The market in the United States is very different from ours. I made frequent visits to Japan to learn what was done there—what were the key success factors. This has been a big help for our business. Just now we are beginning to share with other countries, too, showing them our sales calls, marketing activities, and customer support.[21]

Local innovations can be transferred across borders to markets with similar needs for a greater return on the company's investment. For instance, 3M Singapore employees selling reflective sheeting worked closely with traffic police to develop bright orange license plates for the cars of probationary drivers; this success was shared with Malaysia, which was also looking for a means to reduce accident rates. Singaporean marketers have already sent packages to other countries in the region to communicate success factors. One of them comments, "If we're able to demonstrate success here in Singapore, it helps a lot to demonstrate a proven case to other countries. Not everyone wants to be the first with something new."[22]

The Cascade Effect

■ The Shortfalls of Global Reach

3M managers freely acknowledge that the company's global strengths also beget weaknesses. The vast scope of products can be overwhelming to new subsidiaries. With only a handful of employees trying to serve the needs of numerous 3M divisions simultaneously, some are kept so busy dealing with U.S. or regional headquarters that they lack the time to focus on their customers. As one of them put it, "It is like having many pitchers with just one catcher." Newly hired employees must travel a steep learning curve in order to understand the company, its products, and how to respond effectively to customers. A subsidiary manager remarks:

> We have fifty thousand products, and anyone can pick up the phone. New employees don't yet know what products the company has or what group is selling them. "Tape," for example, could be the Tape Group, or it could be Electrical. . . . Customers get shuffled between departments.[23]

There is also the danger that existing products and procedures can stifle innovation by allowing people to do things the easy way. Another subsidiary manager is critical of employees who want to use someone else's success formula without thinking for themselves:

We are overstructured, working along the lines that the company draws. . . . Instead of copying the U.S. story, we should go down to the fundamentals and look closely. Today having a package of information limits the ability of people. Everyone's waiting for a package so they can push a button. After many years of experience with 3M, I have come to believe that the quality of employee thinking is the most important thing; I would rather train people how to think than give them the solution.

It is thanks to 3M's strong profit discipline that the company can invest heavily in manufacturing facilities around the world. But this can lead to controls that are perceived as excessive: "Every day, directors and auditors are telling us to increase this, decrease that," complains one manager. It also leads to other tradeoffs, both visible and invisible. 3M is masterful at creating new markets, but not always so good at retaining market share. The promise of fresh innovations may lead some subsidiary employees to back away from competitive battles prematurely. They frequently question the balance of profit-taking versus market share in strategic markets or locations:

> The high price gives our competitors room. Other companies start out with a lousy product and a cheap price. But they make progress and become competitors. In the beginning they are in just one location, but later they become regional.[24]

As much as 3M is committed to local manufacturing around the world, issues regarding the pace of investment and global efficiency still cause headaches. Smaller markets may collectively hold large opportunities, but the needs of so many countries will seldom appear as vivid or pressing to project developers in St. Paul as the needs of domestic customers. H. C. Shin, the former managing director of 3M Philippines, observes:

> We don't have a well-established system to collect OUS [Outside of U.S.] customer needs from smaller countries and integrate them into product development. . . . It is too late when a product is at the commercialization stage because it is already 80 percent complete. With Europe and Japan we have established lab operations and can communicate well, but with other subs in Asia, Latin America, or Africa it is difficult to collect information. Now I'm in

St. Paul on the other side of the coin and, frankly, it is physically difficult to collect customer input from abroad because we have limited resources. It may be best to cluster countries and search out their collective needs, reflecting these needs in product development.[25]

Managing for Global Balance

Innovation in a global context generates new sets of creative possibilities and logistical challenges. Indeed, the subtle balancing act that sustains innovation in 3M's research community—providing modest support and encouragement for new ideas while occasionally subjecting them to trial by fire—must be orchestrated with an even more complex set of arrangements in global markets.

Key factors that need to be balanced properly so that subsidiary innovation can flourish include:

• Product range	• Subsidiary capabilities
• Information sharing; cross-border leverage	• Independent thinking
• Local manufacturing	• Global efficiency
• Profit	• Market share
• Headquarters-based design	• Input from smaller subsidiaries

Successful innovation in 3M subsidiary environments does not always draw the corporate thunder and lightning that accompany new product inventions at St. Paul. Still, it is important to remember that technologies leveraged across the globe now garner more than half of 3M's total sales despite formidable cross-cultural hurdles. H. C. Shin claims that in his experience 3Mers from different countries generally respond to the basic McKnight spirit:

Respect the individual, provide boundaries, and get out of the way.

Give freedom to people—delegate. Work hard. Be a good listener and don't act as if you know everything already. Focus on results and intervene only by exception.

This management approach appears to foster innovation in serving overseas customers just as it does in corporate research labs—and with equally important consequences. Shin recalls a special day during his tenure in the Philippines when everything seemed to come together:

I remember driving back after a customer call. We had just reached the one billion peso sales milestone that had been our goal. Five or six people called on my car phone to share their congratulations. In three years we had doubled the size of the company, morale was high, we were all working for the same goal and made it happen. It wasn't a matter of money or glory or fame, but just a true feeling of accomplishment. I stopped to watch the sunset and thought of the phone calls and a good customer visit. It was the best moment of my life."[26]

Key Questions To Ask About Innovation

Global Innovation

1. Is each business unit taking advantage of the seven potential areas of cross-border innovative activity: sales and marketing techniques, product packaging, product adaptation, commercialization of new technologies, acquisition of technical information, co-design, and original invention?

2. Are subsidiaries ready and able, where appropriate, to move up the scale of innovative activity from sales and marketing towards original product development?

3. What are the formal methods by which global innovation is supported: e.g., organizational structure, expatriate assignments, global teams, mentor programs?

4. Are there informal activities that make global innovation easier: e.g., strong cross-border friendships, volunteer activity?

5. Is the subsidiary development sequence managed for optimum product customization and solid local government relations?

6. Is the "cascade effect" being used to disseminate experience from one subsidiary to another?

7. Does global management successfully balance factors such as information-sharing and independent thinking, profit and market share, headquarters-based design and subsidiary input?

6

Sumitomo 3M: Reinventing the Headquarters/Subsidiary Relationship

Are we asking them to be innovative or to just follow orders? Increasingly, we need them to help us drive change.
                                                    —U.S. manager

I want to create new business with my own ideas.
                                                    —Sumitomo 3M employee

Who would think of dispensing Post-it notes from a bright green fish that sings, "Mambo!" to a Latin rhythm? Or an animated pink crab that shouts and waves its claws while offering up pieces of Scotch pop-up tape? Such products are a long way from the staid sandpaper manufacturer of William McKnight's early days. They reflect the extent to which a distinct identity is being developed by Sumitomo 3M—3M's largest subsidiary.

The Tokyo-based joint venture has partnered with a Japanese toy manufacturer to produce these talking sea dwellers, which don't yet exist elsewhere in the 3M world. Sumitomo 3M's ability to reinvent established businesses and product lines in this way makes it a significant model of how a subsidiary can evolve within a global corporate framework. What has been reinvented is more than just products—it is the headquarters/subsidiary relationship itself.

Sumitomo 3M: An Overview

With approximately 10 percent of 3M's total sales, 3,300 employees, 4 factories, and 14 different sales offices and branches, Sumitomo 3M is a substantial organization in its own right. It also earns more than half of 3M's revenues in Asia. Sumitomo 3M was established in 1960 as a joint venture, with 3M holding a 50 percent ownership share and Sumitomo Electric and NEC, two members of the Sumitomo group of companies, each holding 25 percent. Over the years, this joint venture has gained the reputation of being one of the most successful in Japan.

Sumitomo 3M's full complement of operations makes it possible to respond to many customer requests locally: thirty-one out of forty-four 3M Business Units are present in Japan. The Sagamihara research and development operations are 3M's most sophisticated outside of the United States, and its manufacturing operations consistently rival or surpass 3M facilities in the United States on measurements of product quality. The company produces three-quarters of its merchandise locally, and supports its unique product range with excellent technical service. Career longevity in Sumitomo 3M's labs is another advantage. The company has a core of top-quality technical graduates in its research and development operations. Most of its employees have entered the joint venture right out of school. Across the board, employee turnover is only about 2 percent each year.

Sumitomo 3M has the discipline, the climate, and the loyal, hardworking personnel of a good Japanese company. (Some senior employees admit that they joined mostly because of the Sumitomo name.) Use of English is rare outside of meetings with expatriate management, presentations to foreign visitors, and interface with overseas operations. There are just three semipermanent expatriate positions: executive vice president, technical director, and manufacturing director. A Japanese president, presently Hajime Hitotsuyanagi from Sumitomo Electric, handles external relations, while Bill Allen, the current executive vice president from 3M, runs operations.

What makes this joint venture so unique? A veteran employee, now retired, explains by using an episode from the days before Sumitomo and 3M came together:

> It was 1959. At that time, I belonged to Sumitomo Trading, and was a participant in the joint venture discussions with 3M. In the

1950s, Japanese industry was still in a fragile condition compared with the U.S., and there were various rules and regulations designed to protect Japan from the entry of foreign capital firms. So we had shut ourselves away in a single hotel room with executives from the American side, and were preparing for negotiations with the Ministry of International Trade and Industry [MITI]. As we were working, some of the U.S. team members who were at the vice president level within 3M surprised us by making tea. For me, still a very junior member of the group, it was awe-inspiring. And what do you think they said then? They told us, "You know Japanese matters best, and only Japanese can negotiate effectively with MITI. Making tea is the most we can do for you." I was quite moved. As the negotiations proceeded and other executives came and went on the U.S. side, they all continued to make tea and even to cook meals for us. One of these executives was a man by the name of Harry Heltzer. Later the same person was to become CEO of 3M. When Heltzer came to Japan again in the 1970s as CEO, we had a good laugh together about the fact that he had never expected to rise to such a position.[1]

The HQ/Subsidiary Relationship: Stages of Development

Sumitomo 3M's relative maturity, local identity, and corporate culture have opened up intriguing opportunities for cooperation with the United States. Over the last decade, a series of efforts has taken place to examine U.S.–Japan relations at 3M in order to enhance teamwork, customer satisfaction, and competitive advantage. The capacity for marketing and technical innovation at Sumitomo 3M has evolved along with the headquarters/subsidiary relationship.

But in spite of progress in developing synergies between St. Paul and Tokyo operations, Sumitomo 3M's business growth rate and profitability have diminished due to Japan's protracted recession. These difficult economic circumstances have forced a reevaluation of business opportunities and personnel needs. How 3M and Sumitomo 3M navigate the crisis will have major implications for them, and may offer clues to Japanese firms that are restructuring to enhance their own vitality.

Four primary stages of development have distinguished this critical trans-Pacific relationship. To varying degrees all of the stages are still present, although in a more advanced form. It is also important to remember that 3M's structure is based on divisions, and the status of U.S.–Japan relations differs considerably by division.

3M and Sumitomo 3M: Four Stages of Cooperative Action	
Internal	*External*
Trust & autonomy	Serving local customers
Regional leadership	Serving transnational accounts
Strategic integration	Joint product development
Global organization development	Global technical innovation

Trust and Autonomy

Ten years ago Sumitomo 3M's employees sometimes felt like second-class corporate citizens—even working for the company crafted by William McKnight and a joint venture born through executive tea-pouring. They wanted greater trust from their American counterparts in matters large and small, along with the autonomy to respond to the needs of Japanese customers. Two problem areas that reinforced the perceived need for greater trust and autonomy were review meetings and financial authority.

■ Problem 1: Review Meetings

At the beginning of the 1990s, Sumitomo 3M employees participated in regular reviews by regional executives, mostly Americans. The reviews included sector reviews, group VP reviews, division reviews, business manager reviews, and quarterly business updates. For each review, the Japanese presented recent business results, current issues, and action plans, while the reviewers would listen and ask questions. When one Sumitomo 3M division was handling the work of two divisions from the United States, they had to meet more than one set of divisional management.

The Japanese had two main complaints:

1. The inordinate amount of time being spent preparing for review meetings would be better spent with customers.

2. The information presented was not necessarily that good—review formats had become ritualized and the presenters, pressed for time and having limited English skills, would reuse the same canned materials.

In short, the established format was too one-sided to promote a productive exchange of opinions. Two different sources pinpointed the problem:

- Review preparation eats up a lot of valuable time that could be spent with customers. . . . Reviews in our division normally involve the full-time efforts of all of our several marketers plus the general manager for two weeks prior to the review date. We often have as many as five rehearsals over a period of six or seven weeks.

- The U.S. has no idea of how much time is spent for such poor-quality information. . . . Our reviews are too ceremonial. They provide a beautiful format where participants can "be smart" in front of U.S. executives.[2]

After discussion of this problem between Japanese and American executives, a decision was made to reduce the number of review meetings and to change the format to more interactive discussion. The focus of the meetings was also shifted from business results—which can after all be communicated on paper—toward joint planning. A number of the Japanese felt that visiting Americans expected individuals to speak up at meetings, assuming that people who remained quiet had nothing to say. Steps have been taken to schedule more time for one-on-one or informal contacts where junior Japanese team members find it easier to express opinions. Meaningful two-way exchanges provide the foundation for joint innovation.

■ Problem 2: Financial Authority

Japanese managers were feeling restricted by the micromanagement of cost controls and the requirement that they obtain authorization from the executive vice president, an expatriate, to set prices for big-ticket items. Sumitomo 3M managers sought general goals and directions, which they could figure out how to implement, rather than specific instructions. In an ironic twist, the Japanese appeared to be asking for a more global implementation of 3M's basic business philosophy.

> One manager gave me general goals and guidelines and left it up to me to research alternatives and make a proposal with my group. It was tough but rewarding; I gradually learned what was necessary. But if a manager just tells me, "Do this," "Do that," it's easy but I don't have the feeling that I'm involved or learning something. . . . We follow directions but the results are not so good because the directives lack flexibility.[3]

As it happened, a new executive vice president had just been appointed: Tony Gastaldo, who had come up the company ranks at 3M Italy before holding a managing director position in Spain. Gastaldo, a big man with a ready smile and a strong technical background, responded quickly to the most grating Japanese concerns. He granted autonomous pricing authority to the top executives, boosting both their morale and their freedom to innovate with pricing in the field. Sumitomo 3M has proved to be quite expert at the creation of value-added products as well as packages of products and services for which customers are willing to pay a premium above prices in other countries. Indeed, some 3M subsidiaries in Asia have shifted their source of supply from the United States to Sumitomo 3M despite higher prices, due to greater responsiveness and better product fit with Asian markets.

Regional Leadership

At 3M as in other spheres, Japan's position within Asia has long been ambiguous. According to the company's organizational structure, Japan is a region unto itself—China and Southeast Asia constitute separate regions. Although Japan is also part of the general Asia-Pacific area, its unique customer needs, organizational features, and language have led some at 3M to feel that Japan is the most isolated part of the global organization—even given its size and importance.

Such perceptions notwithstanding, the heavy overseas investments of Japanese transnationals in the late eighties and early nineties created a window of opportunity for cooperation with other parts of Asia. Big automotive manufacturers such as Toyota and Honda and electronics giants like NEC and Matsushita were rapidly building up their Asian manufacturing presence. Along with the opportunity to serve Japanese customers in their new Asian locations came the threat that 3M could lose some business altogether if production was relocated away from Japan and supply relationships were not picked up by other Asian subsidiaries. It was vital to act quickly and create new networks within Asia.

To serve transnational customers, a transnational organizational network is very important. For example, if R&D is in Japan, procurement may be in Singapore, and manufacturing in Indonesia, Thailand, or Malaysia. We need to get all of the different countries involved and find someone to work with each office. Eventually there will be mostly R&D in Japan. . . . Singapore is a free port so procurement is easy, and production should take place where there is a market need. The most important thing is how to organize ourselves to cater to these transnational accounts.[4]

Sumitomo 3M is ideally positioned to lead 3M's operations in Asia. Its technical depth, business experience, manufacturing capabilities, and sheer size greatly exceed those of other 3M subsidiaries in Asia, so during this period it was logical for Japan to help smaller Asian subsidiaries to develop and to win sales from Japanese transnational accounts.

Modest technical assistance from Sumitomo 3M to Asia began to gather momentum in the 1980s. By 1992, the company saw the need for it to take on a larger coordinating role. U.S. executives expected Sumitomo 3M to take the initiative and proceed by trial and error in an evolutionary fashion. Sumitomo 3M management, on the other hand, wanted a corporate mandate regarding their role within Asia, together with a comprehensive plan and invitations from Asian counterparts. The Japanese also complained that 3M's reward system didn't support wider cooperation in the sales arena. A Japanese salesperson may have helped Asian colleagues make a sale to a transplant account, yet the sale would be credited to the local subsidiary; moreover, the salesperson could actually lose business as the customer moved production out of Japan and established sources of supply overseas.

Both sides have compromised in drafting a new set of parameters for Sumitomo 3M in Asia. First, expatriate representation has been increased. Twenty or more Japanese have subsequently been assigned to expatriate positions in common transplant locations such as Thailand or Singapore. Indeed, the position of managing director in Thailand was assigned to Atsuhiro Hashida, a Sumitomo 3M veteran with strong automotive industry experience. This was the first such post for a Japanese within 3M, and is hopefully a sign of a wider global role for capable Japanese leaders. Sumitomo 3M employees with experience in Asia feel that, regardless of the high costs, there should be one or more Japanese expatriates based in each of the major Asian countries to serve as a contact window near Japanese customers' sites. One Japanese expatriate's remarks underline the rationale for these assignments:

> I know the future of the market here because I have already seen it in Japan. That's why we can be a market leader and the competitors will always follow. There are many applications from other countries that we can use here. This is a strong point of 3M.

Pan-Asian teams, or APMATS, were created in the early 1990s to focus on particular businesses and customers. More Japanese have traveled to other parts of Asia to provide technical support and training. In the other direction, assignees from China and Southeast Asia have come to Sumitomo 3M for developmental assignments. While these Japan stays have been very instructive for the individuals involved, higher turnover rates in other Asian subsidiaries have meant that a disappointing number of the visitors trained at Sumitomo 3M have left the company.

Sumitomo 3M's sales force now receives compensation on a corporate basis for support lent to Asian subsidiaries. From an outsider's perspective, it would appear that an obstacle to even wider Japanese sales involvement is the fact that Sumitomo 3M profits must be divided among the joint-venture partners. This would make it advantageous for 3M as a whole to emphasize sales in other wholly owned Asian subsidiaries rather than a formula that shares them with Sumitomo 3M. However, that is not how the company operates, counters Ron Baukol, head of International Operations:

> We try to run our joint ventures the same as we would any other

subsidiary. The problem with transnational sales from Japan is how you measure them. If product specifications are set at the home office in Japan it is not so difficult, but what happens when they are not?[5]

While progress has been made in expanding markets and serving transnational customers, further efforts are needed to define a satisfactory system for tracking and rewarding Japanese employees' contributions to sales increases outside of Japan.

Strategic Integration

The historical reality of 3M technical innovation is that most major inventions have originated from St. Paul. During Sumitomo 3M's high-growth years of the seventies and eighties, employees in the Sagamihara labs acquired the habit of adapting research breakthroughs from headquarters to fit the needs of local customers. Likewise, U.S. divisions would devise strategies and only later roll them out to the subsidiaries, with adjustments to local circumstances made as an afterthought. Given the tremendous resources and the close integration of 3M's technical community in the United States, it still too easy to forget about the rest of the world. For their part, the Japanese have perhaps not been sufficiently assertive in securing resources or expressing their real views.

Sumitomo 3M is still not using the technology we have. A smaller country in Europe may demand more information than the Japanese labs. The Japanese try to figure it out themselves. This is admirable but unproductive. They seem to be afraid to tell people they don't know. They should come here and pound on the table more.[6]

Over the past seven or eight years there has been a growing push from Tokyo for closer strategic integration of Sumitomo 3M into technical development processes and business planning cycles. A key vehicle for this integration are the Japanese who are or have been resident in St. Paul on foreign service assignments (see chapter five).

There is now a cadre of several hundred Japanese, including many of its most promising scientists, who have worked at the U.S. headquarters. When Japanese involvement is needed in a high-priority initiative like a Pacing Plus program, there is usually either a Sumitomo 3M employee in St. Paul or a former assignee who can join the project with relative ease.

Such assignments seem to be just as important in establishing personal relationships and overcoming linguistic and cultural barriers as in effecting specific transfers of technology. A two-year assignment in St. Paul makes it far easier for Japanese to get their hands on the information they need and to express their views freely. Foreign service assignments now include people from finance, sales and marketing, human resources, and other non-technical disciplines. An interesting psychological phenomenon occurs with most of these postings, as young Japanese who have realized a personal dream of going overseas to learn will strive extra hard to bring something useful back home:

> They become innovative almost automatically because they feel they have to bring back a kind of gift.[7]

There is a still deeper influence that residence in St. Paul has on Japanese expatriates. With U.S. 3Mers, the Japanese assignees have been able to articulate several common criticisms of Japan-based research, laying the groundwork for future changes:

- *Group-think*: It is often difficult for a Japanese researcher to focus on his or her individual project because of peer pressure to contribute to team efforts. If others are behind in their work or need help, Japanese commonly drop their own work and help out, often to the detriment of personal focus and momentum.[8]

- *Excessive Customer Focus*: Sumitomo 3M's labs are skilled at working closely with customers, perhaps more so than the average research group in St. Paul. But dedication to serving customer needs can become a liability if it means spending large amounts of energy on minor but time-consuming requests. When the voice of the customer is too prominent it can get in the way of setting and maintaining R&D priorities. Preoccupation with tech service activities may preclude more forward-looking innovation when resources are limited.[9]

- *Lack of Diversity:* Innovation often comes from combining two very different technologies like reflective sheeting and abrasives. Japanese researchers, however, tend to become immersed in their technical specialties or loyalties to a particular line of business. Those who come to St. Paul are often astonished at the breadth of technology they find.

- *Limited Technology Sharing:* Oddly enough, in a country famous for its personal networking, Sumitomo 3M's Tech Forum and other networking activities have not taken root in Japan the way they have in the United States.[10] Some Japanese lab members feel that they are too busy to participate; others would like to join in but can't get their manager's permission (maybe the problem is they feel that they have to ask for it). Research teams have close relations within their own circle, but are not so well linked with other teams. A 1994 internal survey of Sumitomo 3M researchers found that more than half had no experience of sharing technology between divisions. Sharing of labs and equipment also appears to be less frequent in Japan than in St. Paul.

- *Over-Seriousness:* Younger Sumitomo 3M employees express longing for a greater spirit of play and of spaciousness in order to foster more creative activity. The vaunted Fifteen Percent Rule is frequently either foregone because people are too busy, or interpreted literally to mean a specific amount of time with a system to support it. One Japanese in St. Paul remarked, "Sumitomo 3M misunderstands 3M culture. We are too serious."

- *Paradigm Shift Versus Continuous Improvement:* The Japanese strategy of making incremental product improvements (*kaizen*) is a relatively low-risk activity; so is creating new applications of existing technologies based on customer input. But there is a much higher failure rate for new product programs, and the more unusual the idea the greater the risk. As Geoff Nicholson says: "We must learn to live with failure. . . . but never to accept it." Some American 3Mers question how ready their Japanese counterparts are to accept greater levels of risk and potential public embarrassment: "Real innovation often requires a certain amount of messiness and chaos. I wonder if the Japanese are ready for this?" The Japanese might in turn question whether Sumitomo 3M is really set up to support risky projects.[11]

Such tough internal criticisms can perhaps be regarded as growing pains and signs of healthy self-reflection. Sagamihara is already the most productive 3M lab in the world in terms of new products generated. The current direction of R&D, combined with the steady influence of former expatriates who have returned to Japan, is pushing Sagamihara to new levels of activity. Technical service and product adaptation are likely to continue to be the mainstays for the time being, but Sumitomo 3M is gradually acquiring the skills and the research culture to enable both full-scale co-design with the United States as well as original invention in Japan. Product areas where Sumitomo 3M strengths overlap with strong world market position for Japanese companies—for instance, the electronics, automotive, and health care industries—could become the focal points for fresh patterns of joint technical innovation.

Another, more radical, proposal from 3Mers who know Japan well is that manufacturing for certain critical new products ought to begin in Japan. In the case of Brightness Enhancement Film, for example, the biggest global customers are Japanese laptop makers, and starting production in Japan might have helped the company gain a firmer market lead over local makers of rival products. In-country manufacturing, when it merits the investment, nearly always enhances a subsidiary's ability to respond to customer requirements. Increasing leading-edge manufacturing in Japan would naturally lend itself to closer and more collaborative product design and development with customers.

Other forward-looking suggestions for closer strategic integration between the United States and Japan include having Sumitomo 3M general managers become members of the U.S.-based Operating Committees for their divisions. This would bring them into the regular flow of divisional information, even if they were not able to attend every meeting, and would make it easier for them to add Japanese input on policy and projects. A second idea is to bring groups of Sumitomo 3M scientists to the United States periodically to comb through the labs there in search of new product technologies with potential applications in Japan. 3M may still have too much good technology sitting on the shelf. A further proposal is for Sumitomo 3M to assume not just regional but global leadership for key Japanese transnational accounts; the aim would be to facilitate long-term R&D collaboration and ultimately joint development activity with customers based in Japan.

Best-practice examples of U.S.–Japan cooperation are becoming more common at 3M as experience and relationships grow. Where they exist, new dimensions open up for shared innovative activity.

> In our area, relations with the U.S. are going very well at the working level. We have a team that communicates regularly. . . . We hold regular discussions on common projects with frequent follow-up. There is joint development and making of test products. They have a positive attitude toward our business chances in Japan. Our young people have a sense of ownership because some programs are led by Japanese, and some by Americans. There is a chance to go to the U.S., which gives us face-to-face opportunities to meet. In areas where Japan is leading, people from the U.S. come here automatically; we collaborate to create products suited for the Japanese market.[12]

Global Organization Development

Sumitomo 3M is a hybrid: it has a divisional structure that mirrors 3M's, but personnel policies more typical of a Japanese company, with annual hiring of college graduates, lifetime employment, seniority-based promotion, and a company union. This hybrid model has functioned well for decades. Now, however, there is greater pressure from 3M and from the external business environment to establish tighter links with the global organization.

The dual heritage of Sumitomo 3M provides it with the opportunity to create a synergistic combination of its parents' best elements: 3M's innovative practices plus Japanese manufacturing and quality control; individual genius plus superb teamwork; flexibility plus attention to detail; freedom plus discipline. The potential for more unfavorable combinations exists, too. For example, Sumitomo 3M has generous wages and benefits along with a standard U.S. retirement age—65 versus the 60 that is normal in Japan—at the same time it practices lifetime employment and seniority. Nor does Sumitomo 3M have the family of subsidiaries to which other Japanese organizations regularly farm out excess senior personnel. So when business growth slows, there is a glut of expensive senior personnel in the management ranks, and promotions for high-potential young employees are stalled. Limited job rotation due to the specialized nature of 3M's many technical fields can create other problems like narrow vision and sectionalism.

Sumitomo 3M continues to outperform real GDP growth and the Industrial Production Index in Japan. Nevertheless, the recent downswing in the Japanese economy has brought Sumitomo 3M's organizational challenges to a head, revealing weaknesses that were masked by previous boom times. Significantly lower profitability in Japan has also brought closer scrutiny from 3M's top management. There is perhaps more change in the wind at present than at any other time in the joint venture's history. But the stern circumstances of the present could turn out to be a blessing in disguise, leading to a new and more flexible Japan–U.S. hybrid.

It is worth looking back at key Sumitomo 3M organizational issues that have become apparent of late to observe just how difficult it is to fully transplant 3M culture overseas.

■ Divisional Barriers

Sumitomo 3M employees will freely acknowledge that barriers between divisions are thicker in their organization than in the parent company. The divisional structure inherited by Sumitomo 3M has come without many of the formal and informal linking mechanisms that are so vital in the United States—as if the bones and muscles of the system were in place without important nerves and arteries. The following comment is perhaps overstated, but nonetheless representative:

> A different division is just like a different company. The only bridge at present is the horizontal connection between people who entered the company the same year. We are caught between the vertical barrier of [traditional Japanese] senior/junior relations and the horizontal barrier between divisions, and can't move.[13]

To complete the project of wiring Sumitomo 3M's organization with more of the linking mechanisms that abound at headquarters, the company got moving in the mid-1990s. A push began to introduce more market- and user-driven organizational forms to supplement the traditional product-out approach of the divisions. Considerable debate and discussion ensued, with advocates of the new methods clashing with others who did not want to sap the entrepreneurial sense of ownership and responsibility that resides in each division. This difference of viewpoints was at least partially resolved by the idea that this was not an either/or issue—that it would be possible to retain divisional strengths and introduce market-driven bridging structures.[14]

These market-driven mechanisms are primarily local versions of 3M corporate marketing initiatives (see chapter four):

- Customer-Focused Marketing
- Industry Centers
- Key Account Program
- Integrated Solutions Initiative

A similar local invention has been the *Kansai Project*, a special cross-divisional response to the rebuilding efforts following the 1995 Kansai earthquake.

Sumitomo 3M is also looking to cultivate multiple routes for launching a new idea, even when one's manager or division does not grasp its potential.

When a salesperson identifies a new idea, he comes back and tells the boss. If the boss doesn't get it, the idea is lost. We could use a more systematic way of capturing new ideas and ensuring that they are taken seriously.[15]

The Sumitomo 3M Technical Council has tried to increase cross-fertilization along the lines of the so-called technical audit process in St. Paul, where managers from unrelated divisions review new product ideas. Fledgling volunteer Tech Forum activities, including poster sessions, are underway. There is a new effort to increase direct customer contacts made by lab personnel; some of these people reportedly have a knack for picking up unarticulated customer needs that divisional marketers might miss.[16] And Sumitomo 3M employees have begun to vocalize their desire for an environment in which they can easily approach executives other than the one to whom they report directly.

■ Human Resources Adapts to Japan's Troubled Economy

Recession has forced Sumitomo 3M to scrutinize its traditionalist human resources policies. A number of 3M personnel systems have been implemented virtually worldwide, with Japan being the notable exception. On the other hand, Sumitomo 3M has thus far avoided the human resources embarrassments that plague foreign capital companies in Japan. Executives in St. Paul have quietly gnashed their teeth and recited McKnight's principles to themselves so long as the Japanese operation was successful. Now, both at the highest company levels and among the younger generation of Sumitomo 3M employees, there are significant pressures toward implementing a more Westernized system.

Specific reform areas where initial steps have been taken include faster promotion of high-potential young managers, more weight on merit in calculating bonuses, and a 360-degree feedback system. Technical employees, especially returnees from the United States, feel strongly that Sumitomo 3M needs a fuller version of the 3M dual-ladder system that creates an independent promotion track for talented scientists who choose not to become line managers.

When dealing with poor performers, Sumitomo 3M has been less severe than some Japanese organizations that find not-so-nice ways to force "voluntary" retirement. The very qualities that make the company an enjoyable place to work, plus the strong work ethic and thriftiness of employees who would rather stay at their jobs than retire, make it difficult to reduce headcount among senior personnel. The company's current dilemma is how to maintain a positive work environment, reduce the number of surplus senior workers, and still bring new blood into the organization. Given the economic situation in Japan and 3M's rising image in the Japanese marketplace, it is now possible to recruit outstanding young graduates. To Sumitomo 3M's credit, it has avoided both the manipulative tactics of some Japanese companies and the drastic downsizings that have brought notoriety to foreign capital firms among the Japanese public. It recently instituted a generous voluntary retirement program that is truly voluntary, and this has met with a good response.

A Company Vision

The Vision 2000 program highlights several of the most promising organizational experiments at Sumitomo 3M. Established in the early 1990s, Vision 2000's goals for 3M are:

- To become a ¥300 billion ($2.1 billion) company by the year 2000
- To satisfy customers by introducing unique products and services to the marketplace
- To be perceived positively by employees, customers, and society in general
- To contribute to global 3M strategies, supporting 3M operations in the Pacific Rim[17]

While the problems of the Japanese economy have hampered the achievement of overly ambitious financial targets, there are signs of progress. Some thirty Vision 2000 product development projects have been launched outside of the existing company divisions, and over fifty marketing and research personnel have been freed up from their divisional responsibilities to participate (some have since returned to roles within divisions). Criteria for Vision 2000 designation are that the projects utilize 3M research and development strengths while having a sales potential of at least ¥1 billion ($7 million) by the year 2000; over half are linked with Pacing Plus activities. These projects simultaneously incorporate innovations in technology, organizational structure, and human resource practices. The most fascinating is the Light Fiber Project, which provides one of the first examples of a 3M product brought to market in Japan before being introduced in the United States.

■ The Light Fiber Project

In the mid-1990s Ken Bartelt, the expatriate technical director in Japan, approached Takaaki Nishijima, a Sumitomo 3M marketing manager, to discuss new light fiber technology that had not been taken up by any of 3M's U.S. divisions. These low-power fibers generate illumination without giving off heat or carrying an electrical charge. The thick acrylic fibers, nearly an inch in diameter, had possible applications in illumination for cars, museums, and swimming pools, and as novel architectural features or alternatives to neon signs. Both Bartelt and Nishijima saw real potential for this product in Japan. During a six-month period in 1996, Nishijima made more than two hundred customer calls and systematically reported the feedback to the lab researchers in St. Paul who were developing product prototypes. Novel applications that he discovered included walkway lighting for tourists in an ancient

Buddhist temple, and illumination for a commercial display of fine wines that could be damaged by the heat of normal electric lighting.

As the project gathered momentum, additional team members were recruited through internal job posting, a system introduced at Sumitomo 3M under the auspices of Vision 2000. There were far more applications than there were positions available; the main trouble was getting approval from divisional managers who were reluctant to part with talented employees. A number of applicants in their fifties, senior to Nishijima himself, wanted to join even though no management positions were available. Several women became key team members. Then, when Nishijima held a project team meeting in June of 1996, he found ten other people in attendance beyond the eight persons on the project team. Nishijima remarks: "All were volunteering their fifteen percent nondirected time to work on this project. It was unprecedented."

To learn about the new technology, a group from Sumitomo 3M spent a month in the United States early in 1997 with the St. Paul team—a highly diverse set of 3Mers, including two corporate scientists who were nominally retired but still working. One of these was the irrepressible Roger Appledorn, who seems to be experimenting with global bootlegging even in retirement. Thereafter the Sumitomo 3M team took over product development responsibilities, creating their own prototypes. The project was further speeded along by the fact that Nishijima chose to use a light source available from an outside U.S. supplier rather than developing an original source as the American researchers wanted to do.

Sumitomo 3M got its light fiber product to market in less than one year. Nishijima was called back to St. Paul to explain his success in the Japanese market. More important for Sumitomo 3M, the charged atmosphere of the Light Fiber Project team has broken some old barriers and created a collective work style that would make old McKnight smile. According to Nishijima:

A "follow me" type of leader is not necessary. Everyone has to exercise their own kind of leadership and ownership—find work they like and do it. We had lots of volunteers. I didn't have to instruct them in detail, or ask them to do overtime. I feel that the others are not subordinates, but colleagues. Everyone wants to make the product succeed. People are flexible, and don't say, "This is my area, and that's yours."[18]

■ Subsidiary Innovation: The Bottom Line

The secret to many Sumitomo 3M success stories seems to be intensive dialogue between headquarters and subsidiary, with the subsidiary employees ultimately winning the freedom to do what they think is best for Japan within the global company structure. Freedom is not casually offered, nor does it mean that anything goes. Lab areas tend to have greater freedom, and the closer one is to daily operations, the narrower the range of personal discretion. As Ron Baukol notes, freedom for a young subsidiary salesperson may mean just the authority to go call on a different kind of customer: "We expect salespeople to go out and find the best opportunities."[19] On the other hand, by starting with a customer need, that salesperson may eventually be able to persuade others with decision-making authority of the viability of a new product idea. There is a progression toward greater freedom that builds over time with the track record and capabilities of each subsidiary operation and the people in it.

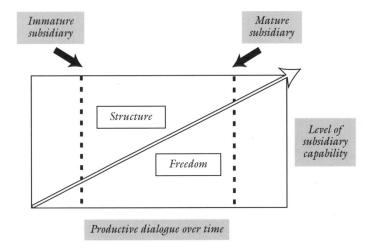

There are many advocates at Sumitomo 3M for expanding the Vision 2000 practice of small project teams engaged in new product development. They feel that such groups, especially when members elect to participate, will have advantages over standard divisional procedures. Comments one enthusiast:

> We need to split up existing divisions in order to create more speed. Ten people is the ideal work unit. We should organize according to

project, and staff up through the internal recruiting system. Middle management is not necessary.[20]

In another example of Sumitomo 3M's increased readiness to make its own choices, corporate marketing has sponsored an advertising campaign that is different from 3M's worldwide theme. In contrast to the standard "1-2-3M" formula—which moves directly from customer "need" to 3M "solution"—Sumitomo 3M has used a series of animated characters. The most recent have been Morphy, a long-eared dog that symbolizes creative thinking, and the perpetually exasperated Professor Hirameki, who hatches one new product idea after another only to find that they have already been turned into 3M products. A 3M marketing manager in St. Paul once lamented, gazing at a Morphy T-shirt: "Could somebody explain to me what this has to do with 3M innovation? 1-2-3M is so clear and simple, and we're using it all over the world. Why can't they just use it in Japan?"[21] But Sumitomo 3M has convinced headquarters that the main corporate campaign would not be as eye-catching for the Japanese public.

Sumitomo
3M Mascots

Yoshihide Inui, the Sumitomo 3M manager who introduced cute green fish and pink crab dispensers to sell Post-it notes and other products, describes a constant process of dialogue with the United States. Pop-up tape, developed in St. Paul, was introduced into Japan under the name "Hari-pop," and Inui suggested the toy concept for its broad appeal to families with children and the female consumers who control most of household spending. Agreement from his American counterparts was not immediate. "Would the products sell through the same channels? How long would their appeal last? Was it a good move to form a strategic alliance with a toy company? Did 3M really want to get into the toy business in Japan?" But finally Inui prevailed, and his creations have since been featured on 3M's corporate web site.

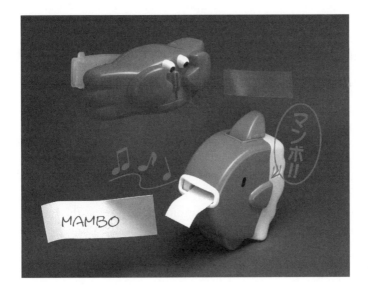

Post-it Dispensers, Japan

■ Indigestion or Innovation?

As Inui did, a subsidiary employee with an innovative idea must win over management both locally and at headquarters. When this employee has to run the gauntlet between an ossified local management structure and unsympathetic counterparts at headquarters, there is little hope for real innovation to emerge. On the other hand, if the headquarters/subsidiary relationship is an open and constructive one, many things become possible, including changes in the local organization and management practices.

There is a vicious circle experienced by many subsidiary operations around the world. Certain of its features are found in other settings as well, including relationships between headquarters and regional offices even within the same country. But cross-border differences in language, communication style, customer needs, and business practices regularly generate misunderstandings that add extra fuel to the fire. Some of the less inspiring examples from Sumitomo 3M hold elements of this circle, although seldom in full-blown form.

Imperatives may be handed down from headquarters to subsidiary without a full understanding of local business conditions, or run smack into the limitations of the subsidiary ("many pitchers and one catcher"), where there may not be the resources, employee skill levels, or buy-in necessary to get the job done.

Emissaries from headquarters, whether they are expatriates or traveling executives, exert pressure on local employees to take on the objectives that headquarters has set. Local employees, constrained by language or unfamiliarity with the headquarters' methods of constructive debate and argumentation, resist in a way that appears stubborn and irrational, making comments like: "It is impossible because this is Japan."

At some point the headquarters representatives, because they have others breathing down their necks to produce results, resort to top-down fiat and impose their will. While local employees may nod in agreement and appear to comply, there are at least two likely consequences: outward signs of cooperation while pursuing the agenda that they thought was best in the first place, and a covert interest in seeing that the headquarters plan does not work. Some subsidiaries become festooned with strings of headquarters initiatives that are kept alive artificially for the benefit of high-ranking visitors—a waste of already

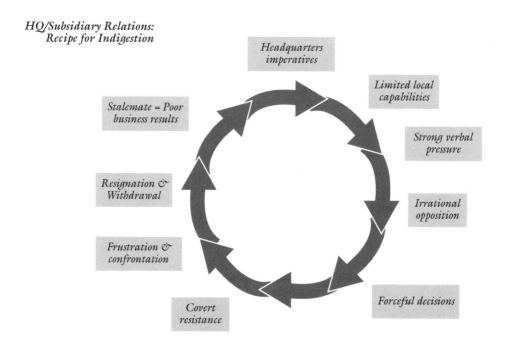

HQ/Subsidiary Relations:
Recipe for Indigestion

Headquarters imperatives

Limited local capabilities

Strong verbal pressure

Irrational opposition

Forceful decisions

Covert resistance

Frustration & confrontation

Resignation & Withdrawal

Stalemate = Poor business results

limited resources.[22] Sooner or later, a headquarters representative will unmask this resistance, with the discovery leading to frustration and perhaps confrontation. At this point local employees may even stop doing what they think is best for the company and woodenly go through the motions of following instructions, a behavior pattern almost guaranteed to affect business results. This stalemate naturally leads to a new round of imperatives from headquarters, which sets off a repeat of this vicious circle.

An opposite, virtuous cycle is exhibited in best practice examples between 3M and Sumitomo 3M. Trust and friendship are at its foundation, with long associations and extensive dialogue between key players providing a reservoir of mutual respect and a willingness to work together toward common goals. The seeds for this cooperation have been sown over many decades of interaction, starting even before the joint venture agreement was signed when a future 3M CEO offered tea in support of a young Japanese who has never forgotten that simple gesture.

Trusting relationships are the basis for innovation together with the U.S. Some of my best friends are people from the U.S. If I know the person, think he's a good guy, and know his family well, it makes everything easier.[23]

An accurate assessment of headquarters and subsidiary capabilities produces objectives that are both realistic and challenging while headquarters demonstrates an ongoing commitment to subsidiary maturation. Rapid and regular communication keeps subsidiary employees up to date on headquarters events and product strategies. Such communication allows for input from local customers to be incorporated into product development, thereby minimizing modification after the product has been launched. Subsidiary personnel are an integral part of the overall R&D effort—indeed, they may be the first to commercialize a new technology.

A flexible attitude toward leadership roles within the development team encourages individual commitment; subsidiary members hold top positions where appropriate. In the event that differences occur, constructive debate takes place using a format that is commonly understood, with all viewpoints being aired and considered. Such actions promote enthusiasm, and a sense of local ownership and responsibility for the project's success. Organizational support systems reinforce successful cross-border cooperation with rewards and recognition. Headquarters representatives take pains to learn from the subsidiary's accomplishments, and the best practices of joint development teams are leveraged throughout the company.

HQ/Subsidiary Relations:
Innovation Begets Innovation

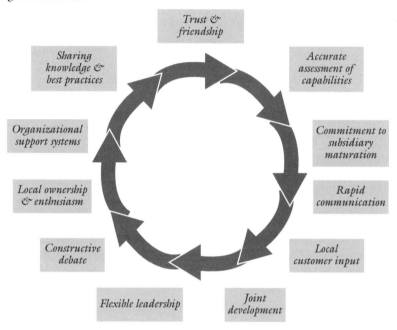

Trust & friendship

Accurate assessment of capabilities

Commitment to subsidiary maturation

Rapid communication

Local customer input

Joint development

Flexible leadership

Constructive debate

Local ownership & enthusiasm

Organizational support systems

Sharing knowledge & best practices

Where an innovative cross-border relationship is in place, other possibilities for innovation multiply. It becomes possible for Pacing Plus programs to actually originate in Japan. There could be not only global management of key transnational accounts by Japanese, but also responsibility for entire product lines in cases where the world market is centered in Japan. Hybrid forms of management might also blend the best of local and the headquarters approaches. What would be the result of a more complete fusion between leading-edge Japanese management practices and McKnight's management philosophy—with delegation and individual initiative at its core? A hint of the future resides in the candid comments of former Japanese expatriates: "Our company needs larger scale changes in its organizational framework. We could be more adventurous." And, "I want to create new business with my own ideas."[24]

It is thoughts like these that will propel Sumitomo 3M to the next stage, and may very well—drawing on 3M's global resources and heritage of innovation—offer fresh possibilities for Japanese society at large.

Key Questions To Ask About Innovation

Subsidiary Relationship

1. Is innovative thinking applied to subsidiary relationships as well as to the invention of new technologies?

2. Has the headquarters relationship with key subsidiaries successfully evolved through the four phases of cooperative action: trust and autonomy, regional leadership, strategic integration, and global organization development?

3. Does each subsidiary enjoy a degree of freedom that fits its particular stage of development?

4. Are the various elements that comprise the "virtuous cycle" of headquarters/subsidiary relationships in place: e.g., trust and friendship, accurate assessment of capabilities, commitment to subsidiary maturation, local customer input, joint development, flexible leadership, constructive debate, local ownership and enthusiasm, mutual learning and best practices?

5. Can an ordinary subsidiary employee with a good idea get it by both local management and overseas counterparts to turn it into a new product, service, or process improvement?

7

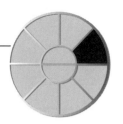

Managing 3M's People System

Innovation comes from a gathering of events to a realization.
—L. D. DeSimone

At the core of 3M innovation is the fusion of active management practices with the stubborn self-direction that wells up from the company's deep-rooted corporate culture. The company's most skilled managers know how to balance discipline with support so that they can direct, facilitate, or get out of the way, as is appropriate for a particular situation. Several additional management balancing acts require equal skill and experience: 1) drawing upon corporate tradition to ignite continuous change, 2) handling successive innovation phases, and 3) nourishing the interdependent elements that make up 3M's innovation system. The full-blown model of 3M innovation and the management practices that go along with it offer a brand of wisdom that transcends more conventional assumptions.

A Tradition of Innovation

Bill Coyne, 3M's chief of research and development, seeks to sustain a tradition of innovation that he cheerfully acknowledges to be paradoxical. He observes, "Innovation needs to be a corporate character trait, one that is built up over time; . . . a stubborn, unchanging habit of embracing the new and surprising." Coyne lays out six straightforward management steps for building such a tradition. For people who seek to benchmark 3M, this is probably the closest thing to a prescription for innovation that the company has to offer. However, taken by themselves these steps are incomplete; they are accompanied by the informal corporate culture elements taken for granted by most 3Mers. The table below integrates Coyne's six steps with a summary of the more informal aspects of 3M corporate culture to show how the whole organization is infused with an innovative mind-set.

Building a Tradition of Innovation	*Coyne's Views*	*Six Key Steps*	*Informal Corporate Culture*
	Innovation needs to become part of a company's self-image, part of its vision. And the 3M vision is explicit on this. We want to be the most innovative enterprise. . . . I constantly remind employees that all their effort should be directed at validating this vision. If it isn't, then they should rethink their work.	*Vision & Values*	Informal values lend heart and hands to vision. Innovation occurs through human qualities—stubborn persistence, curiosity, individual initiative—that are reinforced in various ways. There are also values that are too much a part of the atmosphere to be clearly discerned by insiders: friendship, trust, and efforts on behalf of the common good.
	The second requirement is foresight, figuring out where our customers are going. . . . We know that the returns are often greater when we can find and capture the market for solving an unarticulated need. . . . Our approach is to identify what we call lead users, people who have high demands and might predict where a product category is going.	*Foresight & History*	Corporate history gives 3Mers a sense of direction and continuity, while helping them to understand and accept that unarticulated needs can lead to whole new product lines. Famous stories, told and retold, become both the vehicle for recalling history and a kind of conceptual template for seeking out future possibilities.
	You also need to push yourself to go beyond just incremental improvements. You need to set goals that will make you stretch, that will force you to make quantum improvements. Our ultimate stretch goal is a product that redefines an industry. . . . We think we can cut the time to market by up to 50 percent—another stretch goal.	*Stretch Goals & Security*	Stretch goals are worth reaching for because risk-taking brings generally positive results for both the company and its employees. Employment security makes it easier to stretch beyond known capbilities and limits with minimal fear of punishment. Trust in the acumen and intentions of top management provides a further sense of stability.

Coyne's Views	Six Key Steps	Informal Corporate Culture
The next step in creating a tradition of innovation is to get people in the labs and start them working. The key point here is that managers and executives need to supply the resources and a certain amount of direction and then get out of the way. . . . At 3M, we were practicing empowerment long before it was called empowerment.	*Empowerment & Volunteerism*	Empowerment works because employees are ready to step forward and get things done. Innovative projects gather momentum of their own accord, and an employee who has reached a creative impasse can find help. The trick is how to foment volunteerism without exploiting or smothering it.
The fifth step in creating a tradition of innovation is open and extensive communication. Management needs to communicate broad direction and vision to the labs. Labs need to communicate opportunities to management. And innovators need to communicate with each other. . . . The ability to combine and transfer technologies is as important as the original discovery.	*Communication & Community*	3M's community atmosphere, with its casual contacts and volunteer activities, means that communication can happen through serendipity. Chance encounters bring together information and ideas with unforeseen consequences. Long-term friendships across national borders and organizational lines serve as high-speed "routers" of vital news.
The sixth step in creating a tradition of innovation is a system of rewards and recognition. At 3M, we don't believe in special financial rewards (for innovation). . . . But we do like to see it recognized. With this in mind, we have award programs that include innovation covering most functions in the corporation, for people in marketing, packaging, and administration as well as research.[1]	*Recognition & Reputation*	Individual reputations precede corporate-level recognition and are enhanced when it is given. In fact, the most successful forms of recognition are based upon peer input. Innovators are valued and paid competitive salaries; scientific expertise is recognized through the dual-ladder promotion system. But the best rewards of all are the honor and prestige that come with one's personal reputation as an inventor, colleague, and mentor.

Anyone who seeks to use Coyne's six steps as a checklist should ensure that the informal side of the equation is present as well: stretch goals without some measure of security merely produce skepticism and stress, empowerment without volunteerism is like a cart without a horse, and recognition incongruent with one's reputation among peers can discourage rather than hearten.

The paradoxical virtue of 3M's organizational climate is that it engineers dynamic stability. There is constant pressure to innovate, and each employee must be ready to team up with new colleagues, shift into a new working unit, fight for an idea or possibly give it up. The freedom to volunteer and even to create one's own job makes this dynamism both a top-down and a bottom-up impulse. At the same time, 3Mers can still count on steady jobs, established customer relations, and the technical resources and experience accumulated by tens of thousands of employees over nearly a hundred years. CEO DeSimone intones the corporate management philosophy of balance in all things:

> Balance is extremely important in every area. For example, 3M is a staid company in the sense that it is consistent and steady, with an emphasis on doing everything right, across the board—3M is solid. This also is a company that is always looking for innovation, the next improvement. *We* want to be the ones to make the next breakthrough in every one of our businesses.[2]

Innovation Phases

Although 3M's tradition of innovation is woven into its whole elegant jumble of business units, laboratories, and staff departments, the nature of innovative work and how it is managed also shifts according to the progression of developmental phases. These phases vary in duration from years to months; increasingly they overlap or are deliberately rolled into the same developmental venture. The same people could take part in every phase from beginning to end, or there may be handoffs along the way.

Broadly speaking, the three primary phases of innovation at 3M can be called "innovation by doodling," "innovation by design," and "innovation by direction." These phases have a funnel-like effect on the stream of ideas, being broadly accepting and supportive at first, while gradually producing a more intense and concentrated flow. The fine balance of support and discipline shifts along the way, as more deliberate attention and investment are applied from phase to phase. Discipline becomes progressively tightened so that in the final, most directive phase, measurements of performance according to strategic and financial criteria are paramount.

Innovation Phases: 3M's Innovation Funnel

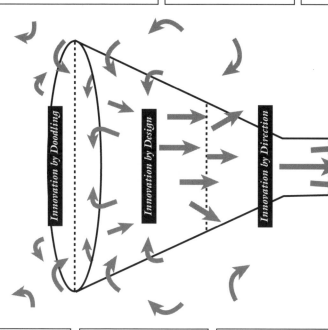

SUPPORT

Lab structure & facilities
Technology platforms
Hiring practices
The Fifteen Percent Rule
Percent of sales from new products
The Benevolent Blind Eye
Tech forum: informal contacts
Technical audit
Volunteerism
Tolerance of failure
Genesis Grants; Alpha Grants
Individual recognition

SUPPORT

CED, Pacing Plus
Cross-functional team systems
Percent of sales from new products
Manufacturing platforms
Marketing initiatives: Industry
    Centers; Customer-Focused Marketing
Team recognition: Golden Step

SUPPORT

Pacing Plus
Manufacturing expertise
Supply chain management
Sales & distribution channels
Key account management
Marketing & sales awards

DISCIPLINE

Lab or individual budgets
Peer reactions
Judgments by supervisors
    and middle management
Top management survey
Trial by fire

DISCIPLINE

Divisional or lab budgets
Judgments by division
    management
Top management review
Project milestones
Trial by fire
Regulatory environment

DISCIPLINE

Top management focus
Strategic planning priorities
Financial targets for:
■ Sales growth
■ Operating income
■ Return on equity
Stock price
Percent of sales from new
    products
Cost control initiatives
Competitive market position
Low tolerance of failure

It is in the tightest part of the funnel that 3Mers see the most room for improving their management performance. While the company's idea pot is still bubbling, and lots of good new technologies are being invented, too many product introductions have not achieved their full commercial potential. The more humdrum, downstream innovation phase is just as vital as the brilliant research insight or the whiz-bang prototype. Full-scale innovative success—the proverbial hit product—requires street-wise market acumen and staying power to select the right application, accurately forecast demand, and implement a sales strategy that gets the product into the hands of paying customers. States Barry Dayton, a protégé of Bill Coyne who works with development groups to improve their innovation practices, "We have to be able to punch through and be successful in the marketplace."[3]

Managing successive innovation phases is a difficult and demanding task because the company must be successful at each one of them without detracting from the others. The 3M equivalent of "tinker, tailor, soldier, sailor" would be "doodler, designer, director," and some of the highest posts within the company go to individuals who have proven over a long career that they understand and can perform in all three areas. Multidexterity, not simply in strategic thinking but in personal capability and experience, is admired and promoted.

Lew Lehr, a former CEO who is still recalled with affection by employees, is famous for an incident early in his career. Lehr was a primary developer of 3M's surgical drapes, one of the first products in its now highly successful health care business. When sales faltered at first and the product began to lose money, Lehr's superiors told him to drop the product line, and he obediently agreed to do so as soon as the inventory was used up. However, Lehr was then afflicted by a sudden, convenient memory lapse, and forgot to tell the factory to halt production until he had built up a substantial inventory. Sitting on this mountain of inventory, he was able to continue his sales efforts and managed to win a large contract from the U.S. military, already an important 3M key account. Because of 3M's commitment to this account, production resumed.[4]

Many things are required from a top executive who wants to build an innovative company. In addition to the compelling vision, management savvy, and people skills that are normally on the list, who is better equipped to know the guts of the innovation process than a former bootlegger? CEO DeSimone provides modest testimony to the strength of 3M's innovation system, saying, "It would take me many years to screw it up."[5] On the other hand, to maintain and enhance this system requires a group of dedicated executives who know every phase of the innovation process inside out and are able to balance the sometimes conflicting requirements of different phases.

3M's People System

Another critical management challenge for 3M as well as for any other innovative organization is to keep the whole innovation system healthy. Innovative practices are a bit like the exotic flora and fauna of a rain forest. They need the other ecological constituents, plus the overall climate that they generate together, in order to thrive.

The Innovation Wheel presented in the Introduction and elaborated upon in each chapter provides a rationalized cross-section of what some 3M employees call its "People System."[6] Of course, innovative activity is in reality more fluid and deeply integrated than the model can portray. A change in one area can reverberate across the rest of the system, with consequences that may be hard to detect immediately. Management needs a sure yet light touch to stimulate and direct innovative activity.

3Mers manage their People System through a combination of caution and uncommon persistence. Although the company has its share of corporate initiatives, the more closely these are linked with core innovation practices, the more conservative managers become about altering them. Human Resources, for instance, is reluctant to embrace faddish trends because its methods for developing, rewarding, and recognizing employees have been established over time and are deeply embedded in 3M's innovative culture—an overly hasty change could have unintended results. By the same token, management is extraordinarily persistent in driving home initiatives once they have been taken up. This gives time for them to sink roots and to develop a positive fit with preexisting organizational elements. 3M's Pacing Plus initiative has been under way in various forms for the better part of a decade, and is only now really beginning to bear fruit.[7]

3M's Innovation Wheel

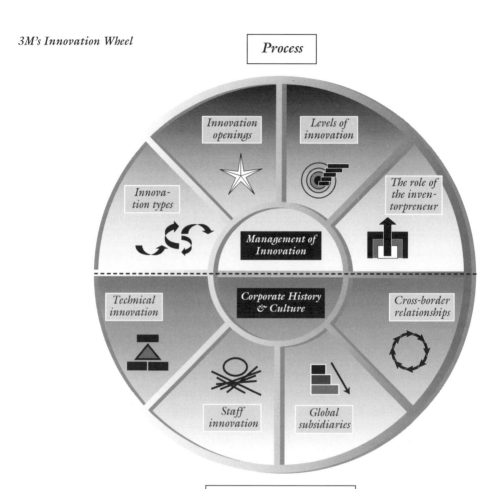

3M Innovation and the Standard Wisdom

The many forms of innovation described in previous chapters make it easier to understand why 3M often flouts the standard wisdom on this subject.

■ Benchmarking

Standard Wisdom, Item 1: Specific innovative practices can be readily benchmarked and imported into other environments.

The notion that specific innovative practices can be readily benchmarked and imported into other environments fails to take into account the complexity of 3M's innovation system. Benchmarkers who are both interested and patient enough to study 3M innovation from various angles will soon realize that it is ridiculous to walk off with a single practice like the famous Fifteen Percent Rule and expect it to flourish back home. At best, it is likely to become one of those sad zoo animals that companies proudly exhibit but which fail to breed in captivity. In a different corporate environment, 3M's Fifteen Percent Rule could easily backfire: it might be misinterpreted as a rigid kind of union clause, encounter derision as the "initiative of the month," or turn into a deceptive charade when undermined by organizational factors that do not support innovation.

The Fifteen Percent Rule works at 3M first of all because people recognize it for what it is: not a literal mandate, but a symbol of the imperfect freedom that each employee has to do what he or she thinks is right. The rule is grounded in the company's history, inspired by a corporate culture with shared values, and preserved by long-established habits of management. Individual work on Fifteen Percent time is channeled by an accumulation of knowledge and experience about innovative processes. Breakthroughs are fostered by impressive technical resources and developmental procedures; corporate staff functions provide a supportive environment both for inventing and for bringing products to market. 3M's global presence introduces cross-border relationships that can help the company to capitalize on a Fifteen Percent time innovation, adapting it to the needs of customers in other markets. And an uncommon degree of camaraderie lubricates this entire system.

An astute benchmarking project will compare complexity with complexity. This means recognizing the various components of 3M's system and their interaction and then tracing the 3M map lightly onto one's own organization, noting points where one or the other is abundant or deficient. The terrain of a different industry may require a somewhat different configuration of elements. A reassuring aspect of 3M's model, however, is that it has been applied successfully to product creation in nearly every major industrial sector.

The primary components of 3M's system—for instance, "Innovation Openings," or "Levels of Innovation"—can find a home anywhere if they are applied by analogy and example rather than force fit. An organization that asks itself how the principles of 3M's Innovation Wheel can be applied to its own circumstances will do even better by examining the symbiotic interactions of these features with one another, both in the 3M model and in the new host environment. Are the different elements of the innovation process deployed in a synergistic way to enhance their common effect? How are they supported by the practices of the technical community or staff departments? Is innovation leveraged on a global basis and routed quickly in all directions by strong relationships?

Comprehensive knowledge of the receiving organization's environment is essential in order to identify exactly what is missing, what the 3M model has to offer, and how borrowed innovation principles should be modified. Based on such a systemic understanding of the "point of highest leverage,"[8] it may even be possible to borrow and carefully adapt a specific practice or two along with the broader 3M innovation principles. However, instead of something obvious and celebrated like the Fifteen Percent Rule, the successful borrowing could be a seemingly insignificant practice that does not even have a direct connection with innovation: an inspiring story, "Show & Tell" time with free donuts, Process Technology Centers, volunteer recruiting teams, a Korean managing director of the Philippines, or the latitude that capable subsidiary managers have to make their own decisions.

■ Market-In/Product-Out

Standard Wisdom, Item 2: Companies need to establish a market-in or product-out innovation strategy that fits the requirements of their market.

There are passionate advocates for both market-in and product-out approaches to innovation; one of their few points of agreement seems to be that a firm's innovation strategy ought to be shaped by the type of market that it serves. A consumer goods company such as Unilever or Procter & Gamble needs to be close and responsive to changing consumer tastes, while a high-technology organization that is inventing a new industry may have to educate end-users about the features of its product before it can even begin to ask for their input.

Market-in advocates assert that the best way to innovate is to listen to customers, understand their needs, and provide products or services that meet these needs better than the competition. It is unsafe, they say, to let engineers and scientists "tinker" with technologies that they find interesting, and later try to link these technologies with product attributes and customer needs. "Usually this sequence doesn't work."[9] Others will defend the opposite position when it comes to major breakthroughs, noting that sometimes the customer can be wrong about a new technology, rejecting it because it does not fit with current ways of doing business, and failing to grasp future possibilities. Companies can make the mistake of staying too close to their customers, giving them the product performance they are looking for, yet ignoring new trends that these customers also fail to see.

> The processes and incentives that companies use to keep focused on their main customers work so well that they blind these companies to important new technologies in emerging markets.[10]

Rather than limit itself to one primary type of innovation, 3M cultivates a number of methods, perhaps due in part to the variety of markets that it serves. Market-in and product-out approaches are each recognized paths to innovation that have venerable precedents in company history: William McKnight directed his salespeople to the shop-floor workers at the base of the smokestacks, but also supported technologies without any immediate market applications that eventually led to products such as Scotchgard. One can glimpse healthy internal tension and swings back and forth between market-in and product-out efforts, with corporate marketing trying to bring more unified attention to customer needs, and 3M's research community pushing for technical breakthroughs into new markets. The distinction between articulated and unarticulated customer needs allows these two paths to coexist.

Market-in and product-out approaches may be joined together to create new and unconventional routes. Marketing has been conditioned to look for unarticulated needs, just as 3M scientists are increasingly urged to get out and make direct contacts with customers. Innovation could thus result from any number of acts, many of which move beyond the market-in/product-out dichotomy: a marketer who identifies an unarticulated need and looks for a technology to meet it;

a scientist who has a sudden insight during a customer meeting; or a cross-functional team that convinces an adventurous customer to sample a new product. Of course there are also the projects that begin with a scientist in a laboratory and happen to collide with a real set of market needs part way along the developmental path, resulting in a happy marriage of tinkering and talking to customers.

■ Established Units/Skunk-Works

Standard Wisdom, Item 3: The best way to foster innovation in a large, established organization is to create an internal "skunk-works"—that is, an entrepreneurial unit insulated from the potentially stifling influence of regular operating procedures, systems, management personnel, and corporate culture.

Current thinking about innovation commonly asserts that companies become victims of their own success. Organizations naturally crystallize around winning products and strategies, gradually moving toward higher levels of efficiency and performance. Over time they build up formal procedures and structures, technical expertise, and seasoned human resources. While all of these features are conducive to incremental innovation, breakthroughs to new products are unlikely. There is a stultifying symmetry between established products and established organizational forms that is hard to break out of, causing revolutionary ideas to be stillborn. "While incremental innovation can be managed within the existing organization, discontinuous innovation cannot."

Contrast this ponderous big company environment with the skunk-works, a radically entrepreneurial organization, relatively small, with decentralized structures, loose work processes, and relatively young and heterogeneous employees. The watchword here is not efficiency but experimentation. Such entrepreneurial groups, in other words, can only thrive with a different set of organizational hardware and software. This is best achieved by creating a work unit that is "physically, culturally, and structurally separate from the rest of the organization." Breakthrough innovations can only be executed through discontinuous organizational change. A key management challenge, therefore, is to balance differentiation with integration; that is, to sponsor, protect, and legitimize distinct entrepreneurial units while also preserving the overall integration of the company as a whole.[11]

3M certainly faces the problem of the established getting in the way of the new. CEO DeSimone acknowledges, "There are pragmatic aspects of every function in the company that suppress innovation." 3M's preferred solution, however, does not seem to be to build up separate skunk-works walled off from established functions, but to drive innovation into every root and branch of the company. Its organizational structure provides natural shelter for technical innovators in its product labs, but, if anything, the trend is to draw these personnel more closely into the daily heartbeat of project implementation and interaction with customers. Ordinary product divisions are frequently the host for intense entrepreneurial activity. A veteran 3Mer reports:

> In my experience it is not uncommon to have an entrepreneurial unit inside of a well-established division. In the divisions I worked in, at any given point in time, there could be one or more groups of a half-dozen people working on something new. Just because you're in an established organization doing incremental product development doesn't mean that you can't have a subgroup doing very innovative things. It's more a matter of creating a climate where you tell them, "Forget about what you were doing and go off and make something of this technology." And off they go. They're well tolerated by the people around them, even when there is very structured work going on side by side with them—in spite of the odd hours and so forth within this group.[12]

Innovation shouldn't be walled off because it is supposed to be everywhere. Innovation heroes become larger-than-life figures, their exploits extolled by corporate publicity and sanctified by awards. Richard Miller, the inventor of Aldara cream, has been appointed global ambassador of innovation, and is regularly called upon to speak to employees. Pat Hager of Scotch Satin Tape fame grouses that there are so many presentation opportunities that it is hard to have time to do work. By broadcasting their achievements, the company seeks to plant another innovative seed in the heart of each employee.

DeSimone speaks of "creating some space in the structure for innovation," but for him, this space is as much a metaphor as an organizational structure. It may be created by the manager who protects an innovative subordinate ("Somebody has to take the bullets"). Indeed, every 3M manager has the right to run an innovative experiment within his or her area. The stronger one's personal credibility and track record, the more slack is allowed. Innovative "space" could also be the ability of an individual to set aside other priorities and follow the gentle tug of an innovative thought. Organizational units are designed to act like small businesses, with the individuals in them serving as entrepreneurs.

For DeSimone, breakthrough innovation results less from isolated activity than from "a gathering of events to a realization." 3M's definition of innovation, which emphasizes both the conception and the implementation of a new idea, necessarily calls for multiple skill sets and different phases of activity. Several key skills may be found in one person—the so-called inventorpreneur—but increasingly they reside in a cross-functional team or a whole business unit. The Pacing Plus programs described previously include original inventors, manufacturing people, scientists from related disciplines, patent attorneys, marketers, and others. Isolation may provide favorable conditions for an idea to percolate, but as soon as that idea shows signs of ripening, 3M's strategy is to pluck it from splendid isolation and leverage it with the resources of the entire organization. Increasingly, breakthrough innovative efforts such as the HFE project begin with high corporate visibility and a concerted cross-functional team push.

3M's relatively simple and flexible organizational structure just doesn't seem to get in the way of innovation as much as other structures. Perhaps this is due in part to the tremendous number of products. With fifty thousand different items, products come and go all the time, and it is hard to get too attached to any of them. Moreover, 3M's organizational structure and corporate culture are so focused on innovation that they make change appear to be the norm. Divisions and technology platforms were created to accommodate growth and transformation. Although particular divisions or platforms may either flourish or be cut loose while new ones appear, the basic structure remains viable because it was built to innovate. 3M's corporate vision, its target for new product introduction rates, the Fifteen Percent Rule, Pacing Plus programs, corporate awards, and any number of other devices all encourage the feeling that innovation is normal. Indeed, businesses or employees are called on the carpet when they don't have new products to replace the old.

Where other companies might seek to innovate by creating differentiated units, and then worry about how to integrate them with the rest of the organization, 3M emphasizes a more radical brand of integration. It sustains a tradition of innovation which permeates the organization in such a way that breakthrough developments could come from anywhere.[13] "Innovation is what makes this a live organism," says DeSimone, and he expects every employee to contribute to its life force.[14]

■ Incremental/Breakthrough

Standard Wisdom, Item 4: Real innovation comes through a revolutionary breakthrough, or paradigm shift.

Incremental improvements in products are often associated in theory with evolutionary product development activities, and incrementalism is said to be incompatible with revolutionary change.[15] To achieve a true breakthrough, the argument goes, it is essential to seize the reins and take a forceful strategic approach, launching new programs with the deliberate intent to cannibalize older product lines.

Major 3M innovations stem from diverse sources that defy common associations between incremental and evolutionary, strategic and revolutionary. Poky, unpredictable evolutionary product development can lead to revolutionary breakthroughs. There is often a product line, such as abrasives, that has been noodling its way along for years, delivering regular line extensions but few breakthroughs. Then it is suddenly revolutionized by combining it with another evolving technology such as microreplication, transforming a tired old technology stream into a pulsing fountain. Revolution occurs through a sharper than usual twist of evolutionary development, and the old is turned inside out to become new.

A multidimensional model better depicts 3M innovation. Innovation occurs in a myriad of ways, but frequently follows a common path, as shown in the chart: developmental activity that is initially incremental and evolutionary (Quadrant A) changes when evolution mutates its way into revolution (Quadrant B); this development is taken up by top management as a strategic priority (Quadrant C), and later utilized strategically as a revenue source even when only incremental improvements are being made (Quadrant D).

Indeed, this is exactly what happened with Post-it notes. Spence Silver was incrementally muddling his way along, having created a failed adhesive and dutifully reported these results to his colleagues, when he got together with Art Fry to invent a revolutionary use for his "not-so-sticky" adhesive. After a good deal of hard work by this pair to demonstrate the new product's potential, 3M made it a strategic priority and created a new global market for it. Over the last two decades, the company has produced seemingly infinite variations on the Post-it notes theme, pursuing a highly successful strategy of making incremental improvements to maintain its dominant market position.

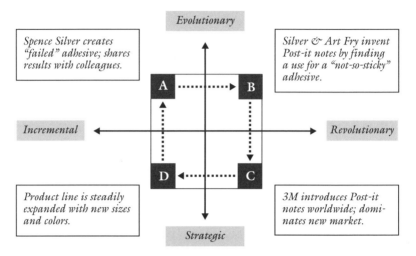

Nor is incrementalism necessarily a long-term death sentence. As the technology evolves, there is always a chance that another radical evolutionary leap will occur, so there can actually be an ongoing cycle of creation and rejuvenation. This is in fact what occurs within and among 3M's technology platforms. Trizact, the revolutionary new abrasive created through an infusion of microreplication technology (see chapter one), is an example of just such an event.

The concepts of innovation that fit 3M best are in fact the ones that reconcile and integrate alleged opposites such as incremental and breakthrough, established organizational systems and entrepreneurial skunk-works. Several of the most famous of these—the "genius of the AND," the notion of "Ambidextrous Organizations," and "Simultaneous Loose/Tight properties"[16]—all ring true in light of the innovation examples cited in previous chapters. 3M is particularly interesting because it is all over the innovation map, and many of its best examples seem to run circles around standard distinctions.

■ Strategic Action/Patient Non-Action

Standard Wisdom, Item 5: Innovation is the product of strategic management actions.

3Mers point out that the kind of strategy which calls for management team scrutiny and debate, large-scale investments, and the building of new organizational structures and systems can get in the way of vital technical evolution (see chapter three). Excessive reliance on this interventionist brand of strategy may be one of the biggest pitfalls of books written by business school savants and consultants who work with top management teams. It looks and feels good to take action, even when that action is misguided or premature.

In fact, strategy at 3M is an animal with many heads. There is a brand of strategy that calls for patient nonaction on the part of top management, letting bright people and good projects simmer in their own juices without such hyperactive intervention.[17] Another subtle strategic function is the support and nourishment of promising evolutionary shoots—creating the right hothouse climate without overfeeding or suffocating new growth. Some technologies are best not rushed to market because they are too far ahead of what customers want, or must await advances in a related scientific field. It may only be at a later stage that more active strategic intervention by top management is helpful. Management must distinguish between "strategic exploration" (an activity that uncovers new ideas by undermining, discovering, or reframing) and "strategic capability" (which advances and extends creative ideas, making them more robust).[18]

L. D. DeSimone likes to point out that it has taken twenty years for the microreplication technology platform to come to fruition: "Sometimes this requires patience, because a lot of small sparks can lead to big ideas five or ten years from now."[19] DeSimone advocates suspending judgment in some cases: "If it's a product that's really unique and different, but I don't know what the heck it is for, don't throw it away; don't give that up."[20]

Managing an Innovative People System

1. Does the organization actively seek to build a tradition of innovation with the six paired steps (derived from Coyne's formula): vision & values, foresight & history, stretch goals & security, empowerment & volunteerism, communication & community, recognition & reputation?

2. Is the balance of support and discipline for innovative activity properly calibrated to fit the three stages of "innovation by doodling," "innovation by design," and "innovation by direction"?

3. Are new initiatives cautiously selected and then persistently adapted and integrated with the entire system of innovation practices?

4. Who is tending to the ecology of the whole system, and do they know what they are doing?

5. Are you prepared to benchmark in a way that compares complexity with complexity? How well do you know your own organization?

6. Can you creatively fuse market-in and product-out approaches, turn any part of the company into a skunk-works, transform incremental improvements into major breakthroughs, and engage in strategic non-action?

8

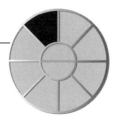

The Future of 3M Innovation

How can we do better?
    —William L. McKnight

Earthquakes are rare in the Midwest. But in November 1995, a shock rebounded through 3M's business world when the company announced the spinoff of its data storage and imaging systems businesses and the discontinuation of its videotape business. This was by far the largest restructuring in 3M corporate history. The cuts eliminated product lines worth nearly $3 billion in sales, or 20 percent of the company's total revenues. More than 11,000 employees eventually left, exiting with the spinoff, through attrition, or via voluntary separation programs.

The 3M spinoff was called Imation Corp. William Monahan, a respected company leader with an excellent track record, took over as Imation's chairman and chief executive in the midst of cheerful speculation about its prospects.[1] But only two years after the spinoff was finalized in July of 1996, Monahan had tough news to report: "We set out to create a new company because we saw significant opportunity. But we also found that we spun off with five distinct businesses with no synergy and poor processes, too much structure and inadequate business discipline." 1997 brought a net loss of $180 million including restructuring charges, along with the elimination of 1,700 out of 9,800 jobs. New high-capacity data storage products plus several strategic acquisitions hold out future promise, but Imation is off to a rocky start.[2]

Nor did the cutting and trimming end there. 3M financial results in 1998 were severely impacted by global economic turmoil, with both sales and income actually falling below the levels of the previous year. Gains in Europe and Latin America were offset by a decline in the Asia-Pacific region as well as currency losses. In August 1998, 3M announced an additional restructuring with three elements:

- Reduction of employment levels by 4,500 (about 6 percent of the company's work force) by the end of 1999
- Consolidation of some manufacturing operations
- Review and cutbacks in product lines with low earnings potential or decreasing strategic fit[3]

3M executives believe they are making the difficult choices that are essential in order for the company to remain in top form. "Our approach both addresses current realities and strengthens our ability to generate future growth."[4] The businesses spun-off to form Imation had lower gross margins than 3M's normal range and were dragging down its overall financial performance.[5] 3M had stood by them a long time—probably too long—and made substantial investments to try to improve results without success. The strategic features of data storage and imaging systems technologies that were once so compelling had also become less important with the advent of digitalization. Just in case, however, the company took the added precaution of arranging for limited technology access back and forth between 3M and Imation.

Products that were dropped altogether had become commodities subject to cutthroat competition. Videotapes, though they represented a high-profile business that 3M helped to invent, are purchased by consumers mainly on the basis of price—various attempts at adding innovative features did not produce sufficient gains in sales or profits. The $350 million worth of product lines now designated for a new round of critical scrutiny have problems similar to those which were spun off or dropped: low returns and decreasing strategic value.

Pressure on 3M top management continued to mount throughout 1998 as financial results fell short of past performance levels.[6] A rare spate of critical articles emerged in the business press in late 1998 and early 1999, exhorting potentially contradictory actions on several fronts: more and deeper cuts, greater investment in R&D, further steps to boost the stock price, and increased employee compensation.

Two researchers sued the company for allegedly violating the dual-ladder principle that top scientists should be paid at a rate similar to that of top managers. Most disturbing—and highly unusual coming from the understated 3M culture—were reports about dissension among executives themselves. Some apparently feel that CEO DeSimone has not been sufficiently tough or decisive in boosting flagging performance. A letter-writing campaign to outside members of 3M's board led to executive interviews by two non-3M directors and rumors of impending changes at the top.[7] In a sense the whole company is undergoing a kind of mid-life crisis. With an average age of nearly 42, 3M employees must struggle like anyone else to keep up with the frenetic pace and gut-wrenching changes that are being wrought by the shift to software, e-commerce, and other industries of the future.

The Temptations of St. Paul

So what will come next? 3Mers generally regard the restructuring efforts to date as unfortunate yet necessary. Top management can draw upon a large supply of goodwill built up through years of prosperity and the commitment to employee welfare that originated in McKnight's era. Recent financial results for both 3M and Imation have improved.[8] Nevertheless, the rising tide of change over the last few years throws several critical issues into relief. Each of these represents temptations that, if poorly managed, will slow the pace of innovation. On the other hand, astute leadership in these areas, focused on both short- and long-term results, will help to lift 3M to new levels of achievement.

■ Temptation 1: Make Lots of Money

3M is a profit machine. In 1997, the year after the Imation spinoff, it had net income of $1.6 billion, or nearly 18 percent of total sales. The 6 percent profit dip in 1998 that provoked the latest round of job cuts still left the company with net income of $1.5 billion. Nobody is talking about losing money here. At a 1998 meeting with security analysts, double-digit earnings growth was projected for the next three years, with an average 8 percent annual increase in sales.[9]

In fact, it would not be that difficult to make more money. Delay certain capital investments, cap R&D spending for a time, or pull the plug on projects or technologies that have failed for too long to deliver, and the numbers will go up—for a while. Some people feel that this is what began to happen in the late eighties under the previous CEO, Allen Jacobson, causing a subsequent drought in the first years of DeSimone's tenure, which began in 1991. In 1989 the company achieved an outstanding return on capital employed of nearly 27 percent, a figure that hasn't been achieved since. "Jake (Jacobson's nickname) was known for cost-cutting," recalls one senior manager.

Today, 3M executives are trying to balance the pressure for stellar financial performance with investment priorities. Having allocated $150 million to Pacing Plus programs, well over a billion dollars to annual capital spending for manufacturing improvements, and another billion to R&D, they can legitimately claim to be doing so. But if you ask some of them in person what keeps them awake at night, you hear answers such as this: "I'm concerned that we focus too much on the investor. We need to make long-range investments. There's too much short-term thinking—too many people doing safe things." Employees in humbler positions put the same point in pithier fashion: "This is a good company that earns money for everyone. We're being jerked around by yuppie investment habits."[10]

Even 3Mers who accept the business rationale for the recent restructurings voice concerns about damage to the company's unwritten social contract. The old rule was, work hard and sacrifice for 3M, and the company will take good care of you. But lifetime employment is certainly no longer a reality for Imation's ex-3Mers, almost 20 percent of whom have lost their jobs. Part of the agreement made in establishing the spinoff was that employees could apply to return to 3M after two years, but now there are scant jobs available for those who inquire and only a few dozen have been hired back. Though most job cuts at 3M are still being made through attrition and voluntary early retirement packages, one hears of people who have been edged out of the company by less genteel methods. "Now in some areas they're saying, your job is gone and so are you."[11]

Any realignment of 3M's social contract with its employees is significant because of the role that stability plays in fostering an innovative climate—maintaining the balance between stretch goals and security. At companies where people are more hardened to cycles of hiring and cutting back, the elimination of a few thousand workers when economic conditions worsen might hardly raise an eyebrow. Yet when a hard-working, veteran 3M employee with many friends in the company suddenly goes on the unassigned list, the swift and informal communication links that are normally such an asset can have an adverse echo-chamber effect, as other 3Mers begin to worry about their own futures. This is particularly true if the positions are eliminated by management edict, without prior consultation with the people involved. "It introduces a nervous element," notes one veteran employee.

A thinning out of intangible assets like friendship, volunteer energy, and fierce dedication to the company could have an impact that is greater than many shareholders imagine. What does it cost when employees become a little less eager to defy their bosses and pursue pet projects, a bit less inclined to donate time to someone else's problem, or not quite as ready to volunteer for an entrepreneurial venture with an uncertain future? Could changing organizational loyalties make people think twice about contributing a promising idea that might also become an independent startup business?

For such reasons, it is vital that measures taken by the company to achieve higher financial performance and productivity goals be seen as fair and properly targeted. 3Mers have already achieved astonishing increases in productivity: in 1984, 89,000 employees had per capita sales of $88,800; by 1994, with 85,000 employees, that figure was $177,000, or more than 100 percent higher.[12] If projected job cuts and sales increases take place as planned, by the year 2001 sales per employee will be over $300,000, an additional 60 percent increase.[13] Such outstanding performance depends on the continued good faith and dedication of 3M's work force. One member of the company's rank and file worries that the behavior of executives is changing now that they have been through more than one bloodletting:

They will tend to say, "Get more profit and get sales up." Somehow they need to tell people, "Here's what we're trying to do. Here's how we'd like you to work differently." But now they cut and don't ask for our plans back. They would be better off saying that 3M's greatest strength is its people, and go to employees. I guarantee you that to a person this company would respond. There's been a degrading of the relationship.[14]

■ Temptation 2: Be Nice to Everybody

Spinoffs, cutbacks, and reductions notwithstanding, 3M is still a pretty comfortable place to work. Compensation and benefits are relatively generous, especially considering the low-cost locations of many company facilities. Working conditions are good. There is a strong corporate commitment to worker safety and to providing employees with the tools they need for their jobs. Some put in long hours, but after 5:30 p.m. or on the afternoon before a holiday in St. Paul, people in the hallways are scarce, and the huge parking lots begin to feel lonely.

A poll of U.S. 3Mers taken in 1996 showed that employee satisfaction was more than ten percentage points higher than the average score for peer companies. Three out of four 3Mers affirmed that they had sufficient authority to make decisions and take action on the job. Ninety percent said they were willing to do more than what was expected to help 3M succeed. But the findings at the other end of the spectrum were interesting, too. The lowest reported score was for the item, "My supervisor deals decisively with poor performance," with only a third of employees responding favorably.[15] Employees said they also want better coaching, practical support in career development planning, and more feedback on job performance.

There may be an opening here for 3M to tighten up its performance standards in a way that is broadly accepted, without doing lasting damage to its innovative climate. Indeed, Human Resources has been implementing a new Employee Contribution and Development Process (EC&DP) to replace its old performance assessment systems. The process was tested in Mexico, France, and Greece as well as in several divisions in the United States. Multisource and supervisor/coach feedback combined with the results of management team reviews provide more information to employees from a wider range of sources. Contributions to meeting customer, team, and corporate expectations have been added as feedback criteria. "EC&DP is designed to better connect an employee's development and contributions to the business needs of 3M."[16]

But when a person's work consistently falls short of expectations, decisive action does not necessarily follow. Changing the EC&DP verbiage from "performance" to "contribution" only muddies the waters in this respect.

We have a long-standing tradition of trying to let people improve their performance, and some of them never do. In some cases, we keep reducing the scope of the job to give them something they can accomplish. Pretty soon it's not a job. Then a new supervisor comes in and says we've got to do something. There is too much tolerance of mediocre performance.[17]

3M's reluctance to deal with questionable individual performance can even extend to the senior level. When an executive is no longer suited for a position, the choice is often made to allow a graceful exit at retirement age rather than intervening earlier with a transfer or reassignment. This can lead to less-visible problems and frustration at more junior levels of the company.

Blanket reductions in the work force are not a good substitute for demanding performance standards. They cost the company high performers as well as less-valuable employees, and foster the view that anyone is vulnerable. Many fine, experienced employees left with the Imation spinoff or have taken early retirement packages. A perverse variant of this phenomenon is occurring at the other end of the human resources pipeline in Japan, where Sumitomo 3M has chosen to minimize the hiring of highly qualified new employees in a slower growth environment while preserving the jobs of senior underperformers. It might be more effective for the company to apply firmer measures both to enhance employee development and to deal decisively with chronic poor performers. This is one area where "Midwest Nice" could be getting in the way.

■ Temptation 3: Declare Victory Too Early

In an off year for 3M it is relatively easy to create a sense of urgency. During normal times, when sales are growing and profits are rolling in from the scores of markets that the company dominates, it really does begin to look omnipotent. Most articles about 3M in the business press are complimentary, depicting pioneering inventors, deep thinking philosopher/leaders, and enthusiastic employees working together to achieve stellar results. It is difficult to imagine anyone who hasn't heard of 3M or doesn't like and admire it. 3Mers can live within an insular bubble of self-congratulation, with little information that contradicts the steady buzz of good news. At headquarters, one can eat in the cafeteria, mail letters, get film developed, do personal banking, have a physical exam, get a haircut, and go for a walk through buildings linked by long corridors—all without stepping outside of the main complex.

This self-satisfied mood is supported by the company's egalitarian definition of innovation. Anyone can be innovative in any discipline, and indeed many people are. But what if you think you're innovative and you're not? How would you know? 3M's divisions, of course, get feedback from customers and track sales performance in competitive markets. Staff departments participate in corporate consortiums, conduct benchmarking studies, and solicit input from expert consultants. However, a critical time lag often exists between activity that is assumed to be innovative and its results. And such results are often ambiguous. How would you find out, for example, whether a product that you chose to invest in was more innovative than the risky idea that you chose to kill? The most revolutionary innovations might actually produce very limited sales for a time until customers discover in them solutions to previously unarticulated needs.

A key 3M measurement tool—percentage of sales resulting from new products—can have unintended side effects. Divisions intent on fulfilling their new product quota of 30 percent of sales in four years and 10 percent every year sometimes resort to quick-fix line extensions that offer new colors or features without any fundamental break-through. Ironically, trying to make everybody innovative may subvert the criteria by which innovation is judged.

In 1996, R&D chief Bill Coyne introduced the Pacing Plus initiative with the following stiff warning:

> Yes, we have a powerful base of technology, but too much of our effort has been devoted to producing small, me-too, "fill-the-bag" products which really do not add value for the customer. In 1995, for example, we set a record for new products, but too many of them—nearly half—produced annual sales of less than $100,000 each. Few of these low-volume products will ever contribute in a meaningful way. These incremental products send the wrong message to the marketplace. They tell our customers that we can only help them to take tiny steps forward and not make the huge strides they need to keep outpacing the competition.[18]

Coyne calls for a focus on truly new products with high sales potential that can be brought to market as fast as possible. "We're going to be interested in 30 percent of the right new products in four years, instead of 30 percent of any new products." The tenor of his remarks could well be extended to nontechnical disciplines as well. His goal is to create a seller's market for novel ideas as well as closer contacts between 3M laboratories and customers, reallocating resources in the process to favor "Big Bang" ideas. For 3M this might ultimately mean thirty thousand products instead of fifty thousand, but it represents an important shift in strategic emphasis.

In short, a distinctively positive feature of 3M is that every employee is invited to become an innovator. However, it is important not to fall into the trap of happy self-deception or to be content with just incremental improvements, declare victory, and go home for a long weekend. "People get complacent and think they're contributing. We've been protected."[19] 3M has to maintain a tough edge of awareness that some things are innovative and some are not, and that too many imaginary or insignificant innovations could weaken rather than strengthen the company.

Technologies of the Future

Over time, 3M has created several new industries and many highly profitable niches. It must continue to anticipate marketplace trends to avoid becoming yet another firm whose once-bustling businesses are bypassed by the new information highway or other changes. In order to gauge 3M's future prospects, it is helpful to consider its mixed progress in areas with high growth potential in the twenty-first century: electronics and telecommunications, eco-efficient products, and software.

■ Electronics and Telecommunications

Electronics and telecommunications are expanding industries in which 3M has already done well. Several Austin-based divisions are dedicated to these markets: Electronic Products, Electronic Handling and Protection, and Telecom Systems. The company doesn't break out its sales by division in its public reports, but these are successful and growing businesses.

To the semiconductor industry, for example, 3M offers a broad array of products. One core offering is Microflex Circuits (seen on the cover of the book), which link computer chips to printed circuit boards. They consist of a tape into which tiny channels are drawn for copper circuitry. These thin, reliable circuits allow for more connections than ordinary rigid circuit boards because they are mass-produced on the tape, and enable manufacturers to bond chips to packages in a continuous process known as tape-automated bonding. They can be used in devices such as phones, pagers, laptops, and printers. Technical requirements are incredible, with projections for the near future that a single chip will require eight hundred to one thousand leads, or connections— more than double the current number—and measurements being made in the tens of microns. Products originating from other 3M divisions are also sold into the semiconductor market, such as HFE cleaning fluids for use in the semiconductor manufacturing process, microabrasives for wafer planarization, and protective equipment for laboratory and manufacturing workers.

3M's Electronics Market Center is working to bring together and apply diverse products and technologies from more than fourteen different business units, including optical films, vibration-dampening components, ceramic wafers, and adhesives. A common 3M approach is to create ancillary but profitable niche components that competitors are less inclined to focus on. By making the connecting package rather than the semiconductor, vibration dampeners for disk drives rather than the drives, or film to enhance the brightness of a laptop screen rather than the screen itself (or the battery), 3M is positioning itself as an integral supplier to the industry without struggling against its star players. Insiders predict confidently that even though most people do not currently think of the company as a major electronics firm, "3M will be a deciding force in this industry in the next three to five years."[20]

■ Eco-Efficient Products

Beyond HFEs and oil sorbents (see chapter one), 3M has begun to make waves with other offerings in the broad and diverse market for environmentally friendly products. CEO DeSimone is a strong advocate of what he calls "eco-efficiency," and has even co-authored a book on the subject under the auspices of the World Business Council for Sustainable Development. In the past, some of 3M's technologies and manufacturing processes have been major sources of pollution due to the nature of core technologies like oil-based coatings and solvents. But over the years 3M's environmental stance has evolved from regulatory compliance, to proactive efforts at pollution prevention, to a newer philosophy of sustainable growth and development of eco-efficient products.

Worldwide, 3M now invests $100 million a year in environmentally related R&D and an estimated $200 million in environmental operations. It is making steady progress toward reducing air emissions, and is striving to cut water releases by 90 percent and waste generation by 50 percent, along with continuous reduction of energy use. Estimated first year company savings from pollution prevention have totaled more than $750 million, not to mention the societal gains resulting from a healthier environment.[21] 3M's achievements received national recognition in 1996, when its Pollution Prevention Pays (3P) program received the President's Award for Sustainable Development in the U.S. Other environmental awards have been granted to the company in Argentina, France, and Germany.

While these environmental benefits, financial savings, and accolades are significant, sales of products with eco-efficient features are equally appealing from a business standpoint. Here are a few examples:

- *Scotchtint Window Film* is applied to windows in cars or buildings to increase their energy efficiency. It cuts heat gain through building windows by more than 70 percent while protecting carpets and furnishings from ultraviolet radiation; new designs also cut heat losses by up to 30 percent.

- *Silverlux Reflective Film* is placed behind fluorescent lights, reducing the absorption of energy by the lighting fixtures and thereby increasing their efficiency. The film enables removal of up to half of the lamps in a room while preserving optimal lighting, and brings additional indirect savings by reducing air-conditioning loads.

- *Safest Stripper* is a water-based remover of paints and varnishes. It reduces toxic risks and is biodegradable and nonflammable. A different use, wallpaper removal, has become the most popular application.

- *3M Space Lens* is part of a new solar power array used aboard NASA's Deep Space I mission. The lens draws on 3M's optics technology to concentrate solar energy on a strip of photovoltaic cells.

Its tiny grooves are able to capture and focus light with such efficiency that only one-seventh of the solar cells generate the same amount of energy as earlier models. Production costs and launch weight are both reduced. Beyond future applications for communications satellites, the technology also has interesting implications for enhancing the efficiency of land-based solar energy collectors.[22]

- *Dryview Laser Imaging* was one other significant environmental success for 3M's product developers. It was transferred to Imation in the spinoff and recently sold to Kodak for $520 million. This product replaces film-based medical radiography, which produces large amounts of wastewater contaminated with hazardous chemicals. It creates substantial savings for hospitals in operating costs and capital investments by using heat application technology instead of wet processing systems, thus eliminating the need for chemical inputs and water rinsing together with the elaborate facilities formerly necessary for water treatment.

Certain eco-efficient products hold out better prospects than do others. While the global market for Scotchtint window film, for example, is estimated at $300 million a year, sales of Safest Stripper have suffered because anticipated government regulations on less-safe products have not been imposed. 3M is hoping that its first attempts here will become the platform for more successful next-generation products. Consumers in some cases still value price and ease of use over environmental or safety concerns—marketers must distinguish between what consumers say they want and what they are willing to pay for. Timing is critical as public awareness evolves, and changing regulatory environments add further uncertainties.

If 3M can build on such early efforts and develop a large portfolio of eco-efficient products, it could open another new door to future growth that is both sustained and sustainable. These types of products fit well with 3M's predilection for profitable niche markets, its mix of technology platforms, and the readiness of its employees to make a positive social contribution.[23]

■ Software

In another major growth industry, software, 3M's approach has been more tentative. It has traditionally been run by chemical and mechanical engineers who like to design and manufacture things. In fact, its first stand-alone software product attempts to reinvent an old hit that applied adhesive chemistry to paper: Post-it notes.

This blockbuster invention has been strategically exploited through a seemingly endless run of line extensions. Nearly two decades after their introduction, Post-it notes are now available in 27 sizes, 18 colors, 20 fragrances, and a multitude of dispensers. In the mid-nineties, however, the business unit's management team began to ask itself what would happen to their aging cash cow in the paperless pastures of the future. Electronic communications were becoming an increasingly viable alternative to paper message conveyers. Could Post-it notes be reconceived to bridge the gap between paper and electronics, leading to a new generation of products?

The Post-it Products Business Unit envisioned a software program that would perform many of the same tasks inside of computers that their paper products do on one's desk. Lacking software expertise, they began to search in the wider 3M community. As coincidence would have it, a two-man team in a corporate research lab had been asked by Larry Eaton, an executive vice president, to explore software opportunities for 3M. The two projects intersected and found that they had much in common: an interest in software, no official status, and no budget. The corporate lab hands, software programmers by the name of Marty Kenner and Mitch Grunes, went back to Eaton, reported that they had found a promising software opportunity, and talked him into providing a small amount of seed money to build a prototype.

Kenner and Grunes enlisted the assistance of a 3M specialist in computer/human interfaces. Through a series of interviews with potential end-users, the desired features of electronic Post-it notes became clearer. They then built the first prototype, circumventing the divisional product development sequence which had assigned their project a zero priority rating and therefore zero budget. There were lots of questions about the product's commercial viability—many asked whether 3M should be in the software business at all. Advocates countered with arguments that a software product would bring greater exposure to the Post-it brand, protect it against electronic competitors, and give 3M valuable software experience. One thing everyone agreed upon was that further marketing input would be needed to demonstrate that commercialization made sense. Another modest infusion of nondivisional financing from Eaton kept things going, and an experienced marketer agreed to help out part-time.

Market studies eventually included numerous focus groups, 110 one-on-one end user tests, and a series of three Beta tests, the last with 500 participants. From a starting point where people invited into 3M's software lab were simply asked what they would expect an electronic Post-it note to do, the researchers began to observe prototype users, incorporate their responses, and ask for suggestions regarding additional features. Kenner and Grunes discovered needs that they had anticipated from computer users, such as the desire to create electronic reminders. Less straightforward or even unarticulated needs for functions such as self-organization and messaging were ferreted out as well. Some features were added for both function and fun, such as the ability to crumple up a note and throw it away, with sound and graphics to match—not to mention the ability to rummage through the trash and dig out an old note. End-user research eventually resulted in software program functions that correspond to the findings in the diagram here.

Post-it Software: End-User Research Results	**Behavior**	**Feature**	**Scenario**
	Remind	Create	• Written phone messages • Write down an idea in the middle of doing something else
		Alarms	• Need to remember to look at the note you created
	Organize	Memo-boards	• File several notes on one subject in the same place
		Find	• Cannot remember where you put that important note
	Communicate	E-mail	• Need to quickly inform someone else of information on your note
		Attach	• Use note to draw attention to a section of another document
		Print	• Need to take a note with you • Use a note to remind someone else

The work that was going on in the software lab attracted the attention of Jerry McAllister, a lab manager for paper Post-it notes. He liked the software concept but felt that the most commercially viable application would be to enable users to print out notes, thereby also enabling 3M to sell them the paper consumables. He launched a parallel bootlegging operation to develop the software for this printing process. Another proposal was to print signs the size of normal paper that could be attached and detached like Post-it notes—these would not require special software but could be equally lucrative. McAllister's ideas did not meet with immediate agreement either, as the first demonstration of the prototype printing system for executives produced chuckles, the opinion that it was unlikely to sell, and the slightly barbed jest that the lab staff must have too much time on its hands.

Although the projects continued separately for some time, what eventually carried the day in 3M's internal discussions was the idea of uniting them into the product family that now includes Post-it Software Notes, Post-it Notes for Ink Jet and Laser Printers, and Post-it Signs. The intriguing linkages between software and paper products began to remind people of the razor and razor blade formula that has been so lucrative for 3M in areas such as commercial graphics. Meanwhile, McAllister's team had been able to detail the handsome sums competitors were earning for consumable media that are run through printers. After several attempts at gaining additional funding were turned down, the expanded product family concept was finally anointed with Pacing Plus status. Post-it Software Notes were introduced in the spring of 1996, while the paper products for printers came out the following October.

One distinctive aspect of the Post-it notes software development process was its combination of direct customer research with a deliberate attempt to seek out both articulated and unarticulated needs as the product was built. Kenner and Grunes systematically searched out software user needs that only became clear after multiple prototypes were put through successive testing phases. Each model incorporated user input from the previous phase, with features that gradually took shape as the user needs themselves were better defined. This represents a fourth type of innovation process that can be added to the three already described in chapter one.

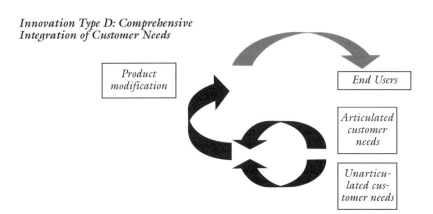

A second distinctive aspect of the effort to reinvent Post-it notes was the quantity and quality of teamwork involved. Overlapping team efforts extended from the software development team to the business unit to the global marketing team. Sub-teams were formed for each of the three major product areas (Post-it Software Notes, Post-it Notes for Ink Jet and Laser Printers, and Post-it Signs). Another type of team, focused on the new product commercialization process, had already done a study of 3M best practices that all of the teams adopted to compress their cycle times. Such best practices spurred the two teams making the printer products, for example, to follow an intense schedule featuring concurrent product development, lab tests, pilot runs, and marketing planning. They were thus able to go from product definition to introduction in a mere nine months. All of this teamwork was facilitated by a move toward co-location, with marketers sitting alongside with lab and manufacturing colleagues.

*New Generation Post-it Notes:
Team Functions*

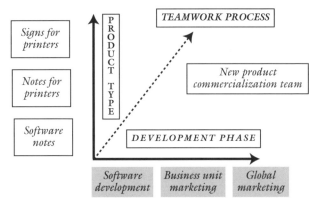

Team members claim not to know who invented their new products. One of the business unit leaders observes that the magnitude of the project was sufficiently large that it could not have been carried out effectively by any individual. A would-be candidate for product champion who prefers anonymity says:

> It wasn't me. I was just part of it. . . . When you get into a team-based organization and you go beyond a single product concept, and you're talking about a whole system, you recognize teams and not individuals. It's a sign of the times. The beauty of it is that there are multiple champions now. . . .

But no one would deny that it took a small group of individuals with great energy, enthusiasm, and courage to get the project going. And someone like Marty Kenner, who has migrated from being a software programmer in a corporate lab to leading barnstorming public relations tours for the new product across North America and Europe, still looks a lot like a classic 3M inventorpreneur.

Kenner's chief worry now is how to make money on the Post-it Software Notes that he helped to invent: "We're still struggling. We're not profitable yet." He is currently working together with others to develop marketing and sales techniques that are new to 3M. Among these are internet advertising: a new deal with Netscape will put Post-it Software Notes on its web site, and a successful launch on The Dilbert Zone home page produced 754,000 hits when the product was introduced. Unusually intense public relations efforts are targeting "techie" lead users, package deals are being negotiated for companies, and licensing to OEM (Original Equipment Manufacturer) computer makers such as NEC is underway. Internet orders from overseas locations have caused 3M to accelerate licensing efforts in major markets where the product is vulnerable to piracy without such agreements; translations are already available in nineteen languages.[24]

The fate of 3M's fledgling software efforts is very much up in the air. It is hard not to admire the persistence and ingenuity of Kenner and his colleagues. At the same time, mighty Microsoft has been pushing a competing offering that, while currently inferior, is integrated into its Microsoft Exchange software at no additional cost to the user. Microsoft's "notes" are yellow and look strikingly similar to Post-it notes. (The instructions begin: "Notes are the equivalent of paper sticky notes.") Should the Northwest software giant choose to do to

Post-it Software Notes what it has done to the products of much larger industry rivals like Novell or Netscape, it is difficult to see what would stop it. Kenner claims not to be too worried because of strong 3M patent protection for its new technologies and partner developer status with Microsoft, but he sounds a bit like a man whistling bravely as he passes a graveyard in the dark.

3M, with its limited software offerings, must somehow build a bridgehead into this highly competitive field. Pockets of software expertise exist elsewhere within the company,[25] but not yet enough to make 3M a significant industry force. The jury is still out on whether or not it will be able to thrive as fully in an information-based economy as it has in manufacturing environments.

3M's Organization of the Future: Two Examples

The restructuring that 3M has undertaken in recent years has aimed to improve the company's economic performance and competitive position. As the following examples show, 3M is also increasingly part of a global economic order, and needs to continue its process of reinvention so as to maintain its position as an innovation leader around the world.

■ Research and Development

From a long-term perspective, 3M's most critical organizational challenge will be to transform its research laboratories so that they can meet global customer needs. At present, with almost half of the company's sales made domestically, it is natural to have a research establishment still focused on U.S. market needs. Yet this is somewhat dysfunctional in serving major overseas subsidiaries, and a decade or two from now, when more than three-quarters of 3M sales revenues are likely to come from abroad, such a setup will be far more problematic. Even now, 3M is regarded in some countries as a high-cost foreign vendor rather than the friendly preferred supplier it would like to become. This perception may be reinforced by the company's general strategy of introducing new products and technologies and creating markets rather than slugging out price wars with competitors.

But adapting to a higher proportion of international sales will take more than simply setting up a laboratory in every major market. Given the tremendous complexity and variety of 3M products and technologies, successful R&D depends upon the critical mass of large-scale facilities like those in St. Paul and Austin. In contrast to the five thousand US researchers, the highest concentration of 3M scientists anywhere else in the world is the five hundred Japanese at Sagamihara; most of the others are scattered in smaller, specialized facilities across Europe and elsewhere.

The need for critical mass creates tensions with the need for greater research focus on overseas customers. How could a subsidiary laboratory possibly perform the duties of the Electronics Market Center, which is adapting technologies from a dozen or more different platforms to the fast-evolving needs of the electronics industry? And even in places such as Japan or Germany, where the number and sophistication of researchers is increasing, can 3M's tradition of innovation be transplanted in a way that leads to breakthrough inventions?

3M's response to this conundrum has been to steadily cultivate its global R&D presence, placing additional resources in the countries with the most promising local markets. As far back as the 1970s, a decision was made to increase the company's investment in R&D from 4.5 percent to 6.5 percent of revenue. About half of that increase has gone into building labs overseas. A lab has recently been completed in Germany adjacent to the 3M headquarters in Neuss; there is a new customer technical center at Sagamihara in Japan; Mexico and Brazil are also receiving substantial investments.

Interaction between U.S. and overseas laboratories has also increased. Joint R&D activities are on the rise, particularly in connection with Pacing Plus programs. For instance, there are now thirty-seven Japanese researchers participating in Pacing Plus programs in Japan and St. Paul. Bill Coyne outlines four additional steps the company is taking to integrate its global research community more closely:

1. Using the latest computer and network technologies to create real-time linkages between 3M scientists around the world.

2. Ensuring that researchers overseas know what resources are available in the United States and how to access them.

3. Sending U.S. corporate scientists outside of the United States to build mentor relationships with talented research personnel.

4. Continuing the pattern of foreign service assignments that bring overseas researchers to work in the United States and dispatch people from the United States to overseas posts.

3M's research establishment will have attained full global status when its whole range of innovative activities becomes the norm outside of the United States—commercialization of new technologies, co-design, and original inventions in addition to product adaptation, repackaging, or novel sales and marketing approaches. What seems feasible to shoot for in the short term could perhaps be termed "co-invention" by cross-functional teams with global membership, and simultaneous introduction of key products in major world markets.

■ 3M Europe

3M was one of the first companies in Europe to undertake organizational innovations in response to the gradual economic unification of the region. Changes made by 3M's European operations in the 1990s may hold clues to what other regions will look like in the future.

As customers began to organize themselves on a pan-European basis, the traditional 3M independent subsidiary structure was becoming outmoded. Customers would purchase centrally and shop around for the best price: if one 3M subsidiary offered better terms than another, savvy customers would purchase their entire European supply through that country. Moreover, with operations in seventeen different countries, each with its own management structure, internal 3M coordination of product development and sales activities was difficult. Every country wanted its own product modifications and had to be convinced to sell a new product. Yet market penetration for many 3M products in Europe was only half the levels attained in the United States.

In 1991, a volunteer group of European country managers and staff representatives began to meet periodically to define a more harmonized European business strategy. They would get together once every six weeks in Brussels after work in the late afternoon, have dinner, and then meet again until ten or eleven in the evening. All of 3M's European businesses were asked to present a new organizational scenario—some proposals were more centralized, while consumer-oriented businesses had a more local emphasis.

Through this consultative process emerged a matrix between eighteen "European Business Centers" (EBCs) consisting of one or more business units, and ten "Regional Subsidiary Organizations" (RSOs) that were either major European nations or combinations of smaller countries such as the Nordic Region. This brought a major shift of power and responsibility to the businesses, with basic profit-and-loss responsibility residing in the EBC product-line structures rather than in the regions or countries. Product rollouts were implemented by the individual businesses themselves. Unlike many of the multinational companies that have centralized their headquarters operations in one European country, different 3M EBCs have chosen to establish their headquarters in the United Kingdom, France, Belgium, Germany, or Italy.

The EBC/RSO structure immediately enhanced speed and efficiency in responding to customers. Under the previous structure a business would have had to persuade and cajole seventeen different country contacts; now it was free to set strategy and make resource decisions for all of Europe. It could thereby present a single face to the customer, add or move people with greater ease, delegate complementary responsibilities to different countries, and eliminate redundant manufacturing or distribution facilities. 3M's abilities to serve customers were further heightened through pan-European linkages of sales and marketing, research, manufacturing, and tech service. Input and support from the United States was also streamlined, with the EBC serving as a primary point of contact for divisions in St. Paul and Austin.

Problems do remain with the new European structure. It is not easy to coordinate teams of people who are dispersed in facilities across the continent. EBC heads must still drive their sales forces across ten different regions. There is also the desire of less independent-minded personnel to be in close, daily contact with a manager: "The country subsidiary management before the change . . . played the role of the godfather to the organization. There was someone to whom you could refer for your career, a job rotation, a new opportunity, as well as for sensing the level and motivation of the people and infusing them with energy."

To address these issues without creating a set of business center silos to replace country silos, regional managing directors have retained responsibility for country-based resources and are tasked with developing European key account management programs. Customer

Focused Marketing, laboratory poster sessions, and regular meetings including all EBC technical heads have been implemented to promote contact across business lines. All of this was accomplished without hiring outside consultants, and even ignoring expert advice against setting up such a cross-border matrix structure. EBC and RSO heads were trained on shared leadership, with numerous meeting forums available to air potential conflicts.

> We created a true matrix and gave the local managers real power. Some people think that's impossible, but we tried to establish this principle of shared leadership in order to ensure a balance of Euro management and strategy with local input and customer interface.

The practical reality has been that some businesses, such as chemicals, were easily adapted to a pan-European structure, while others like office supplies remain more country-based. Some business centers continue to struggle with regional versus country identities. 3M has realized that ideal organizational structure doesn't matter as much as looking carefully at each business, with its distinctive distributor arrangements, market pressures, and sales force requirements.

3M is still trying to get its European structure balanced properly and is not in a hurry to export it to other parts of the world. Over time, however, similar issues are bound to arise in other regions undergoing economic integration such as Latin America or Southeast Asia. Putting an effective regional structure in place may help local subsidiaries to sell or service products more effectively. As Doug Hanson, head of 3M Europe at the time of its reorganization, notes, the company can draw on experience and personal relationships to bring it through such times of radical organizational transformation.

> I did not expect this change to be as huge as it is in terms of business process and management style changes—no one did. We knew there would be adjustments to be made, but we did not anticipate the hundreds of managers in new jobs and what that really meant. . . . Yet, we know each other, trust each other and rely on each other. I think we have the kind of willingness to adapt to change as is necessary with the new business conditions.[26]

Conclusion: The 3M Way of Innovation

Even though 3M has repeatedly broken new ground in its pursuit of innovation, recent events have brought the company to another turning point. Perhaps at no time in the organization's modern history has the resilience and adaptability of its tradition of innovation been more severely tested. Top executives are being forced to weigh their own commitment to 3M's unique tradition and culture against the expectations of Wall Street.

The obvious imperative for 3M—or for that matter, any company with a history of success plus a long list of challenges—is to stay focused on its strengths while also fomenting and acquiring new ideas and technologies. This may seem like a plain vanilla strategy, but it is also the sort of steady course that is typical of 3M. In fact, once you examine the finer points of choosing what to preserve and what new ideas to embrace (not to mention the compatibility of old and new), this apparently simple path develops wickedly complex twists and turns. It is far too easy either to ignore outside advice or become overly dependent on it, to focus exclusively on in-house inventions or to reject valuable nuggets of home-grown experience.

3Mers once again must strike a balance, and that balance ought to include a full and careful appreciation of the company's own innovative strengths. Because any process of change requires countless independent decisions made at every level of the organization, the danger exists that some of the decision-makers may have their hand on just one part of the innovation elephant without grasping what the whole animal looks like in full stride. 3M's rich store of best practices has still not been fully distributed or leveraged within the company. And while its climate of innovation is something that every employee imbibes over time through stories and personal experience, this is not readily conceptualized or described.

One thing that may help each 3Mer is to consider the company's innovation system in its entirety, applying the kinds of questions found at the end of each chapter to their own business efforts (see Appendix A for the complete list of questions). The same exercise will also be valuable to other companies who need to stimulate innovative activity, or who may simply want to supplement their existing strengths with other models.

There are encouraging signs that 3M's patient investments to support innovation through the Pacing Plus programs have finally begun to produce results. In the midst of 1998's uncharacteristically mediocre financial performance, these programs broke the $1 billion mark in sales, an increase of about 50 percent from 1997. A similar steep rise has taken place thus far in 1999, with yet another 50 percent increase in Pacing Plus revenues projected for the full year.[27] Several programs have gained so much momentum that they appear likely to transcend the parameters of Pacing Plus altogether and grow into full-fledged business units. And impressive new products keep emerging to demonstrate the fundamental health of 3M's innovation infrastructure: technologies for deciphering the human genome; a new fiber optic cabling system, a potential oral treatment for hepatitis C; a dry cloth that traps dust, water, and oils; and "not-so-sticky stickers" for kids that easily peel off walls and furniture.[28]

Indeed, there is a shared sense of anticipation that 3M is overdue for a new hit product or two. Missed financial targets seem to have stemmed not from a lack of ideas but from issues related to commercialization, as well as volatility in international markets. For the immediate future, company insiders predict a concerted push in several areas that will recharge 3M's innovative batteries: 1) improved commercialization practices for new products, 2) technology acquisitions to fill the gaps in 3M's portfolio, and 3) greater speed in all processes, including executive decision-making.

Increased commercial success is already being sought in part through constructive self-criticism. At a recent management gathering, brutally frank comments aired by Pacing Plus participants included a confession by Trizact abrasives team members that they had missed a fundamental point about factory employee work habits. Acceptance of this superior new 3M technology was delayed because the team failed to notice that factory workers consistently sought better results from standard abrasives by applying pressure to them, an action which unfortunately had the opposite effect with the Trizact line, with its unusual microreplication structure. The product team's belated discovery of this "fact of factory life" was a painful reminder that commercialization has to complete the circle between invention and product users (the people at the base of McKnight's smokestacks).

3Mers are also attempting to embrace new technologies and practices from outside the company. Numerous plans for strategic acquisitions are now in the works, although critics contend that 3M has missed opportunities in the pharmaceutical industry and other fields. A recent memorandum from top management to employees estimates that acquisitions could account for as much as 20 percent of the company's growth on an ongoing basis. 3M's financial health gives it a relatively free hand in shopping for technologies; thus far the scale of acquisitions is still not large enough to pose significant organizational difficulties. In addition to technology acquisitions, the company promises greater openness in hiring outside talent.[29]

3M's most deep-seated challenge is to accelerate the internal pace of innovation. Speed is an ever more prominent factor in information-age technical development, yet the evolutionary forms of innovation at 3M have traditionally proceeded at their own, more leisurely, pace. Here, patience must be increasingly infused with urgency, and 3M's entire research community is being exhorted to pick up the pace without choking off spontaneity or sacrificing the long-term product pipeline. On the management side of the equation, 3M has eliminated a layer of management and reorganized itself around six primary markets in order to focus more fully on customer needs and growth opportunities.[30]

R&D chief Bill Coyne says, "I'm bullish. We've had a very good year for new products. We've got the capability to grow for the next fifty years. We're strong financially, good technologically, and capable of participating in many different industries so we're not dependent on any one trend."[31] Others see adversity as an opportunity: "Financial pressures force you to reexamine everything and further commit to the things that are contributing. . . . The process is a necessary one."[32] Still others have had their confidence shaken by the string of sub-par business results, but are anxiously ready to do what needs to be done. Critics of the company regard CEO DeSimone's patient approach as maddeningly indecisive rather than courageous. Yet regardless of what one's view of 3M's future prospects might be, its long record of accomplishment and its enlightened human resources and ethical practices are such that even most critics wish it well.

If you ask present 3M executives what legacy they want to leave, the answers are a characteristic mix of modest pragmatism and far-reaching aspiration. DeSimone says he would like to see the creation of a couple of new technology platforms, adding, "These things last a century sometimes." Ron Baukol, head of International Operations, refers to a global company where everybody talks to everybody else, and where national boundaries are not an obstacle: "We need to get the customer in Osaka as close to our best experts as the customer in Atlanta." Bill Coyne is focused intently on preserving 3M's culture of innovation and the intelligently applied passion of the individual innovator. "Innovation," Coyne observes, "is an intensely human activity. . . . No other species can adapt to changes with such speed and inspiration."[33]

Innovation is both the touchstone of 3M's past and the intricate pattern of adaptation that will shape its future. The organization that began in such an inauspicious manner has become an astonishingly resourceful and sophisticated global enterprise which is evolving further every day. 3M employees manifest an enthusiasm, energy, and collective ingenuity that are contagious. "I don't want 3M ever to get to be just a place for people to come to work. I want it to be a place where people have joy in coming to work." This unusual ambition was voiced by a company executive twenty-five years ago, and employees today echo this view. Like any other company, 3M contains a human measure of ineptitude and discontent, but it is still a place where even ordinary people are stimulated to perform in extraordinary ways.[34]

3M's climate of innovation is, among other things, an ambitious social experiment that seeks to apply the values of freedom, tolerance, and individual initiative in a business context. In this sense, the company is one of the more promising human endeavors of our era. If 3M is around a century from now, as this author is willing to wager along with Collins and Porras, it will be because similar core values continue to inspire innovation in new and changing environments. Innovation in the service of prosperity and freedom is a worthy cause.

Key Questions To Ask About Innovation

The Future of Innovation

1. Can you successfully handle the three temptations brought on by innovative success: "Make Lots of Money," "Be Nice to Everybody," "Declare Victory too Early?"

2. Are you positioned to be a major player in industries of the future such as electronics and telecommunications, environmental products, and software or e-commerce?

3. Does your company practice the fourth major innovation type: Comprehensive Integration of Customer Needs (articulated and unarticulated)?

4. Have your product development teams incorporated best practices from other team efforts to compress cycle time and improve overall performance?

5. Can your organizational structure accommodate future requirements for higher levels of cross-border technical innovation or regional integration of company operations and product offerings?

6. Do you understand and continue to cultivate what you are good at while simultaneously embracing new ideas and technologies?

7. Do you still have the vision and the courage to continue blazing your own trail?

Key Questions To Ask About Innovation

The Innovation Process

1. Does everyone in your organization know how to define innovation: new ideas + action that produces results?

2. Are you utilizing all four innovation types: A) Creating a New Market or Industry, B) Changing the Basis of Competition, C) Line Extension, and D) Comprehensive Integration of Customer Needs (introduced in chapter eight).

3. Are you practicing the five innovation openings: bridge, association, stimulation, reversal, combination?

4. Is innovation occurring at all levels: original, adaptation, organizational, customer relations, regulatory environment?

5. Who are the inventorpreneurs in your workplace? How can you or your team do the work of an inventorpreneur or find ways to support such activities?

6. Do managers know how to balance support for innovation with healthy discipline—e.g., the "benevolent blind eye" and "trial by fire"?

CHAPTER 2

Origins of Innovation

1. Does your organization have an oral history of stories that helps employees to learn about innovation?

2. In what way have key corporate leaders contributed to creating an innovative heritage?

3. Are there established corporate values that enable innovators to flourish: stubborn persistence, creative use of failure, curiosity, patience, individual initiative, and so on?

4. How deep do these values run and what sustains and renews them?

Forging Technical Innovation

1. What are your technology platforms?

2. Are long-term research groups in touch with customers and flexible enough to support short-term development when necessary? Do research projects with a short-term focus leave room for longer-term efforts?

3. Can you implement the radical innovation practices necessary for Type A Innovation—that is, Creation of a New Market or Industry: intelligent accident, direct customer contact, resource bootlegging, volunteer recruitment, market creation, and staff contributions?

4. Are you familiar with Appledorn's prescriptions for organizational culture (freedom, never give up), communication (opening doors, interface with customers), and management style (being a servant, breaking the rules)?

5. Does your style of technical innovation simultaneously integrate individual research efforts with laboratory resources, marketing ideas, global employees and customer input, product and vendor systems, and strategic partners?

6. Is your approach to innovation dominated by strategic planning or a more evolutionary model? What is the proper balance between the two ("manage technology" vs. "let it show us where to go")?

7. Do you have process innovation to better enable product innovation?

8. What volunteer employee activities foster innovation and how can these be encouraged without being suffocated?

9. Does the company recognize innovative achievements in a meaningful way?

Innovative Staff, Innovative Company

1. How can staff functions best support innovation? Areas to explore include:

   • For human resources: recruiting; corporate TV; leadership competencies.

- For finance: balance sheet management to reduce capital costs; rapid response to international crises; procurement reengineering.

- For marketing: coordinated approaches to customers; global data warehouse; analysis of customer data.

2. Are staff functions innovative themselves in their support for innovation? Do they successfully balance steady support for new product invention and commercialization with calculated risk-taking?

3. Are staff departments in subsidiary operations able to contribute significantly to global business expansion? How can headquarters staff resources be leveraged to augment subsidiary performance?

CHAPTER 5 ————————————————————————————

Global Innovation

1. Is each business unit taking advantage of the seven potential areas of cross-border innovative activity: sales and marketing techniques, product packaging, product adaptation, commercialization of new technologies, acquisition of technical information, co-design, and original invention"?

2. Are subsidiaries ready and able, where appropriate, to move up the scale of innovative activity from sales and marketing towards original product development?

3. What are the formal methods by which global innovation is supported: e.g., organizational structure, expatriate assignments, global teams, mentor programs?

4. Are there informal activities that make global innovation easier: e.g., strong cross-border friendships, volunteer activity?

5. Is the subsidiary development sequence managed for optimum product customization and solid local government relations?

6. Is the "cascade effect" being used to disseminate experience from one subsidiary to another?

7. Does global management successfully balance factors such as information-sharing and independent thinking, profit and market share, headquarters-based design and subsidiary input?

Reinventing Headquarters/Subsidiary Relationships

1. Is innovative thinking applied to subsidiary relationships as well as to the invention of new technologies?

2. Has the headquarters relationship with key subsidiaries successfully evolved through the four phases of cooperative action: trust and autonomy, regional leadership, strategic integration, and global organization development?

3. Does each subsidiary enjoy a degree of freedom that fits its particular stage of development?

4. Are the various elements that comprise the "virtuous cycle" of headquarters/subsidiary relationships in place: e.g., trust and friendship, accurate assessment of capabilities, commitment to subsidiary maturation, local customer input, joint development, flexible leadership, constructive debate, local ownership and enthusiasm, mutual learning and best practices?

5. Can an ordinary subsidiary employee with a good idea get it by both local management and overseas counterparts to turn it into a new product, service, or process improvement?

CHAPTER 7

Managing an Innovative People System

1. Does the organization actively seek to build a tradition of innovation with the six paired steps (derived from Coyne's formula): vision & values, foresight & history, stretch goals & security, empowerment & volunteerism, communication & community, recognition & reputation?

2. Is the balance of support and discipline for innovative activity properly calibrated to fit the three stages of "innovation by doodling," "innovation by design," and "innovation by direction"?

3. Are new initiatives cautiously selected and then persistently adapted and integrated with the entire system of innovation practices?

4. Who is tending to the ecology of the whole system, and do they know what they are doing?

5. Are you prepared to benchmark in a way that compares complexity with complexity? How well do you know your own organization?

6. Can you creatively fuse market-in and product-out approaches, turn any part of the company into a skunk-works, transform incremental improvements into major breakthroughs, and engage in strategic non-action?

CHAPTER 8 ————————————————————————————————

The Future of Innovation

1. Can you successfully handle the three temptations brought on by innovative success: "Make Lots of Money," "Be Nice to Everybody," "Declare Victory too Early"?

2. Are you positioned to be a major player in industries of the future such as electronics and telecommunications, environmental products, and software or e-commerce?

3. Does your company practice the fourth major innovation type: Comprehensive Integration of Customer Needs (articulated and unarticulated)?

4. Have your product development teams incorporated best practices from other team efforts to compress cycle time and improve overall performance?

5. Can your organizational structure accommodate future requirements for higher levels of cross-border technical innovation or regional integration of company operations and product offerings?

6. Do you understand and continue to cultivate what you are good at while simultaneously embracing new ideas and technologies?

7. Do you still have the vision and the courage to continue blazing your own trail?

3M Chronology

1902	Minnesota Mining and Manufacturing founded in Two Harbors, Minnesota.
1904	"Corundum" production begins.
1905	Edgar Ober and Lucius Ordway purchase 60 percent of 3M stock and take control of the company.
	3M moves from Two Harbors to Duluth, Minnesota.
1906	Sandpaper production begins.
1907	William McKnight hired as assistant bookkeeper.
1910	3M moves from Duluth to St. Paul, Minnesota.
1914	First product innovation: invention of synthetic abrasive Three-M-ite.
1916	First quality laboratory established by McKnight.
	3M pays first dividend to stockholders.
1920	Ober implements profit-sharing practice with key employees.
1921	Wetordry waterproof abrasives developed at 3M labs by Francis Okie.
1924	First product innovation failure: Restul car polish is discontinued only a decade later after slow sales growth.
1925	Dick Drew, lab assistant, works on his own initiative to invent Scotch masking tape, 3M's first nonabrasive product.
	Richard Carlton, lab manager, publishes technical information manual to encourage high quality standards and cooperation between sales and manufacturing.
1929	McKnight, newly elected president of 3M, establishes policy of devoting money to research.
	3M and 9 other U.S. abrasives manufacturers form Durex company to manufacture and sell their products in foreign countries.
1930	First commercial shipments of Scotch brand cellophane tape, invented by Dick Drew.
1932	McKnight pioneers one of the country's first company-financed unemployment insurance programs for 3M employees.
	Production of Colorquartz aggregate artificially colored roofing granules begins.
1937	Central Research Labs established to conduct long-term scientific research.
	General profit-sharing plan implemented for all 3M employees.
1939	First reflective sheeting for highway signs developed.
1940	New Products Department organized to study new product ideas.

	Product Fabrication Lab established to develop new manufacturing methods.
1944	Magnetic sound recording tape research begun. 3M becomes the first U.S. company to master the manufacturing process, and succeeds in bringing Scotch magnetic tape to the mainstream.
1948	McKnight's principles of delegating responsibility and encouraging individual initiative are written down.
	Company restructured into separate business divisions with near-autonomous status.
1949	Nonwoven fabric invented. Becomes the basis of hundreds of 3M products including face masks, absorbent materials for oil and air filtration, medical tapes, and Scotch-Brite cleaning products.
1950	U.S. government orders dissolution of Durex company. 3M begins solitary overseas expansion.
1951	Technical Forum founded by 3M scientists with the purpose of "encouraging a free and active interchange of information and the cross-fertilization of ideas."
1954	Scotch magnetic video tape first used to record television programs.
1956	Scotchgard fabric and upholstery protector developed.
1959	Scotch-Brite cleaning pads introduced to consumers.
1960	First surgical tape, Steri-Strip tape for wound closures, invented.
1962	Scotch magic transparent tape introduced.
1963	Carlton Society formed to honor extraordinary scientific and technical contributions.
1964	Dry Silver technology invented. Allows for reproduction of images by heat process.
1972	3M data cartridge technology revolutionizes computer data storage.
1973	Disclosure that corporate funds have been used to make illegal political contributions generates shock waves throughout the organization.
1975	Pollution Prevention Pays (PPP) program introduced to reduce or eliminate pollution during 3M manufacturing processes.
1979	Lightweight Thinsulate insulation material introduced, providing warmth without bulk.
1980	Post-it notes introduced.
	Scotch Very High Bond (VHB) tapes introduced.
1985	Invention of first successful optical disks for information storage.
	First refastenable diaper tapes developed.
1989	Introduction of Maxair Autohaler asthmatic inhaler for delivering accurate doses of medicine triggered by breathing.
1992	APC adhesive-coated orthodontic brackets introduced: first brackets with pre-applied adhesives.
1995	3M microreplication technology leads to development of structured abrasives, the first abrasives with a precise surface.
	Spin-off of Imation Corp. and other restructuring steps eliminate $3 billion in product revenues and 11,000 employees.
1996	Innovator Award introduced to reward employees for non-directed projects resulting in new and profitable technologies and products.

Dual Brightness Enhancement film invented based on microreplication technology. More than doubles the brightness of computer screens.

HFEs (hydrofluoroethers) developed to replace harmful chlorofluoro-carbons (CFCs) and other ozone-depleting substances.

1997   Major new product introductions: Aldara cream and 3M Volition Fiber Optic Cabling System.

1998   Pacing Plus programs pass $1 billion in sales for the first time.

Negative impact of turmoil in international markets and currency losses; flat growth in sales and profits.

Additional restructuring announced to reduce employment by 4,500 and cut back on product lines with low earning potential.

1999   Organizational realignment eliminates group vice-president level of management and creates six market-based organizations.

Renewed focus on successful commercialization, outside acquisitions, and speed in decision-making and product development.

3M Technology Platforms

Adhesives	Ceramics	Chemical Power Source
Coated Abrasives	Composites	Copper Interconnects
Dental & Orthodontics	Diamond-like Films	Displays
Electro-luminescence	Electromechanical Systems	Electronics & Software
Films	Filtrations & Separations	Fluorochemicals & Fluoropolymers
Health Information	Imaging	Inks & Pigments
Mechanical Fasteners	Medical Devices	Microreplication
Mineral Granulation	Molding	Nonwovens
Optical Fibers & Connectors	Optics & Light Management	Particle & Dispersion Processing
Pharmaceuticals & Drug Delivery	Polymer Melt Processing	Porous Materials & Membranes
Precision Coating	Radiation Processing	Skin Health
Specialty Chemicals & Polymers	Surface Modification	Vibration Control

3M Nonwovens Technology Platform: A Sample

TAPE BACKINGS

HOOKIT
WRIST REST

Fire Barrier
Insulation Tape
Conformable NVH Tape
Interam
Removable Highway Marking Tapes
Floppy Disk Liners
Dampening Sleeves
Tapes and Ribbons
Filament Tape
Sasheen Decorative Ribbons

LOW DENSITY ABRASIVES

Never Scratch Pads
Never Rust Pads
Mill Rolls
Surface Conditioning Pads, Brushes, Disks, Belts and Wheels
Rescue Soap Pads
Buf-Puf Pads
Food Service Cleaning Pads
Clean 'n Strip Pads
Scrubbing Pads
Floor Pads
Nomad Entry Mats
Scotch-Brite Pads

MEDICAL PRODUCTS

First Aid Dressings
Medical Electrode Backings
Surgical Gowns
Membranes
Steri-Strip and Surgical Tapes
Surgical Masks
Breathable Tapes
COBAN
Masks and Drapes

INSULATION AND FILTERS

LITE LOFT
Acoustic Insulation
Chemical Spill Sorbents
Furnace Filters
Cabin Air Filters
Vacuum Bags
Thinsulate
Thermal Insulation
Air Filters
Doodleduster
Liquid Filters
Filtrete Electrets
Face Masks and Respirators
Melt Blown Webs
Oil Sorbent

1940   1950   1960   1970   1980   1990

3M Executive History

COB = Chairman of the Board
CEO = Chief Executive Officer
COO = Chief Operating Officer

1902	Henry S. Bryan	President
1905	Edgar B. Ober	President
1906	Lucius P. Ordway	President
1909	Edgar B. Ober	President
1929	William L. McKnight	President
1949	William L. McKnight Richard P. Carlton	COB President
1953	William L. McKnight Herbert P. Buetow	COB President
1963	William L. McKnight Bert S. Cross	COB President
1966	Bert S. Cross Harry Heltzer	COB & CEO President
1970	Harry Heltzer	COB & CEO
1972	Harry Heltzer Raymond H. Herzog	COB & CEO President
1973	Harry Heltzer Raymond H. Herzog	COB & CEO President & COO
1974	Harry Heltzer Raymond H. Herzog	COB CEO
1975	Raymond H. Herzog Lewis W. Lehr	COB & CEO President, U.S. Operations
1979	Raymond H. Herzog Lewis W. Lehr	COB Vice Chairman & CEO
1980	Lewis W. Lehr John M. Pitblado	COB & CEO President, U.S. Operations
1981	Lewis W. Lehr James A. Thwaits	COB & CEO President, International Operations & Corporate Staff Services
1984	Lewis W. Lehr Allen F. Jacobson	COB & CEO President, U.S. Operations
1986	Allen F. Jacobson	COB & CEO
1991	Livio D. DeSimone	COB & CEO

3M Trademark Products

The following are trademarks of the 3M Company:

Aldara™ (imiquimod) Cream
Maxair™ Autohaler™ (pirbuterol) Inhaler
Post-it® Notes
Post-it® Notes for Ink Jet and Laser Printers
Post-it® Signs
Post-it® Software Notes
Scotch® brand Tape
Scotch-Brite™ Cleaning Pads
Scotchgard™ Fabric and Upholstery Protector
Scotch® Magic™ Tape
Scotch® Masking Tape
Scotch® Pop-Up Tape and Dispenser
Scotch® Satin Tape
Thinsulate™ Thermal Insulation
3M™ Antibacterial Di-Noc™ Film
3M™ Brightness Enhancement Film
3M™ Colorquartz™ Aggregate
3M™ Floor Pads
3M™ Fluorinert™ Liquids
3M™ HFE (hydrofluoroethers) Fluids; now called
3M™ Novec™ Engineered Fluids
3M™ Light Water™ Aqueous Fire Fighting Foam
3M™ Microflex Circuits
3M™ Oil Sorbents
3M™ Optical Lighting Film
3M™ Safest Stripper™ Paint and Varnish Remover
3M™ Sasheen™ Decorative Ribbon
3M™ Scotchban™ Paper Protector
3M™ Scotchlite™ Reflective Sheeting
3M™ Scotchprint™ Electronic Graphic System
3M™ Scotchtint™ Sun Control Window Film
3M™ Scotch-Weld™ Structural Plastic Adhesive DP–4000
3M™ Silverlux™ Reflective Film
3M™ Space Lens
3M™ Steri-Strip™ Adhesive Strips
3M™ Three-M-ite™ product line
3M™ Trizact™ Abrasive Belts
3M™ Unitek APC Adhesive Coated Bracket
3M™ VHB™ Tape
3M™ Volition™ Fiber Optic Cabling System
3M™ Wetordry™ Waterproof Abrasives

- Breathe Right® nasal strips are a product of CNS, Inc. 3M holds an exclusive licence to the international distribution rights to this product until June 30, 2000.
- DryView™ Laser Imaging Products were acquired from Imation Corp. by Eastman Kodak Company.
- Teflon® is a registered product of E.I. du Pont de Nemours and Company.
- Microsoft® Exchange and Excel are products of Microsoft.

NOTES

Introduction

1. Miller, James, "Private R&D Spending Seen Rising 9.3%," *The Wall Street Journal*, December 31, 1998: A2. This article suggests that strong private industry support for R&D will continue into the next decade, barring a major economic downturn.
2. Richard Lidstad, personal interview, November 1998.
3. Two examples of recent works are: Tushman, Michael, and Charles O'Reilly, *Winning through Innovation: A Practical Guide to Leading Organizational Change and Renewal*. Boston: Harvard Business School Press, 1997; Kanter, Rosabeth Moss, ed., Fred Wiersema, and John Kao, *Innovation: Breakthrough Thinking at 3M, DuPont, GE, Pfizer, and Rubbermaid*, New York: HarperBusiness, 1997.
4. Collins, James C., and Jerry I. Porras, *Built to Last: Successful Habits of Visionary Companies*. New York: HarperBusiness, 1994; paperback HarperBusiness, 1997: 150.
5. Financial results for 1998 provided in *3M Annual Report*. These actually reflect a tough year for 3M. The 1997 annual report shows annual operating income of 18 percent of sales, and return on invested capital of 18 percent.
6. "3M Fights Back," *Fortune*, February 5, 1996: 94.
7. Study by Research Strategies Corporation, Princeton, New Jersey. The sample of executives was drawn from the one thousand largest manufacturing and five hundred largest service companies in the United States. Interviews were conducted in fall 1997 and analyzed forty-eight company reputations.
8. Richard Lidstad, personal interview, November 1998.
9. "The Idea Factory Stumbles: 3M Tries to Recover on Its Own Terms," *U.S. News & World Report*, December 21, 1998 (online version).

Chapter 1

1. From internal presentation materials used by Roger Appledorn.
2. Dave Braun, the nonwovens scientist, gave one version of these three innovation types in a May 1998 interview.
3. *3M Technology Platforms*, internal 3M publication, 1996: 30–35.
4. Simon Fung, personal interview, May 1998.
5. Dave Braun, personal interview, May 1998.
6. Based upon "Reinventing 3M's Oldest Business," *3M Today*, 14, 1 (January 1997); internal 3M publication, 1996: 6–11; *3M Technology Platforms*, 6–11; May 1998 interview with Robert Finocchiaro; 1996 and 1998 interviews with Roger Appledorn.
7. This section is based on 1997 and 1998 interviews with 3M Specialty Chemicals Division employees, including Richard Minday, Tim Sullivan, and Kathy Williams; also, "How to Clean up on the Competition," *3M Sales Forum*, Fall 1996; "High-Performance Teamwork Brings New Products to Market in Record Time," *3M Stemwinder*, September 4, 1996; *3M Ovation*, second and third quarter report, 1996; *3M Specialty Fluids*, April 1996, 2, 2; October 1995, 1, 2; and Winter 1997, 3, 1.
8. From a collection of overhead slides used by Roger Appledorn to instruct 3M employees in the practice of innovation.

9. Miller's story is summarized in *3M Stemwinder,* August 27, 1997; further information on this new form of treatment is provided in *3M Today,* 13, 6 (November 1996): 4–5.

10. Collins and Porras call this "the genius of the AND," a fortuitous label to which we will return later.

11. Roger Appledorn, innovation presentation notes: 36.

12. Tom Peters refers to this phenomenon in the chapter "Simultaneous Loose–Tight Properties" in *In Search of Excellence.* New York: Harper & Row, 1984 ch. 12: 318–25.

13. Personal interviews in 1996 and 1998; Coyne, William, "Building a Tradition of Innovation," *The UK Innovation Lecture,* March 5, 1996: 9–10.

14. Coyne: 11.

15. *3M 1997 Annual Report:* 5.

16. Sutin, Lawrence, "Searching for the Innovators," *3M Today:* 3. December 1996, 13, 7: 1–3.

Chapter 2

1. Among the various source materials cited in the bibliography, this chapter draws most heavily on the 3M corporate history, *Brand of the Tartan: The 3M Story* by Virginia Huck. New York: Appleton-Century-Crofts, 1955.

2. Ibid.: 93–94.

3. Ibid.: 231.

4. Ibid.: 159–65. There is another, similar 3M legend about Dick Drew and the invention of Scotch brand Cellophane Tape. In 1929, a packaging customer told 3M that he was looking for a waterproof, transparent sealant for DuPont's newest product: cellophane. The clear material had become extremely popular for packaging foods but proved impossible to seal shut, particularly with wet foods such as meat. Drew thought up the perfect solution: simply coat the cellophane with adhesive in order to make a tape.

   Unfortunately, manufacturing the tape turned out to be more difficult than Drew had anticipated. The cellophane had a tendency to snap when coated with adhesives. Also, the tape would stick to itself on the rolls. After overcoming many technical difficulties, Drew and his fellow lab workers finally created a viable product: Scotch brand Cellophane Tape. And all this happened in a little over one year.

   The marketing department expressed concern about demand, especially since the tape was released during the first year of the Depression. But they could not have been more wrong. New ideas for how to use the tape came up almost every day and sales grew at an explosive rate. The tape was 3M's most famous early invention, earning the company a reputation as an innovator. (Ibid.: 166–81.)

5. Huck, 291.

6. *Our Story So Far.* 3M Public Relations Dept., 1977: 13.

7. Huck, 260–76.

8. "Fluorochemicals: Forever Young," *3M Technology Platforms.* St. Paul: 3M, 1996: 18–23. Robinson, Alan G., and Sam Stern, *Corporate Creativity: How Innovation and Improvement Actually Happen,* San Francisco: Barret-Koehler, 1997: 214–38. Robinson and Stern provide an enlightening corrective to the official 3M historical accounts, showing how many actual events have been glossed over or simplified. One of the points that they make, citing Mullin's frustrating experience, is that "even when people know each other and work relatively near each other, it can be difficult to bring their ideas and expertise together at the right time and in the right way to spark a creative act." Robinson and Stern go on to provide several sensible suggestions for building an environment conducive to what we labeled as "Structured Serendipity" in chapter one.

9. "Fluorochemicals: Forever Young": 18–23.

10. 3M corporate web site (www.mmm.com).

11. 3M also has a more contemporary and conventional list of corporate values that focuses on major stakeholders:

- Satisfy customers with superior quality, value, and service.
- Provide investors with an attractive return through sustained, quality growth.
- Respect our social and physical environment.
- Be a company employees are proud to be part of.

Chapter 3

1. This list was provided courtesy of Dr. Bill Coyne, senior vice-president and head of research and development.

2. Stewart, Thomas, "3M Fights Back," *Fortune*, February 5, 1996: 96.

3. This outline of 3M's former laboratory structure is courtesy of Geoff Nicholson; the innovation types in the right-hand column were added by the author.

4. Bill Coyne, personal interview, May 1998.

5. Robert Finocchiaro, personal interview, May 1998.

6. For more on the role of storytelling in 3M's corporate culture, see Shaw, Gordon, Robert Brown, and Philip Bromiley, "Strategic Stories: How 3M Is Rewriting Business Planning," *Harvard Business Review*, May–June 1998: 41–50.

7. Appledorn, Roger, "Creating a Climate for Innovation," February 1996: 34–51. The original account has been slightly edited and abridged.

8. Patrick Hager, personal interview, May 1998.

9. Joseph Ward, III, personal interview, May 1998; 3M Commercial Graphics web site (www.mmm.com).

10. The notion of evolutionary spinoffs is referred to in presentation materials shared by Geoff Nicholson; Collins and Porras also emphasize this idea in *Built to Last* (see note 14).

11. Stewart, *Fortune*, February 5, 1996: 99.

12. Appledorn spent considerable time and money, for example, in the admirable but commercially unsuccessful effort to make more energy-efficient materials for greenhouse construction.

13. Oslund, John, "More than Meets the Eye," *Star Tribune*, May 8, 1995.

14. Collins and Porras developed this evolution metaphor for 3M innovation in "The 3M Story: Making Big Money on Little Ideas," *Audacity*, 4, 2 winter 1996.

15. Bill Coyne, personal interview, May 1998.

16. From presentation materials shared by Bill Coyne.

17. David Hagen, Director, Tape Process Technology Center, personal interview, August 1998.

18. 3M web site (www.mmm.com), "3M's Major Innovations."

19. Simon Fung, personal interview, May 1998.

20. Patrick Hager, personal interview, May 1998.

21. From 3M Intranet web site on the Tech Forum (www.mmm.com).

22. Ibid.

23. Simon Fung, personal interview, May 1998.

24. In the popular management classic *In Search of Excellence*, Tom Peters quotes MIT Professor Edward Roberts on the subject of career progress for a 3Mer who is part of a successful venture team. The quote links changes in employment and corresponding compensation categories with sales of a new product, citing movement through the following steps: first-line engineer, product engineer, product-line engineering manager, and finally departmental manager of engineering or R&D. Although this is an interesting concept, according to 3M Human Resources "it is not true now and has never been true. It may have been somebody's idea at one point." See *In Search of Excellence: Lessons from America's Best Run Companies.* 227.

25. From 1998 3M Innovator Award Launch Kit.

Chapter 4

1. M. Kay Grenz, vice-president, Human Resources, personal interview, May 1998.
2. "3M Human Resources Mission," company pamphlet, 1995.
3. "Hiring Innovators," *3M Staffing and College Relations*, 1994; "3M Develops a Way to Find Future Innovators," 3M corporate web site (www.mmm.com).
4. George Kiperts, personal interview, May 1998; "3M Develops a Way to Find Future Innovators," 3M corporate web site (www.mmm.com). See also "Searching for the Innovators," *3M Today*, 13, 7, December 1996: 1–2.
5. Arlan Tietel, 3M TV, personal interview, May 1998.
6. Margaret Alldredge, personal interview, May 1998.
7. Giulio Agostini, senior vice-president and chief financial officer, personal interview, May 1998.
8. At a recent meeting for investors, 3M executives began wondering what was wrong with their presentations as one person after another headed for the door clutching their cellphones. At the break the outside hallway was a buzz of conversation, with some analysts wearing dark expressions and others seemingly gasping for air. At that point 3Mers not already aware of what was happening were informed that the problem was not their presentations but the fact that the stock market was dropping like a stone. On that day, August 27, 1998, the market plunged more than 350 points.
9. Quotes throughout this section are from Guilio Agostini, personal interview, May 1998.
10. "3M Mexico Teamwork Turns Mexican Economic Crisis into an Opportunity," *3M International Ambassador*, third quarter, 1996: 8–11; personal correspondence from 1997 forwarded by Bill Allen.
11. Chuck Harstad, staff vice-president, Corporate Marketing and Public Affairs, personal interview, May 1998; internal presentation documents shared by Corporate Marketing personnel.
12. Wendy Stanton, Reengineering Manager, 3M Procurement Operations; personal interview, May 1998; internal publication, "3M Procurement's 'Future State Vision,'" 3M Procurement, Revision 3, reprinted in March 1998.
13. Michael Linnerooth, sales and marketing analyst, Construction and Home Improvement Markets, personal interview, May 1998; internal 3M presentation notes from Linnerooth: "Kmart Financial Analysis Modeling Tool."
14. Unfortunately, several of the employees brought into the United States for developmental assignments have been transferred to completely different functions on their return, in some cases due to poor performance in St. Paul. Likewise, in the case of one American staff manager sent abroad, it was noted wryly that after several years in the country he still couldn't pronounce the name of the street on which he was living.

Chapter 5

1. H. C. Shin, personal interview, May 1998.
2. 3M Korea, personal interview, spring 1995.
3. Ronald Faas, personal interview, fall 1998.
4. Jean Waller, personal interview, fall 1998.
5. 3M China, personal interview, 1995.
6. Nicholson also cites the development of acrylic foam tape, an industrial technology originally invented in the United States. "When the technology was transferred to Europe through our German laboratory, our customers there needed a product with different properties. The laboratory developed the product and was able to file several patents to protect 3M's invention. This technology was subsequently transferred to Japan, where, again, the customer requirement was different. This led to the invention of patentable new products." Eventually this technology came full circle back to the United States, as the improved German-Japanese products were reimported. "Searching for the Innovators," *3M Today*, 13, 7, December 1996: 1–2.

7. Birla 3M, personal interviews conducted by Hiroshi Kagawa, fall 1998. In yet another Birla 3M case, a leading Indian petrochemical manufacturer mentioned to one of Mr. Kumar's fellow Birla 3M employees that it had a problem with PVC (polyvinyl chloride) granules escaping during transport. A cross-functional team from Birla 3M investigated the problem and found that the customer was packaging the chemical in bags that were sewn shut. The team drew upon 3M's wealth of tape technology and products to develop 3M Bag Sealing Tape, a product with high tack and adhesive properties. This self-adhesive tape, easily dispensed from a machine at the customer's site, could be applied on top of the stitches to fully seal the bag and make it tamper proof. For their efforts, the Birla 3M team received a Pathfinder Award, given out to acknowledge those in the company whose innovative efforts guide new products, services, or ideas through the first critical stages of development. They are currently looking for other applications for their new tape in the packaging of commodities such as cement, flour, and batteries. See "1997 Pathfinder Awards Honor International Innovation," *3M International Ambassador*, first quarter, 1998: 16–17.

8. Antonio Pinna Berchet, personal interview, August 1998.

9. Gene Shipman, personal interview, May 1998.

10. Ellis, Kristine, "The Soviet Connection," *3M Today* 15, 3, March–April 1998: 1–3.

11. Alphonsus V. Pocius, personal interview, May 1998. Pocius recounts a breakfast meeting that Albozsta held with Russian scientists from a major technical institute who pleaded, with tears in their eyes: "We have all of this training, we know what to do. Please give us something useful to do!"

12. Ikuko Ebihara, personal interview, May 1998.

13. "Catalyst for Growth," *3M International Ambassador*, first quarter, 1998: 6–9.

14. "1997 Pathfinder Awards Honor International Innovation," *3M International Ambassador*, first quarter, 1998: 18.

15. St. Paul, personal interview, spring 1994.

16. The author was involved in the study of best practices in a 3M JMAT in 1992.

17. "Catalyst for Growth," *3M International Ambassador*, first quarter, 1998: 6–9.

18. Sumitomo 3M, personal interview, October 1990.

19. Milind Sabade, personal interview, May 1998; "Exploiting the Power of Multicultural Teams," *3M Today*, 13, 7, December 1996: 10. A similar volunteer movement is now underway by resident Chinese and Chinese Americans to provide support for 3M China.

20. 3M Singapore, personal interview, spring 1995.

21. 3M Korea, personal interview, spring 1995.

22. 3M Singapore, personal interview, spring 1995.

23. 3M Singapore, personal interview, spring 1995.

24. St. Paul, personal interview, spring 1995.

25. H. C. Shin, personal interview, May 1998.

26. H. C. Shin, personal interview, May 1998.

Chapter 6

1. "Lefty" Satoh, personal interview, June 1998. Satoh is retired but serving Sumitomo 3M as a consultant and advisor.

2. Sumitomo 3M, personal interviews, 1990.

3. Sumitomo 3M, personal interviews, 1990.

4. Sumitomo 3M, personal interviews, 1995.

5. Ron Baukol, personal interview, August 1998.

6. St. Paul, personal interviews, 1996.

7. St. Paul, personal interviews, 1996.

8. St. Paul, personal interviews, 1996. "It is hard to become an individual product champion when there is so much emphasis on consensus. It hurts to have people

worry too much about stepping on others' toes. What if all the nails could be standing up instead of the one that gets hammered down?"

9. St. Paul and Tokyo, personal interviews, 1996. "Particularly for the technical departments, their essential role is to develop new things for their division and for the company. But in reality they're so busy with requests from sales and from customers that their time is taken up with customer service, and they have their hands full just supporting the existing business. There seems to be no time for exercising their creativity."

10. Japanese expatriate, St. Paul, personal interview, spring 1996. "There are people who question the purpose of the Tech Forum. They feel that those who participate have too much free time, and want to know what the business result is. But maybe we shouldn't emphasize output too much."

11. St. Paul and Tokyo, personal interviews, 1996.

12. Sumitomo 3M, personal interview, February 1998.

13. Sumitomo 3M, personal interview, 1996.

14. In an interesting case of life imitating art, Japanese executives seized on the phrase, "genius of the AND," coined by Collins and Porras in their book, *Built to Last,* and wove it into their solution. *Built to Last: Successful Habits of Visionary Companies,* was translated into Japanese under the title, *Visionary Companies,* and has sold briskly in business circles.

15. Sumitomo 3M, personal interview, 1996.

16. St. Paul and Tokyo, personal interviews, 1996. Interviewees favored "technical marketing," or the combination of technical depth and listening for customer needs, rather than focusing on product performance and specifications. "It is not easy to ask the right questions of customers. You need both technical ability and good questioning techniques."

17. "Aggressive Product Development and Integrated Solutions Keep Sumitomo 3M Growing in a Flat Economy," *3M International Ambassador* (third/fourth quarter, 1997): 3–6.

18. Takaaki Nishijima, personal interview, February 1998. See also "Aggressive Product Development and Integrated Solutions Keep Sumitomo 3M Growing in a Flat Economy," *3M International Ambassador* (third/fourth quarter, 1997): 3–6; and "Multicultural Teams," *3M Today,* 13, 7 (December 1996): 8–9.

19. Ron Baukol, personal interview, August 1998.

20. Sumitomo 3M, personal interview, 1999.

21. St. Paul, personal interview, fall 1996.

22. Sumitomo 3M, personal interview, spring 1996. "We think that because the U.S. is doing a program, Japan has to do it. But we eat without properly digesting. It's better to make sure that new programs are worthwhile. We should watch, wait, and bring in the good points."

23. Sumitomo 3M, personal interview, spring 1996.

24. Sumitomo 3M, personal interviews, spring 1996.

Chapter 7

1. The words in this column are Coyne's. A few liberties have been taken with phraseology and word order for the sake of readability. Coyne, William, "Building a Tradition of Innovation," the U.K. Innovation Lecture, March 5, 1996.

2. "The Road Ahead Is Clearer," *3M Today,* February 1996, 13, 1: 2–5. Other quotes in this segment are from a personal interview conducted in August 1998.

3. Barry Dayton, personal interview, February 1999.

4. The Lew Lehr story is recounted by Coyne, William, "Building a Tradition of Innovation," the U.K. Innovation Lecture, March 5, 1996: 11.

5. Stewart, Thomas, "3M Fights Back," *Fortune,* February 5, 1996: 99.

6. This term is taken from materials provided by Kim Johnson, an organizer of 3M's Grass Roots Innovation Team activity, which goes by the acronym GRIT.

7. The Pacing Plus initiative was preceded by a similar set of so-called Pacing Programs. When the latter grew too numerous, Pacing Plus was inaugurated in order to restore greater focus.

8. Senge, Peter, *The Fifth Discipline: The Art and Practice of the Learning Organization*. New York: Doubleday Currency, 1990.

9. Cohan, Peter S., *The Technology Leaders: How America's Most Profitable High-Tech Companies Innovate Their Way to Success*: 110–11. San Francisco: Jossey-Bass, 1997.

10. Bower, Joseph, and Clayton Christensen, "Disruptive Technologies: Catching the Wave," in Brown, John Seely, ed., *Seeing Differently: Insights on Innovation*: 123–25. Boston: Harvard Business School Press, 1997.

11. Tushman, Michael, and Charles O'Reilly, *Winning through Innovation: A Practical Guide to Leading Organizational Change and Renewal*: 167–76. Boston: Harvard Business School Press, 1997.

12. Richard Lidstad, former Human Resources vice-president, personal interview, November 1998.

13. Sumitomo 3M, where the Vision 2000 programs have been run according to a different organizational setup, is perhaps an exception that proves the rule. Vision 2000 work units were at first organizationally differentiated and sheltered in the manner that innovation gurus describe and prescribe. As this subsidiary operation grows in its technical capabilities and organizational sophistication, however, the trend is to integrate experimental Vision 2000 thinking and practices back into the rest of the company.

    3M's Pacing Plus programs are a fast-forward version of what happens elsewhere in St. Paul or Austin, functioning like hot spots in a larger conflagration; Vision 2000 is a smaller flame, a promising attempt at a new organizational beginning. It may be that other subsidiaries, too, will need to go through such a "differentiated phase" on the way to building the fully integrated innovation whirligig that one finds at headquarters.

14. L. D. DeSimone, personal interview, August 1998.

15. Tushman, 35–37.

16. Peters, Tom, *In Search of Excellence: Lessons from America's Best Run Companies*, chapter 12; Tushman, Michael, and Charles O'Reilly. *Winning through Innovation: A Practical Guide to Leading Organizational Change and Renewal*, chapter 7. Collins, James, and Jerry I. Porras, *Built to Last: Successful Habits of Visionary Companies*, 43–45.

17. For this reason, to juxtapose strategy in the 3M sense with evolutionary innovation as in the previous chart is not entirely accurate.

18. Brown, John Seely, ed., *Seeing Differently: Insights on Innovation*, xxiv–xxv.

19. "The Road Ahead is Clearer," *3M Today*, February 1996, 13, 1: 2–5.

20. L. D. DeSimone, personal interview, August 1998.

Chapter 8

1. "The Road Ahead is Clearer," *3M Today*, February 1996, 13, 1: 3.

2. *Imation Corp. 1997 Summary Annual Report*: 2–4.

3. "3M Targets Double-Digit Earnings Growth: Outlines Plan for Growth, Productivity Improvement," 3M corporate web site, August 1998. "3M Reports Second-Quarter, First-Half 1998 Sales and Earnings," 3M web site, July 23, 1998.

4. Quote from L. D. DeSimone cited in "3M Targets Double-Digit Earnings Growth: Outlines Plan for Growth, Productivity Improvement," 3M corporate web site, August 1998.

5. See, for example "The Road Ahead is Clearer," *3M Today*, February 1996, 13, 1: 2–3.

6. The previous accolade that the company was "the Cal Ripken of corporate consistency" (Stewart, Thomas, "3M Fights Back," *Fortune*, February 5, 1996) began to take on an ironic bite. Cal Ripken's amazing streak of consecutive baseball games has finally come to an end, and 3M's 1998 economic results didn't look quite as

stellar either. Never in modern memory has the company had such a flat performance as in 1998, and five straight quarters of missed financial targets.

7. See for example "3M: The Heat is on the Boss," *Business Week*, March 15, 1999: 82–84. The outside directors conducting the interviews are said to be Allen Murray, retired CEO of Mobil Corp., and Edward Brennan, former CEO of Sears Roebuck & Co.

8. As of mid–1999, the most recent financial reports posted on 3M's corporate web site indicated that second quarter sales were up 2.5 percent over the previous year, and earnings were up 9.6 percent. Asia–Pacific volume rose 11 percent, a strong indication that the economy of that region is starting to come back. Imation reported modestly positive income for the first half of 1999 as opposed to a loss in the same period for 1998 (www.Imation.com).

9. "3M Targets Double-Digit Earnings Growth: Outlines Plan for Growth, Productivity Improvement," 3M web site, August 1998.

10. St. Paul, personal interviews, May 1998.

11. St. Paul, personal interviews, May 1998; Tokyo, April 1999.

12. Stewart, Thomas, "3M Fights Back," *Fortune*, February 5, 1996: 97.

13. The $300,000 figure assumes flat 1998 sales and a 10 percent annual increase for the 3 years thereafter, from roughly $15 billion to $19.97 billion, divided by 66,000 employees.

14. St. Paul, personal interview, May 1998.

15. "1996 3M Poll: An Overview of Results," *3M Today*, April/May 1997, 14, 4: 9–15.

16. "EC&DP Spells Growth for Employees and for 3M," *3M Today*, December 1996, 13, 7: 16–19.

17. St. Paul, personal interview, January 1999.

18. Owen, Henry, "Going for the 'Big Bang,'" *3M Today*: 6–7.

19. Tokyo, personal interview, January 1999.

20. *3M 1997 Annual Report*: 9–13; *3M Technology Platforms*: 78–83; 3M web site.

21. DeSimone, Livio D., and Frank Popoff, *Eco-Efficiency: The Business Link to Sustainable Development*: 2.

22. 3M web site, "Sky's the Limit for 3M Space Lens," March 1999.

23. DeSimone, Livio D., 218–31.

24. Miller, Marilyn, ed., *3M Ovation*, May 1997: 1–23 (special edition devoted to electronic applications of Post-it products); Marty Kenner, personal interview, May 1998.

25. For example, another promising software area is Health Information Systems. 3M has developed medical records software that captures clinical data and merges it so that hospitals receive proper reimbursements.

26. The information in this section on 3M Europe, including the quotes, comes from Ackenhusen, Mary, "The 3M Company: Integrating Europe (A,B,C)," case study, INSEAD, 1994. See especially Part C, 1–12. A second source was a personal interview with Rainer Goldammer, European Human Resources Director, August 1998.

27. *3M 1998 Annual Report*: 2.

28. 3M corporate web site, *3M 1998 Annual Report*: 12–13.

29. Message to employees from L. D. DeSimone, 3M Chairman and CEO, August 30, 1999. In this memorandum, DeSimone provides a preliminary report on the results of 3M's "Millennium Planning Project," undertaken with the help of consultants from McKinsey. The first part of the memo affirms core 3M attributes and strengths, while the latter part addresses four major issues of accelerating growth.

30. Ibid. The group vice-president level has been eliminated, with division heads now reporting directly to executive vice-presidents in charge of six market areas: consumer and office markets, electro and communications markets, health care markets, industrial markets, specialty material markets, and transportation, graphics and safety markets.

31. Bill Coyne, personal interview, December 1998.
32. Tokyo, personal interview, April 1999.
33. L. D. DeSimone, personal interview, August 1998; Ron Baukol, personal interview, August 1998; Bill Coyne, personal interview, May 1998.
34. *Our Story So Far*. St. Paul: 3M Company, 1977: 117. The quotation is attributed to Jim Thwaits who was formerly president of 3M's international operations. A former personnel executive named Lyle Fisher is also quoted as saying, "Our advance will stem from providing for our people a better climate for achievement—a climate which stimulates ordinary people to produce extraordinary performances. The extent to which any one of us can produce beyond his or her rated capacity may be small indeed, yet the sum of these, when added together, will make the difference between a great organization and an indifferent one."

BIBLIOGRAPHY

Ackenhusen, Mary. "The 3M Company: Integrating Europe (A,B,C)," case study, INSEAD, 1994

Argyris, Chris. *Knowledge for Action: A Guide for Overcoming Barriers to Organizational Change*. San Francisco: Jossey-Bass, 1993.

Bartlett, C., and Ghoshal, Sumantra. *Managing Across Borders: The Transnational Solution*. Boston: Harvard Business School Press, 1989.

Brown, John Seely (ed). *Seeing Differently: Insights on Innovation*. Boston: Harvard Business School Press, 1997.

Cohan, Peter S. *The Technology Leaders: How America's Most Profitable High-Tech Companies Innovate Their Way to Success*. San Francisco: Jossey-Bass, 1997.

Collins, James C., and Porras, Jerry I. *Built to Last: Successful Habits of Visionary Companies*. New York: HarperBusiness, 1994.

Comfort, Mildred Houghton. *William L. McKnight, Industrialist*. Minneapolis: T. S. Denison, 1962.

Davenport, Thomas, and Prusak, Laurence. *Working Knowledge: How Organizations Manage What They Know*. Boston: Harvard Business School Press, 1998.

De Bono, Edward. *Lateral Thinking: A Textbook of Creativity*. London and New York: Penguin Books, 1970.

Denison, Daniel R. *Corporate Culture and Organizational Effectiveness*. New York: John Wiley & Sons, 1990.

DeSimone, Livio D. and Popoff, Frank. *Eco-Efficiency: The Business Link to Sustainable Development*. Boston: MIT Press, 1997.

Frost, Peter, et al. *Organizational Culture*. Newbury Park, CA: Sage Publications, 1985.

Hampden-Turner, Charles. *Creating Corporate Culture: From Discord to Harmony*. Reading, MA: Addison-Wesley Publishing Company, 1990.

Huck, Virginia. *Brand of the Tartan—The 3M Story*. New York: Appleton-Century-Crofts, 1955.

Imation Corp. Annual Reports, 1996, 1997, 1998.

Kanter, Rosabeth Moss. *The Change Masters: Innovation and Entrepreneurship in the American Corporation*. New York: Simon & Schuster, 1985.

——. *The Challenge of Organizational Change: How Companies Experience It and Leaders Guide It*. New York: The Free Press, 1992.

Kanter, Rosabeth Moss, ed., Wiersema, Fred, and Kao, John. *Innovation: Breakthrough Thinking at 3M, DuPont, GE, Pfizer, and Rubbermaid*. New York: HarperBusiness, 1997.

Kao, John. *Jamming: The Art and Discipline of Business Creativity*. New York: HarperBusiness, 1996.

Kotter, J., and Heskitt, J. *Corporate Culture and Performance*. New York: Free Press, 1993.

Meyer, Christopher. *Relentless Growth: How Silicon Valley Innovation Strategies can Work in Your Business*. New York: Free Press, 1998.

Nadler, David, and Tushman, Michael. *Competing by Design: The Power of Organizational Architecture.* Oxford: Oxford University Press, 1997.

Nonaka, Ikujiro. *The Knowledge Creating Company.* Oxford: Oxford University Press, 1993.

——. *3M no chōsen* (3M's Challenge). Tokyo: Nihon Keizai Shinbunsha, 1987.

Peters, Thomas J. *The Circle of Innovation: You Can't Shrink Your Way to Greatness.* New York: Knopf, 1997.

——. *In Search of Excellence: Lessons from America's Best-Run Companies.* New York: Harper & Row, 1982; paperback New York: Warner Books, 1988.

Plsek, Paul. *Creativity, Innovation, and Quality.* Milwaukee, Wisconsin: ASO Quality Press, 1997.

Ray, Michael and Meyers, Rochelle. *Creativity in Business.* New York: Doubleday, 1986.

Robert, Michael. *Product Innovation Pure and Simple: How Winning Companies Outpace the Competition.* New York: McGraw-Hill, 1995.

Robinson, Alan G., and Stern, Sam. *Corporate Creativity: How Innovation and Improvement Actually Happen.* San Francisco: Berret-Koehler, 1997.

Schein, Edgar. *Organizational Culture and Leadership.* San Francisco: Jossey-Bass, 1985.

Senge, Peter. *The Fifth Discipline: The Art and Practice of the Learning Organization.* New York: Doubleday Currency, 1990.

Smith, Douglas. *Taking Charge of Change: 10 Principles for Managing People and Performance.* Reading, Massachusetts: Addison-Wesley Publishing Company, 1996.

Tokuda, Kiyoshi, and Kaneda, Shin'ichirô, eds. *Akarui kaisha* (The Cheerful Company): *3M Tokyo.* Nikkei Business, 1998.

Tushman, Michael, and O'Reilly, Charles. *Winning through Innovation: A Practical Guide to Leading Organizational Change and Renewal.* Boston: Harvard Business School Press, 1997.

Van de Ven, A., Angle, H., and Poole, M. *Research on the Management of Innovation: The Minnesota Studies.* New York: Harper & Row, 1989.

Wick, Calhoun W. *The Learning Edge: How Smart Managers and Smart Companies Stay Ahead.* New York: McGraw-Hill, 1993.

Journals/Newspapers/Magazines

Begley, Sharon. "The Houses of Invention," *Newsweek.* Special issue, winter 1997/1998: 26.

Collins, James C., and Porras, Jerry I. "The 3M Story: Making Big Money on Little Ideas," *Audacity,* Winter 1996, 4, 2.

Greenwald, John. "Spinning Away," *Time.* August 26, 1996: 30–31.

Kelly, Kevin. "High-tech Tape Unravels at 3M," *Business Week.* November 27, 1995: 49.

Loeb, Marshall. "Ten Commandments for Managing Creative People," *Fortune.* January 16, 1995: 135–37.

"The Mass Production of Ideas, and Other Impossibilities," *The Economist.* March 18, 1998, 334, 7906: 72.

"McKnight, Westbee Resign From Board," *St. Paul Megaphone.* August 1973: 1.

Miller, James. "Private R&D Spending Seen Rising 9.3%," *Wall Street Journal.* December 31, 1998: A2.

"Minnesota Mining in Motion," *Fortune.* March 1949: 93.

O'Brien, Robert. "3M Leads Indiscriminate Sell-Off; Mobil, IBM and Alcoa Also Drop," *The Wall Street Journal.* June 16, 1998, 231, 116: B4.

Oslund, John. "More than Meets the Eye," *Star Tribune.* May 8, 1995.

Shaw, Gordon, Brown, Robert, and Bromiley, Philip. "Strategic Stories: How 3M Is Rewriting Business Planning," *Harvard Business Review.* May–June 1998: 41–50.

Stewart, Thomas A. "3M Fights Back," *Fortune.* February 5, 1996: 94–100.

——. "How to Lead a Revolution," *Fortune,* November 28, 1994.

——. "A New Way to Wake Up a Giant," *Fortune,* October 22, 1990.

"3M to Trail Forecasts, and Its Shares Fall," *New York Times.* June 16, 1998, 147, 51190: D9.

Tully, Shawn. "Why to Go for Stretch Targets," *Fortune,* November 14, 1994.

3M Publications

Appledorn, Roger. "Creating a Climate for Innovation," February 1996.

Coyne, William. "Building a Tradition of Innovation," The UK Innovation Lecture, March 5, 1996.

Our Story So Far. St. Paul, Minnesota: 3M Company, 1977.

3M Annual Report, 1997.

3M Innovator Award Launch Kit.

3M International Ambassador, first quarter, second quarter, third/fourth quarter, 1997; first quarter, 1998.

3M Ovation, second/third quarter, 1996; special edition, May 1997.

3M Sales Forum, fall 1996.

3M Specialty Fluids, 1, 2, October 1995; 1, 2, April 1996; 3, 1, Winter 1997.

3M Stemwinder, April 22, 1995; September 4, 1996; August 27, 1997.

3M Technology Platforms, 1996.

3M Today, February 1996, 13, 1; March 1996, 13, 2; May 1996, 13, 3; July 1996, 13, 4; September 1996, 13, 5; November 1996, 13, 6; December 1996, 13, 7; January 1997, 14, 1; February 1997, 14, 2; March 1997, 14, 3; April/May 1997, 14, 4; June 1997, 14, 5; July/August 1997, 14, 6; September 1997, 14, 7; October 1997, 14, 8; January 1998, 15, 1; February 1998, 15, 2; March/April 1998, 15, 3; March/April 1999, 16, 2.

3M Website (www.mmm.com).

INDEX